AF574622

REVEALING CHARACTER

TEXAS TINTYPES *by* ROBB KENDRICK

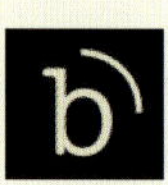

BRIGHT SKY PRESS
BOX 416, ALBANY, TEXAS 76430

10 9 8 7 6 5 4 3 2 1

LIBRARY OF CONGRESS CATALOGING-IN-PUBLICATION DATA

KENDRICK, ROBB, 1963—
REVEALING CHARACTER : TEXAS TINTYPES / BY ROBB KENDRICK ; WITH ESSAY BY JOHN GRAVES.
P. CM.
ISBN 1-931721-57-2 (ALK. PAPER)
1. COWBOYS—TEXAS—PORTRAITS 2. TINTYPE—TEXAS 3. COWBOYS—TEXAS—BIOGRAPHY
4. COWBOYS—TEXAS—PSYCHOLOGY 5. CHARACTER. 6. TEXAS—BIOGRAPHY—PORTRAITS
7. TEXAS—SOCIAL LIFE AND CUSTOMS—PICTORIAL WORKS I. GRAVES, JOHN, 1920-
II. OLD JAIL ART CENTER III. TITLE

F383.K46 2005
976.4—DC22

2005045365

JACKET AND BOOK DESIGN BY DERRIT DEROUEN, MCGARRAH-JESSEE, INC.

PRINTED IN HONG KONG THROUGH ASIA PACIFIC OFFSET

ACKNOWLEDGMENTS

Without patronage, talent is oftentimes unshared. Recognizing Robb Kendrick's skill and sensitivity with a camera, executives of Frost Bank commissioned him to undertake a Texas "expedition" to document the character of the land as seen in the faces of its truest men and women, those we call cowboys. Furthermore, they had the foresight to realize that the resulting tintypes should be shared broadly, in a book and in museums, funding the entire project. With support from Dick Evans, Chairman and CEO, and Tom C. Frost, Senior Chairman, Pam R. Thomas, Executive Vice President for Marketing, has supervised the "Character of Texas Expedition." Sallie F. Newman, Vice President, Marketing, and Renée Sabel, Vice President, Marketing, have assisted her in the overall project. *Texas Monthly* magazine soon became a partner, with David B. Dunham, Associate Publisher, as chief champion of the expedition and Amy Saralegui, Texas Advertising Manager, as facilitator. Robin Stauber of Dublin & Associates helped publicize the project.

The subjects of the tintypes posed for their portraits willingly, a situation that demands time and concentration. Snapshots, these are not, yet these busy men and women graciously gave Robb their time and hospitality. He's grateful to each and every one.

Robb's assistant, Jason Bryant, himself a documentary photographer, traveled thousands of miles and spent hundreds of hours preparing chemicals, setting up and breaking down equipment, working out logistical arrangements and interviewing the subjects. He was a welcome companion and invaluable right hand.

The inimitable John Graves, a Texas treasure, contributed his insights into the character of Texas cowboys—and by extension, the character of the state. Buster McLaury, a working cowboy and wordsmith, has had the last word. We are grateful to them for spinning out words to envelop the silent tintypes.

McGarrah/Jessee, an innovative advertising agency, helped Frost conceive the overall project and manage the details. Principals Mark McGarrah and Bryan Jessee enthusiastically steered the course, supported every aspect of the work and lent their friendship to all involved. Many in their shop worked tirelessly and creatively on this project over a short deadline, among them are: Meredith Gunthorp, Account Manager; Derrit DeRouen, Designer; Brooks Jackson, Copywriter; and Lisa O'Neill, Communications Director.

Robert Workman, of Robert Workman & Associates, helped shape the exhibition and book project and marketed the exhibition. Frost Bank contracted with the Old Jail Art Center of Albany, Texas, to oversee the book project and organize the exhibition. Margaret Blagg, Executive Director; Patrick Kelly, Preparator; Shelly Crittendon, Registrar; Kathryn Mitchell, Education Director; and Daniel Alonzo, Archivist/Librarian, did so, including creating a Web site: revealing-character.com.

Rue Judd, publisher, Bright Sky Press, has moved mountains and all individuals involved to get the book published on schedule. Watt M. Casey Jr., an Albany photographer who ranches with his father, documented Robb and Jason at work to help all of us better understand the sublime tintype.

Additionally, Robb would like to thank many people for their friendship, support, and sharing of knowledge in this project: John Coffer, inspiring mentor, who introduced him to this arcane process; William Dunniway, who has answered the seemingly unanswerable; Milan Zahorcak, who walked him through early lens design to overcome or take advantage of early design flaws; Shawn Henry and Bill Kennedy for their insight into making the best possible scans for reproduction; and lastly his wife Jeannie and two boys Gus and Jeb for putting up with absence from home to make this dream possible.

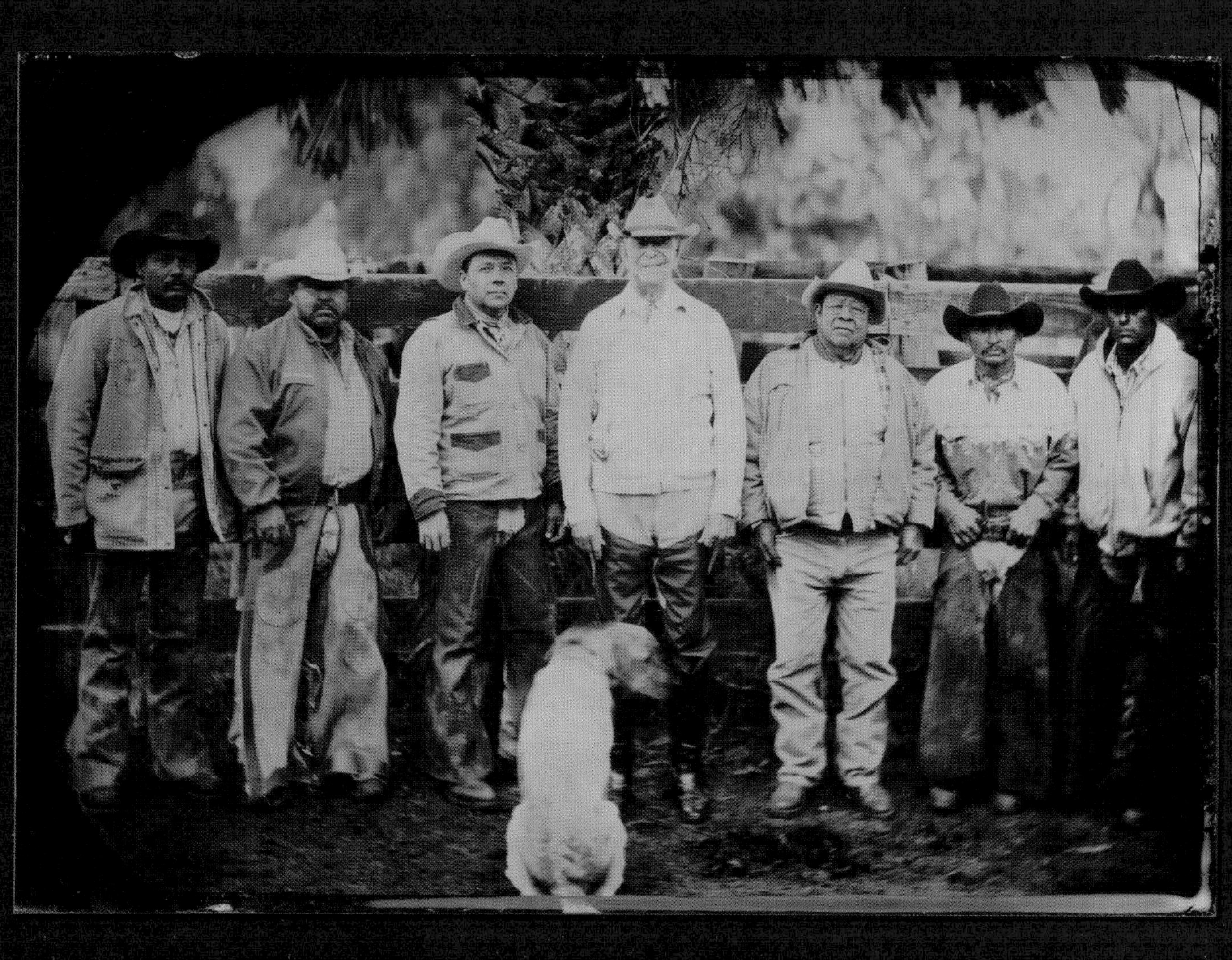

CONTENTS

PRECEDING PAGE: ELIODORO PAZ, ERNESTO JIMENEZ, ROMERO MEDELLIN JR., TOBIN ARMSTRONG, ROMERO MEDELLIN SR., ROBERTO FERNANDEZ, ROBERT LEE HINOJOSA AND ALFIE, ARMSTRONG RANCH

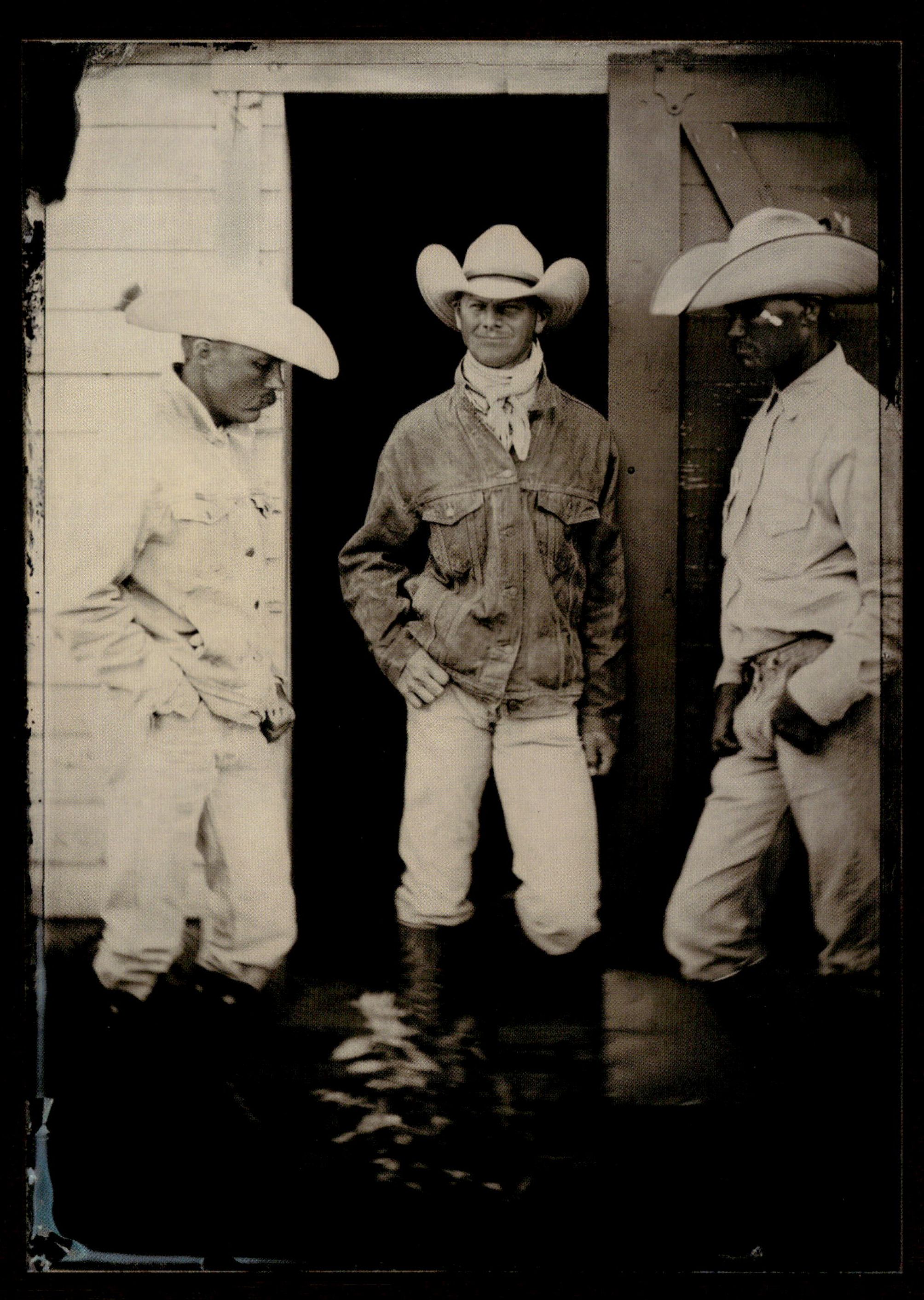

PREFACE

by TOM FROST

"Man's chief purpose is the creation and preservation of values: That is what gives meaning to our civilization."

– LEWIS MUMFORD

My great-grandfather, Colonel T.C. Frost, founded Frost Bank in 1868 based on his personal dedication to the values and moral qualities that formed his life story. In fact, the 2002 book documenting his life and genealogy is entitled *Character Endures*. The character he instilled in his family and those who worked in his fledgling mercantile company and bank has lasted through the years. And it still guides me today, in my 52nd year as a Frost banker.

Character involves all the features and traits that form the individual nature of a person and yes, a business.

To honor our company's heritage and remind us all that character is just as important today as it was in the 19th century, we asked renowned photographer Robb Kendrick to travel around the state to photograph working cowboys and cowgirls, using an 1800s photographic technique called tintype.

In Robb Kendrick's tintypes, we saw a reflection of the character that built the great state of Texas, the same persistent character that built Frost Bank. Now, it may seem unusual for a bank to be drawn to a project involving old-fashioned photography and Texas cowboys. But, to us, it seemed like just the right fit. After all, the cowboys of the 19th century gave Texas its character. Their honesty, sense of humor, work ethic and determination remain as our indigenous values. We honor their values through this collection.

These images that Robb so meticulously captures resonate with me for another reason. Back in the 1800s, the Colonel's earliest customers were ranchers and farmers, who came into his mercantile store to buy bits and saddles, boots, wagons and rope—and for help in warehousing their wool and financing their purchases. In the faces of these men and women Robb has photographed, I can see those early Texans who helped settle the state.

In our 21st century world of immediate information and gratification, the slow, often tedious tintype method may seem strangely out of synch. Yet through this unhurried process, the photographer captures the soul of the subject.

Many of these images first appeared in the pages of *Texas Monthly* through our partnership with the magazine. We were pleased to bring these photographs to the citizens of Texas and beyond, and we are proud to present them in this book.

Tom Frost

TOM C. FROST – SENIOR CHAIRMAN, FROST BANK
MARCH 2005

PRECEDING PAGE: RHETT CAUBLE, BUCK MCLAIN AND R. D. HORN, JA RANCH

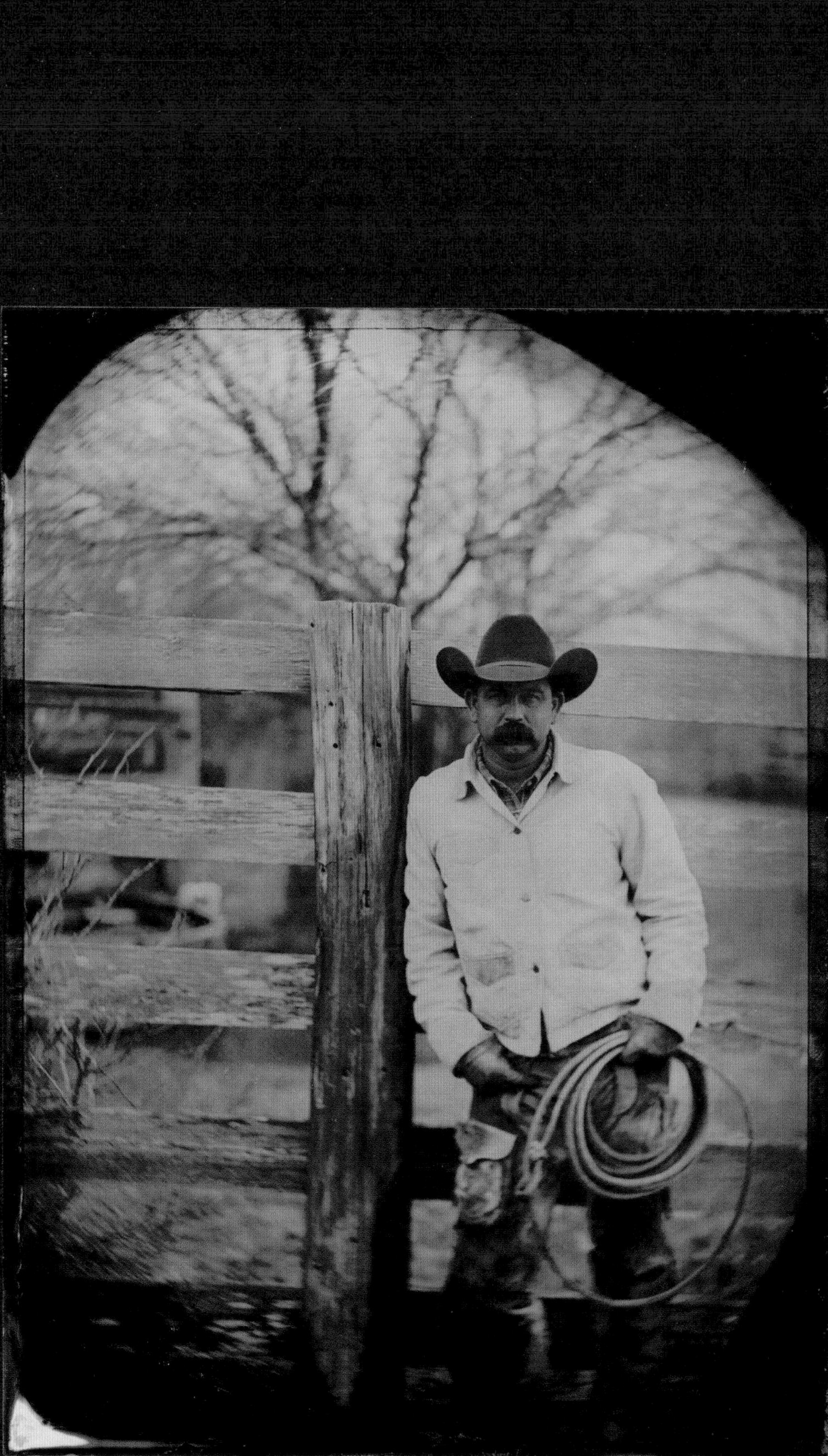

PHOTOGRAPHER'S PREFACE

by ROBB KENDRICK

When THIS PROJECT CAME TOGETHER 18 MONTHS AGO, I WAS ENTHUSIASTIC ABOUT THE CHANCE TO CAPTURE WORKING COWBOYS AT THE START OF THE 21ST CENTURY USING A PHOTOGRAPHIC PROCESS THAT DATES BACK TO THE EARLY DAYS OF RANCHING IN TEXAS. THE POINT OF THIS PROJECT HAS NOT BEEN TO ROMANTICIZE THE COWBOY AND TRANSPORT HIM BACK TO THE 19TH CENTURY, BUT TO DOCUMENT THOSE WHO STILL CARRY ON THE TRADITIONS, VALUES, AND LIFESTYLES THAT MANY TODAY WOULD FIND ISOLATING, LONELY, OR SIMPLY TOO HARD.

The images in this book represent a small percentage of the people I photographed while driving 18,000 miles through Texas. Even though I'm a visual person, it was important to me to include the cowboys' stories along with their images. I wanted readers of the book to enjoy the photographs while meeting these very special people, focusing on one person at a time, to reflect the experience I had with the subjects when shooting in the tintype process. This process, which dates back to the dawn of photography, is slow and requires patience and commitment from both the subject and the photographer.

My biggest regret now that I've concluded the project is that each and every person I photographed cannot be included in the book or exhibition. They all deserve to be part of this, but the reality of book editing and exhibition curating dictated the cuts. I know that those not included will understand, as they are accustomed to tough realities in their own lives. My second and only other regret is missing many great cowboys. I would have loved to have met them, heard their stories, and photographed them.

As I went along, I came to realize that the tintype process was the perfect approach to photographing the cowboys for reasons I hadn't imagined. The nature of tintype-making resonates with them in ways digital photography never can. Photographers had visited many of the ranches before. I was told by more than one cowboy, "Most photographers are nice people, but a little high maintenance—always telling you how to pose, do this, do that." When I drove up to each ranch carrying a camper in my truck and pulling a 12-ft. trailer, which houses my portable darkroom, I'm sure I looked like a squatter. The cowboys probably weren't sure what they had signed on for.

The process, described later in the book, builds an intimate relationship between photographer and subject. Posing for a tintype requires more time than modern point-and-shoot photography and instructions must be followed carefully—"hold still for seven seconds," "try not to blink"—or the photo can be ruined. It's a dance like no other that I have experienced in 21 years as a photographer. The fact that no two plates are ever the same speaks to the individuality of each cowboy I met, the handmade aspects of the process, and the variances of the 19th-century lenses I use.

In most cases the cowboys leaned on a wall, a post, or whatever we could find to steady them. With the long

PRECEDING PAGE: SAMMY FALCON, KING RANCH

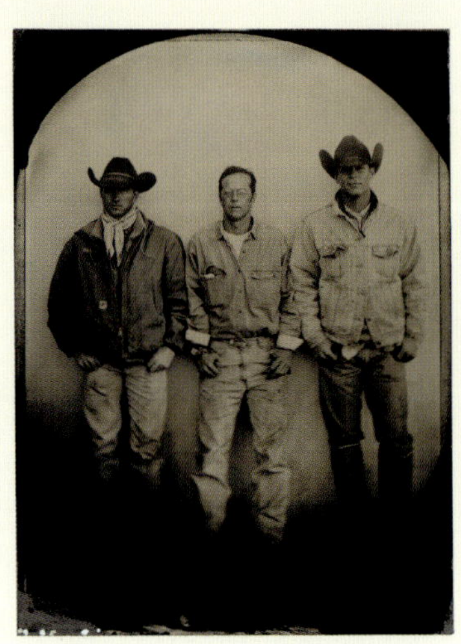

"They define the highest qualities of character: honesty, incredible work ethic, self-reliance, and a respect for the wonders of the unflinching nature they deal with year-in and year-out trying to eke out a living as cowboys."

exposures, steadiness is a must. I gave very little, if any, art direction, and I never styled anyone. Every person conveyed his own sense of style in what he chose to wear and how he wore it. Cowboy hats—which essentially define the man—are probably the most distinctive piece of attire, with each person creasing his hat to his own particular taste. Hats can also have a regional flair, such as the "taco hat"—curled up brims like a taco—seen widely in the Panhandle.

After exposing the tintype plates, I invited each person into the darkroom trailer to see the developing process. Those who could stand the smells of the chemicals came in for several looks. Invariably, everyone was interested in and stunned by what he saw. When the plate is taken out of the last water bath, under amber darkroom lights, it is a bluish plate resembling a negative. Then, under normal lights, I put it in a clear tank of potassium cyanide. The magical moment comes when, within 30 seconds, the blue plate is transformed into a positive image, almost always eliciting a gasp or a "Wow!" I'm pleased many of them felt the same sense of wonder I do every time I put a plate in the cyanide. Even after shooting some 3,000 tintype plates, it's still amazing to me. Many of the cowboys were glad to see that I struggled to make each plate, that it was not an automated process. One observed, echoing the sentiments of others, "What you're doing is a lot like what we're doing. It's not the easiest way to get the job done, but it's probably a lot more rewarding." The sense of being accepted by these people and the respect that I was given were incredibly satisfying—particularly because I have so much respect for them and their work. I've never been around people as a whole who love life and family more, and are more tolerant and considerate of others, than cowboys. They define the highest qualities of character: honesty, incredible work ethic, self-reliance, and a respect for the wonders of the unflinching nature they deal with year-in and year-out trying to eke out a living as cowboys.

I grew up in a small Texas town in the Panhandle, and have photographed on several of the big Texas outfits for more than 20 years. I've heard a lot of people say that cowboys are a dying breed, that they won't be here much longer. After completing this project, I beg to differ. Cowboys are evolving with the times. No, things aren't done the way they were in the 19th century, and, yes, many cowboys have cell phones and satellite TV. But even though they may choose to make their lives a bit easier and more efficient, cowboying still tests a man each day. Boots O'Neal of the 6666 Ranch, a 72-year-old cowboy, talked to me about times before the introduction of the gooseneck trailer, crew-cab trucks, and roads that cut through the ranches. "Gathering a pasture and branding might take eight to 12 cowboys three days; now we can do it after dinner in five hours or so. That's not bad; it's just evolution." Ranching has become more efficient, but replacing the cowboy will be tough to do. If you've seen some of the rough country that the cowboys work, you'll understand that there will be no substitute for a man on horseback to round up cattle. And there will be no shortage of men and women eager to fill the shoes of those who retire. When you read the thoughts of young kids like Chance Stout or Gage Moorhouse, you quickly realize that the current generation is passing on a life that still means something to kids who have been lucky enough to grow up on a place that spans 300 square miles or more. They are the ones determined to carry the torch forward. I hope they keep passing it on for generations to come.

THIS PAGE: JIM TACKETT, ROBB KENDRICK AND KC GREEN, SPIKEBOX RANCH FOLLOWING PAGE: BUBBA SMITH, TONGUE RIVER RANCH

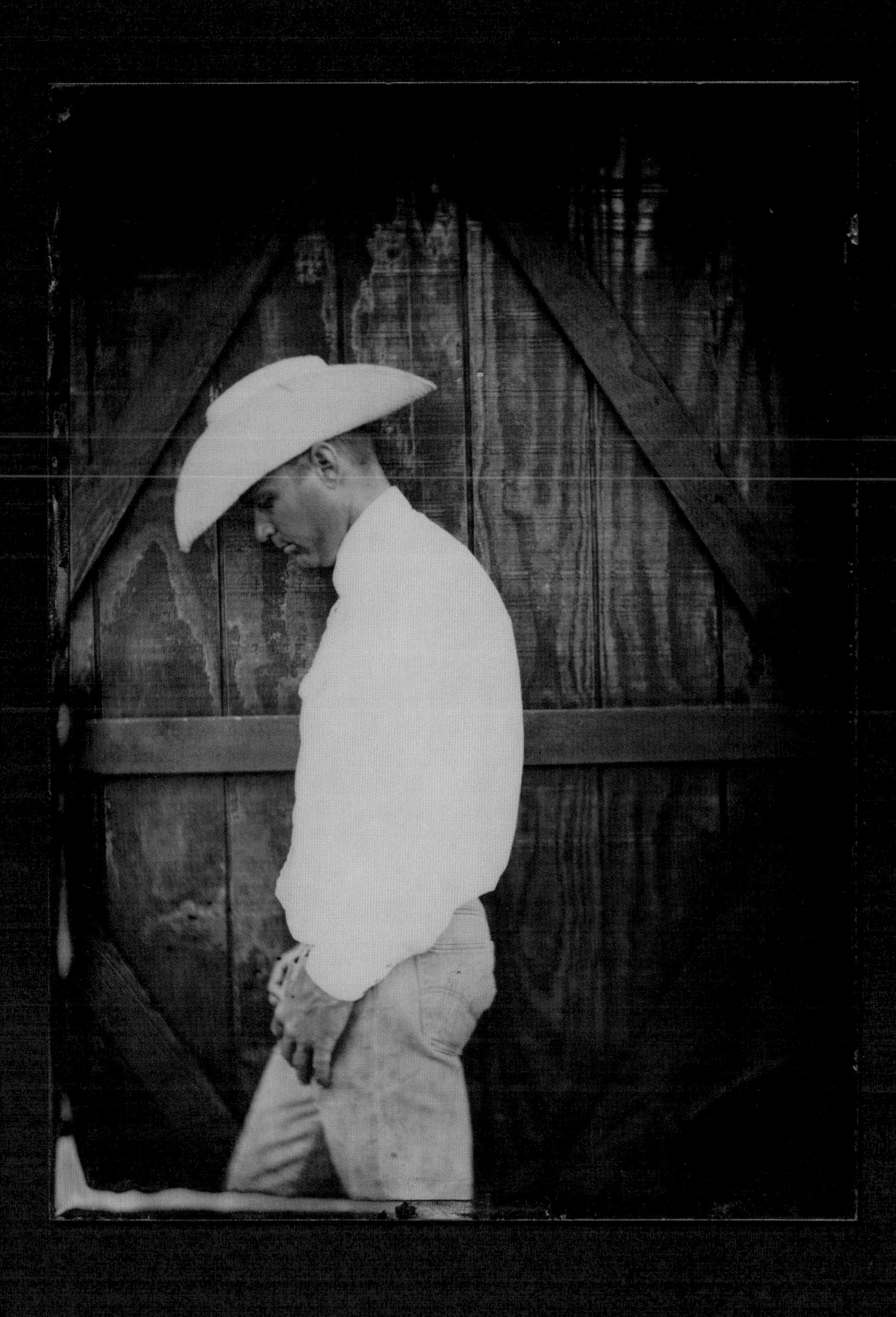

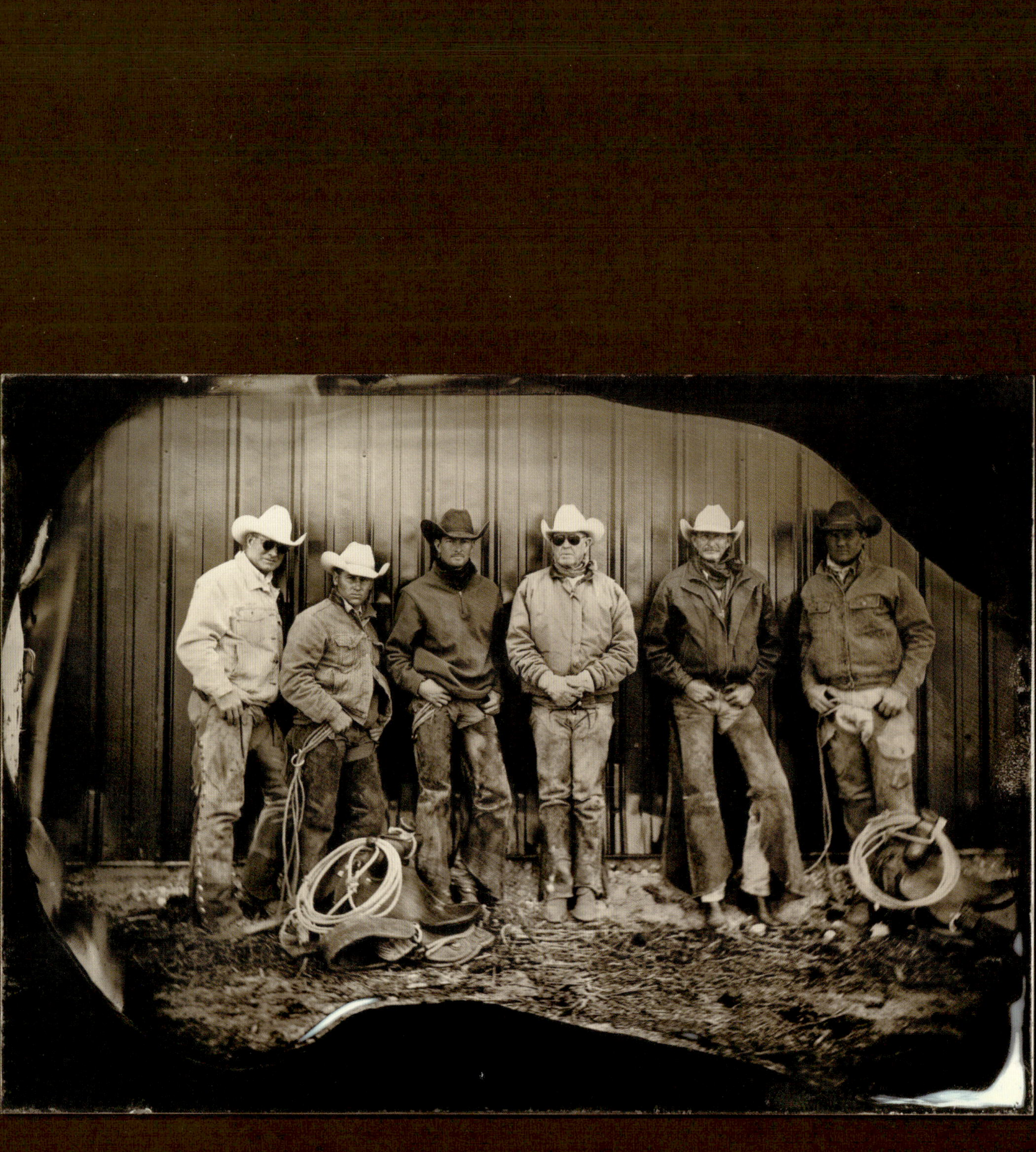

ASPECT & ESSENCE

by JOHN GRAVES

When I WAS GROWING UP IN FORT WORTH IN THE 1920S AND '30S, OIL AND ITS LORE AND ITS PEOPLE WERE WELL ALONG TOWARD STATUS AND EVEN ROMANCE IN THE PUBLIC'S MIND. BUT CATTLE AND THOSE WHO TENDED THEM, RANCHERS AND COWBOYS, WERE MUCH MORE WARMLY REGARDED, FOR THERE WAS STILL A PERVASIVE AWARENESS THAT, AS THE OLD SENTIMENTAL VERSE HAD PUT IT, "TEXAS GREW FROM HIDE AND HORN."

The city had definitely grown in that way, having served as a way station and supply point for the huge trail herds of longhorns pointed toward Kansas and beyond in open-range times, and having possessed its full share of rowdy saloons, prostitutes, gamblers, and tough men on both sides of the law, who were adept at using Colt's revolvers and other weapons on one another.

By my time, of course, the trail herds and most of that colorful violence were history. But the city, while tamed down, was still essentially a cow town, with a stockyards area on what was always called "the North Side," to which West Texas ranchers shipped great numbers of cattle by rail, and large packing plants where many of the animals were converted into meat. The smell of that neighborhood enveloped just about the whole city at intervals during winter when northerly fronts blew in, but most of us got used to it.

There were always cowboys on the North Side, seeking fun after their rail-borne charges had been delivered, and thus there were also plenty of the kinds of places that furnished such fun, if with a minimum of gunfire. The annual rodeo was held out there, and its participants were likely to be real working cowhands from the ranches, rather than the rodeo professionals of today.

In such an atmosphere, many of us Fort Worth kids grew up with horses and cattle and lariats on our minds. When we played cowboy, while we might stage a few cap gun battles in emulation of Tom Mix and other early heroes of the silver screen, we also had a sense of the actualities of ranch life and its tasks. We wore out our share of cotton-clothesline lassos on fence posts, dogs, cats, cars, and one another. And as adolescents, old enough not to be liabilities for ranch and farm owners, we often had low-paying summertime country jobs, the best of which involved a little horseback herding and corral work, though not on a basis of equality with the capable riders and ropers—some not much older than we—who really knew what they were doing. These were heirs to an array of skills coming down from three or four hundred years of open-range grazing in Mexico and the Caribbean, and later in Texas and the whole West up to Canada. On the whole, they were a leathery lot, and some were a bit bowlegged from long years in the saddle. They were proud men because they were good at what they did, regardless of the pay.

In more recent years, with the advent of squeeze chutes, calf cradles, improved fencing patterns, and other innovations, the era of true cowboy skills has been winding

PRECEDING PAGE: GEORGE BRUTON, LUKE LUCERO, MATT JENNINGS, BOB HOLLOWELL, JOE LEATHERS & JARED JEWKES, 6666 RANCH DIXON CREEK

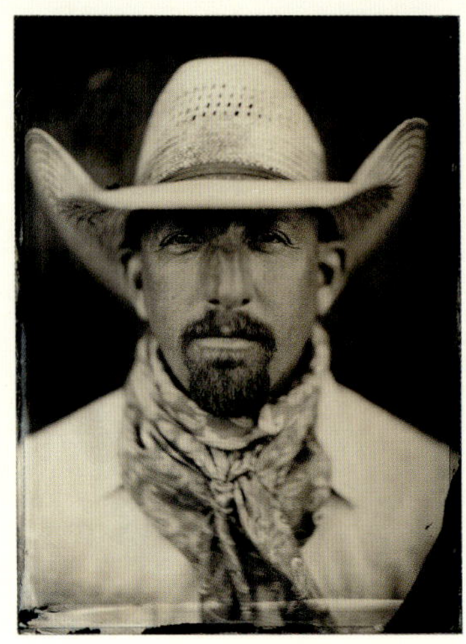

"Their faces are not 21st century faces, those of people who get their pleasures watching games and manipulating electronic gadgets, and who work...for corporations in jam-packed office buildings, pecking at computers each day."

down, but it refuses to die. Few if any ranches these days hire the sizable contingents of hands that were standard during my youth and for many years before that. But when such skillful folk are needed, as they often are—especially in the rough country to which much ranching has been relegated as smoother Western terrain has increasingly been turned over to tractors and plows and spray-irrigation systems—they are still available, and are valued.

At demanding times, when steers are being corralled and loaded and shipped (mainly now in 18-wheelers) or calves are being brought in for branding, castration, dehorning, doctoring, and shots against disease, a lot of the competent help a ranch receives comes from other nearby ranches' operators and their families, including capable women and girls, a favor that will be repaid when they themselves have need of assistance.

And much also comes from "hired men on horseback," working cowboys who, despite all the changes, do still exist. Most grew up in ranch families and have stayed with the life because it is what they know and like. Not many these days are bowlegged unless they were born that way, for they spend more time in pickups than saddles and have done much fence and windmill work. Great prosperity does not loom in their futures unless they happen to excel at the rodeo game. But when the ancient skills are called for, they have them, and they feel the same satisfied pride in having them that the old-timers felt.

Robb Kendrick, a cameraman as qualified in his occupation as these cow people are in theirs, has rendered their portraits not on film or digitally but using the laborious nineteenth-century medium of tintype, with results that are reproduced in this handsome book. Tintype was a startlingly appropriate choice, for it places strong emphasis on the link between Kendrick's subjects and their forerunners in open-range times of long ago. It is a link that exists in the minds of those subjects and it shows in their clothing and mien.

Their faces are not 21st century faces, those of people who get their pleasures watching games and manipulating electronic gadgets, and who work in factories or stores, or for corporations in jam-packed office buildings, pecking at computers each day. Kendrick's tintype portraits give us the faces of people who do physical outdoor labor that change throughout the year as the seasons and the weather dictate, labor with and for living creatures and the wide land itself.

The faces and the personalities they convey are quite varied, as those of any aggregation of human beings must necessarily be. Young, mature, old, male, female, Anglo, Hispanic... Some are impassive, but others look mean as hell, types you would not want to tangle with, while still others are clearly affable and outgoing, so that you know you could have a good talk with them if the chance arose.

Despite these differences, however, they have one big thing in common, and that is the work they do. In a sense the work is them and they are the work, able users of fencing tools and windmill wrenches and pickups and horses and lariats and corral chutes and calf-pullers and all the other things required for handling cattle in our times. They do it because it is what they know and they love it, nearly regardless of recompense and the parts of it they love best are those that link their horseback dexterity to those long centuries of ranching experience in the Americas.

Such people may well be obsolescent, ultimately to be supplanted by some form of the corporate and bureaucratic sameness toward which our era pushes everyone. But I hope that takes a long, long time to happen. Because I place high value on the kind of people they are, and I'm glad that they're still here. And that Robb Kendrick has so rightly preserved their aspect and their essence in these pictures.

THIS PAGE: JUSTIN JOHNSON, JA RANCH FOLLOWING PAGE: KIDS, JA RANCH

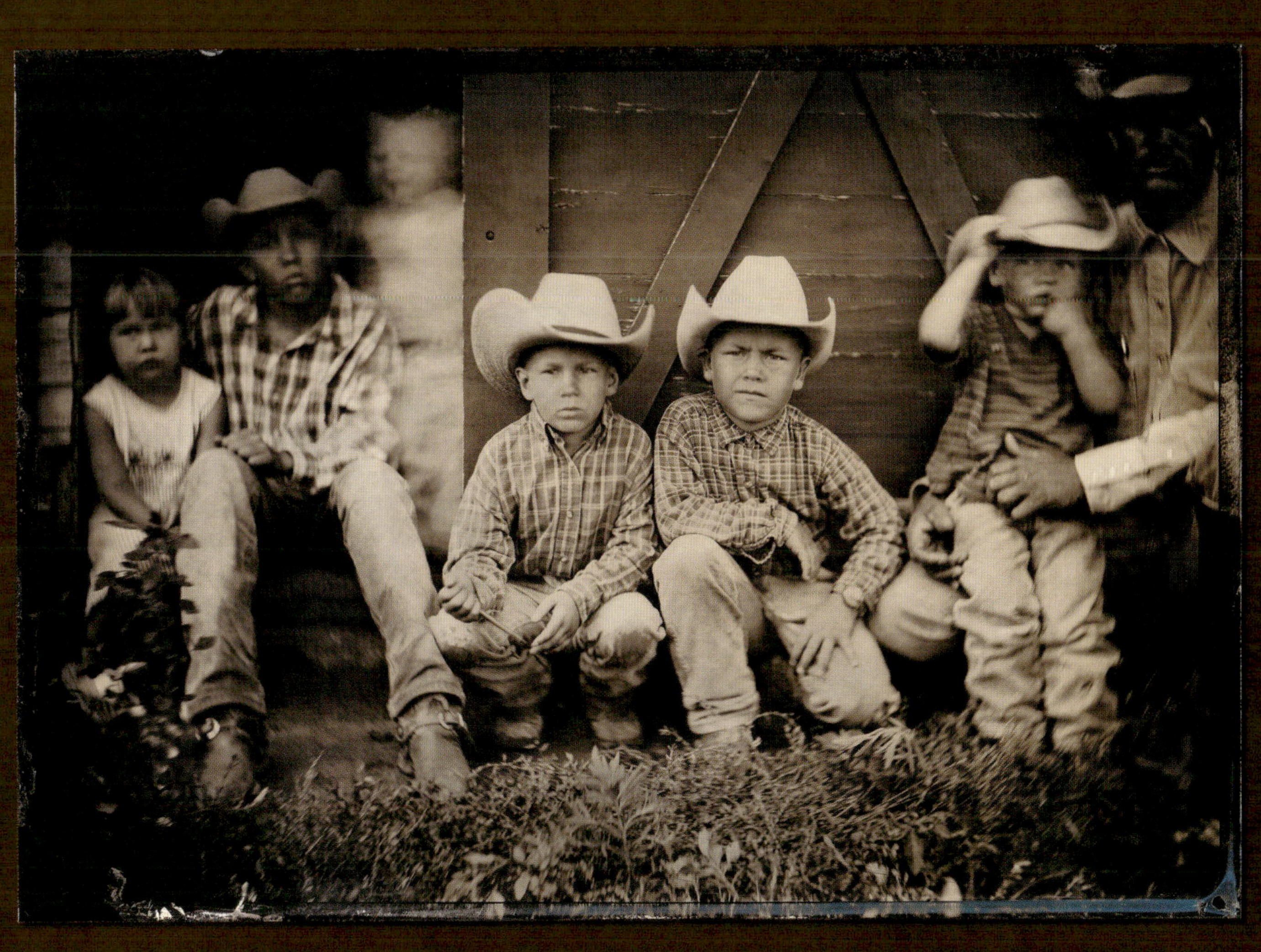

PLATES

by ROBB KENDRICK

FOLLOWING PAGE: BOB MOORHOUSE, PITCHFORK RANCH

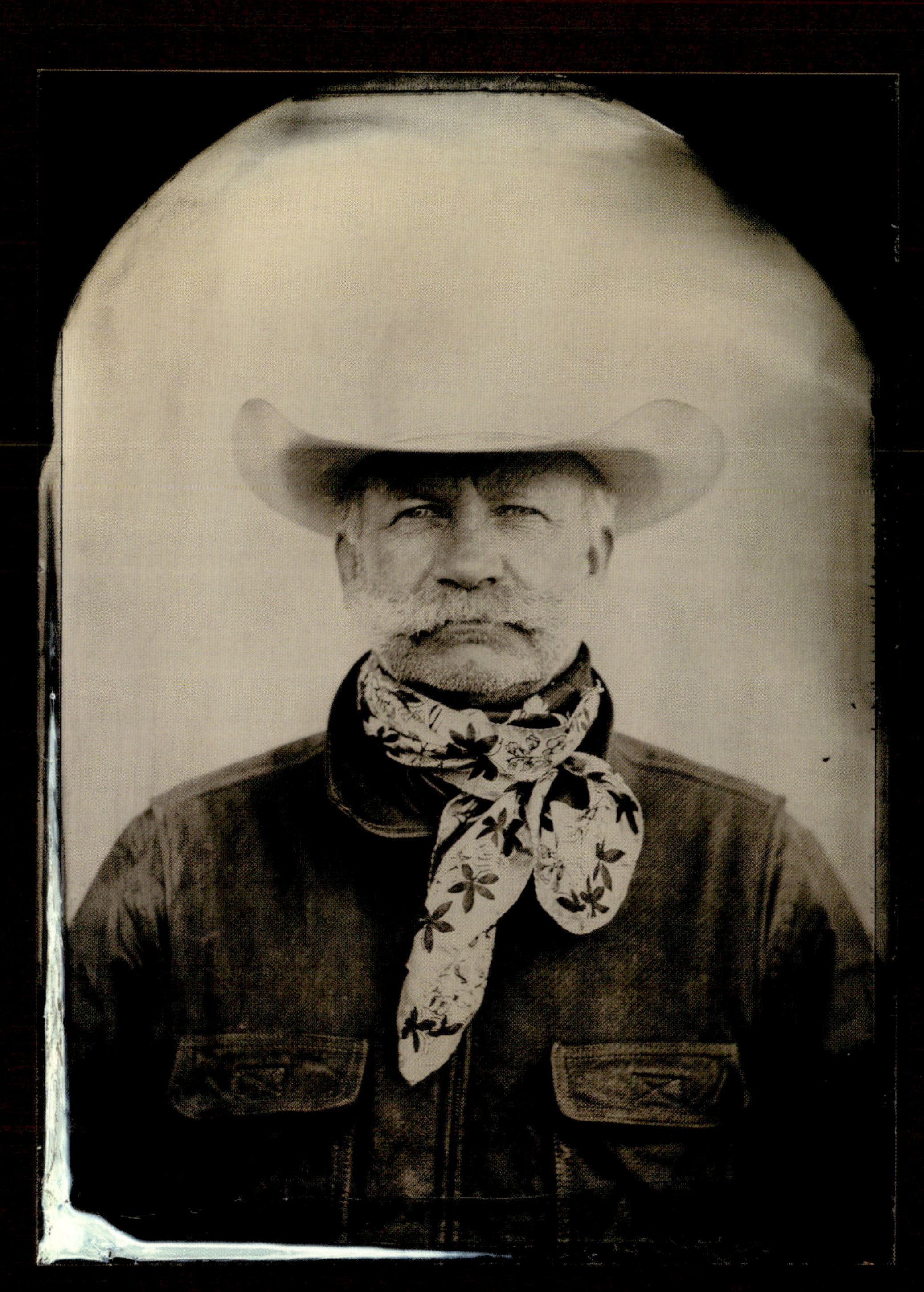

PLATE 01

JIM TACKETT

SPIKEBOX RANCH

Jim is 32 years old. Grew up day working. Always rode colts. He says he takes great pride in the work, so no matter if it's 110 degrees or 10 degrees, the job has got to be done, and done right. "Working with other great hands and joking around makes the hard work fly by."

"I won't have another job. I'm where I want to be."

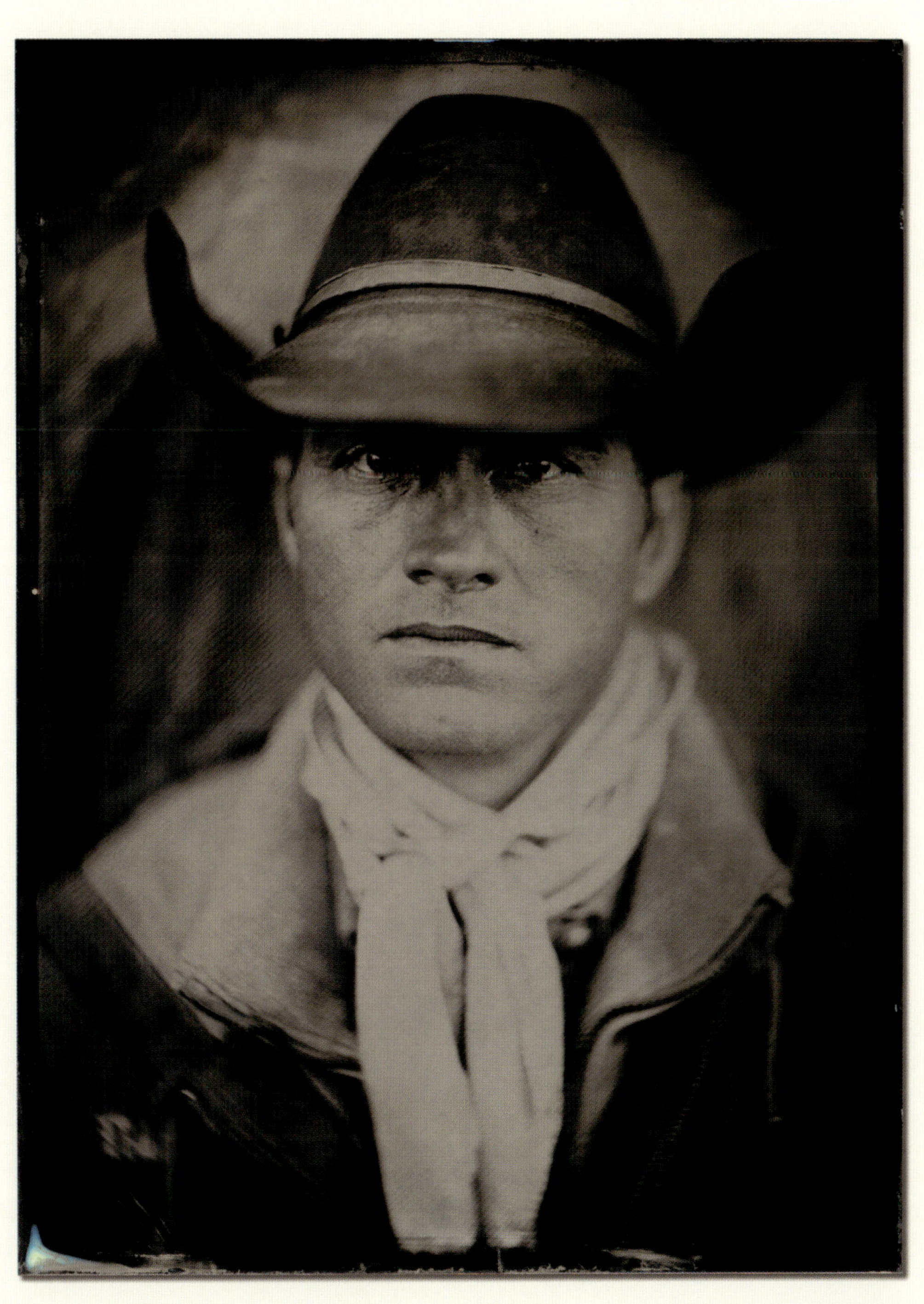

PLATE 02

IGNACIO HSANTILLAN

LONG X RANCH

Many consider the life of a cowboy to be a hard one, but not Ignacio.

"If you like this work, being outside with the cows and the beautiful mountains, it's not hard at all. Not even when it's cold or raining."

Find something you like, and then do it for the rest of your life, that's his motto. And it's something he'd like to impart to his three kids.

"I won't mind if one of them follows me into the cowboy life, as long as it's what they really want to do and it will make them happy."

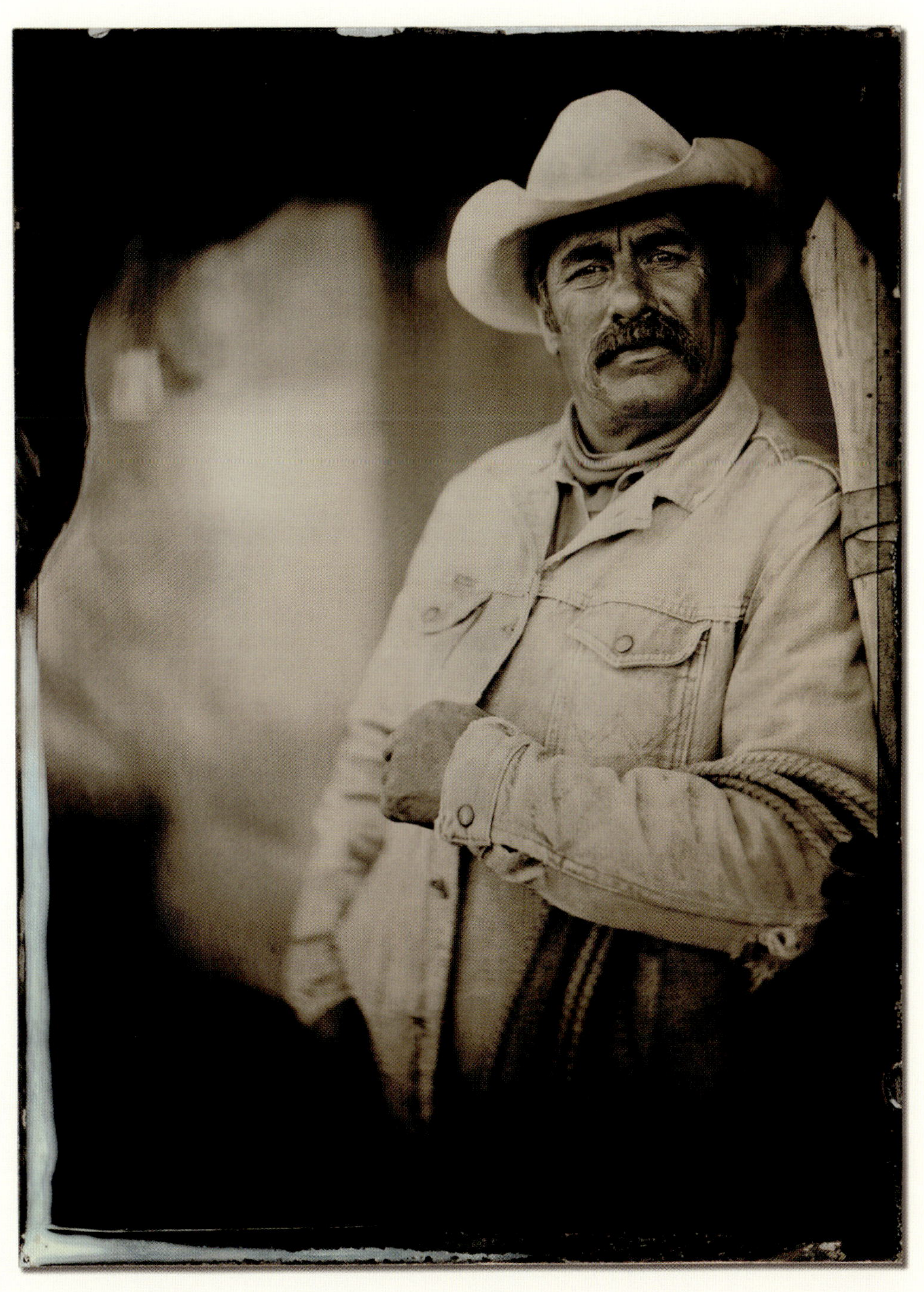

PLATE 03

TIM BYERLY

SILVERBROOK RANCH

Tim's 42, married, with a six-year-old son. Born and raised in Virginia; came to Texas at 27. He's been a cowboy for 20 years. He does it for a few simple, noble reasons.

"Ranching keeps me outside and horseback."

He never had ideas about making a ton of money. Figures this is the best way to raise his son and be close to the people he cares about.

"My wife rides with me; we do this as a family."

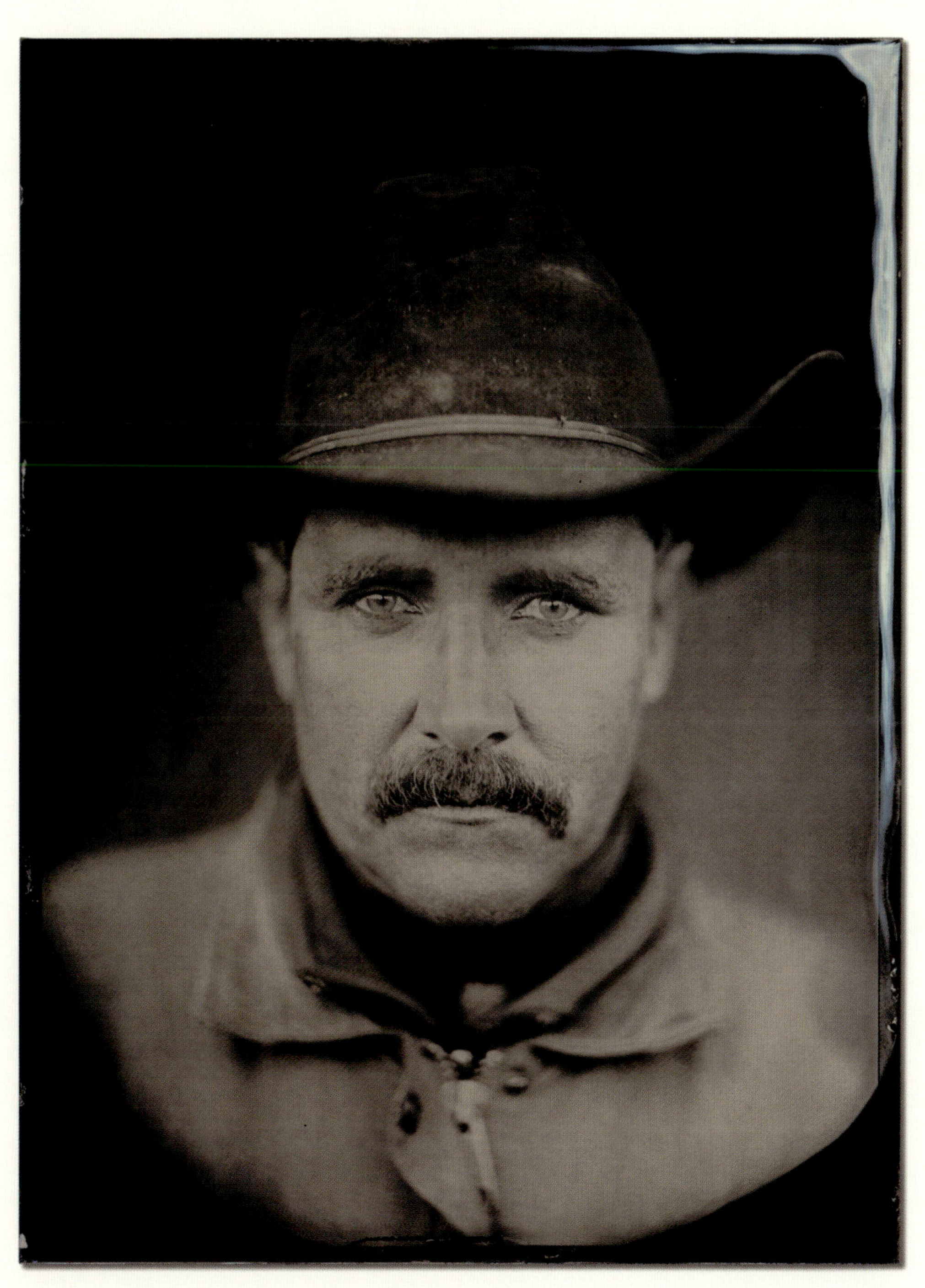

PLATE 04

JAMES GHOLSON

PITCHFORK RANCH

To James, wagon boss at the Pitchfork, cowboying is not something just anybody can do. You have to have a good head on your shoulders. "This is a large-scale, unpredictable routine that requires a lot of thinking."

The work is rough. "I'm greedy for punishment!" Says it was bred in him. But he'll tolerate the hard work to enjoy spring.

"Spring replenishes you, seeing colts looking at the future. It's like you get a new lease on life."

He says the best place to be during tough times is in a saddle. "You can forget about your troubles when you're on a good horse."

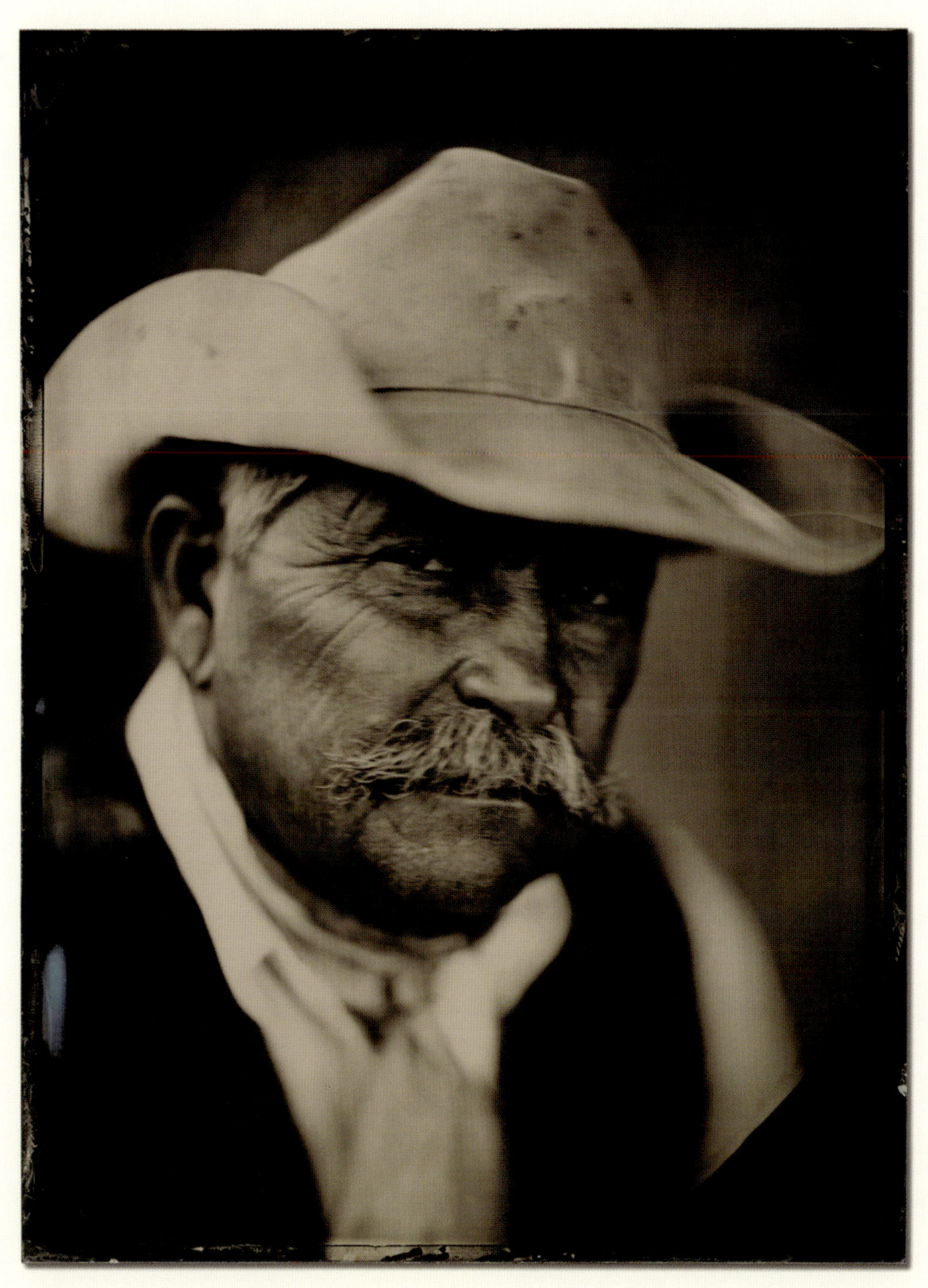

PLATE 05

RICKY CLARK

LONG X RANCH

Ricky has been on a ranch since he was born. "It's my life. I don't know anything else and don't want to know anything else."

Tradition runs deep in his family. "My boys are both cowboys. They're 23 and 21, and I couldn't be prouder of them. My boys are the fifth generation of cowboys. It's true blood."

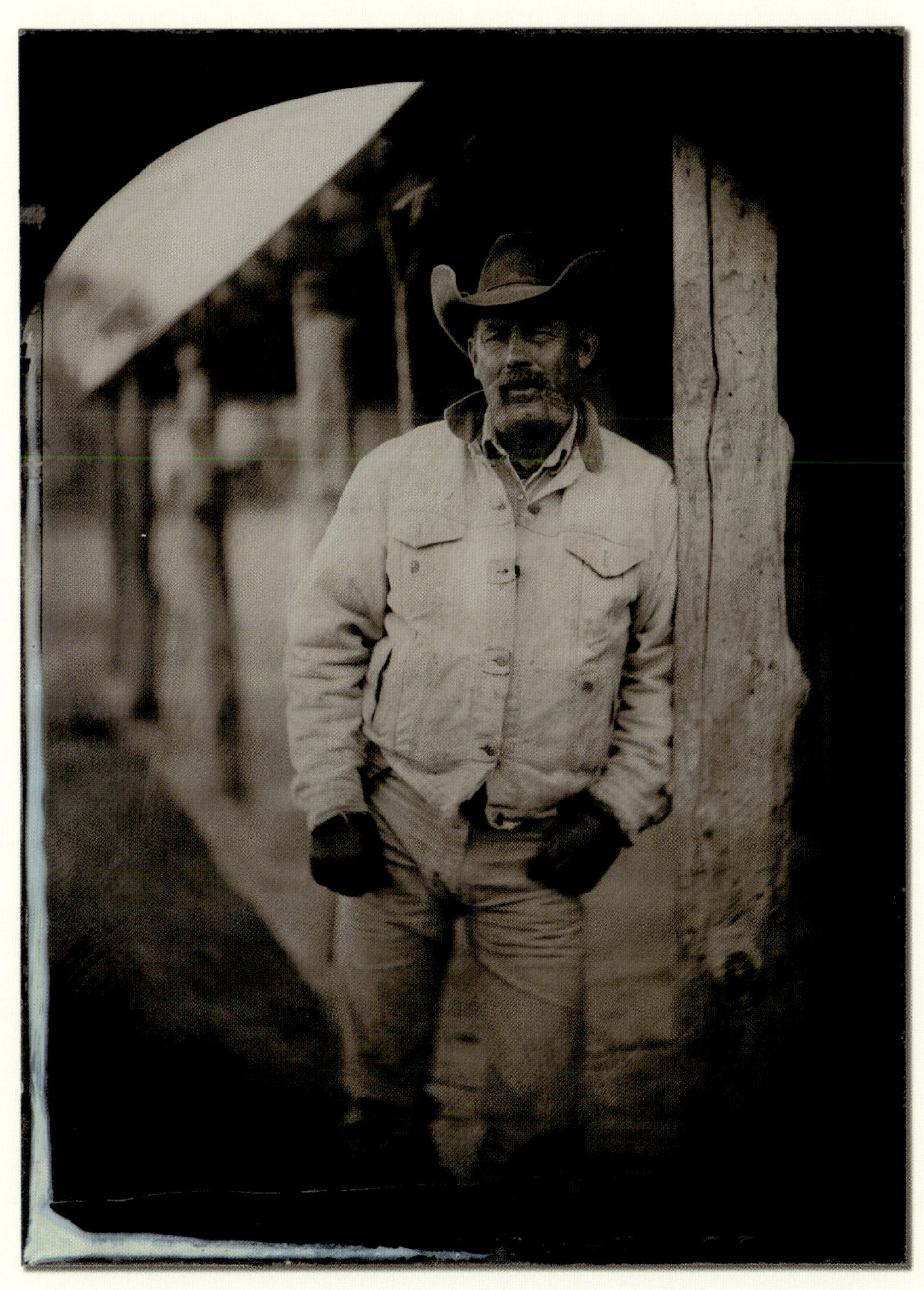

PLATE 06

MIKE SHEEDY

SPIKEBOX RANCH

As ranch manager of Spikebox Ranch, Mike says no matter what year it is, the traditions that cowboys have always upheld will be preserved and passed down through the generations.

"Time may change lots of things, but it can't change a lot of us. That's the way we feel about our way of life, and the things we do."

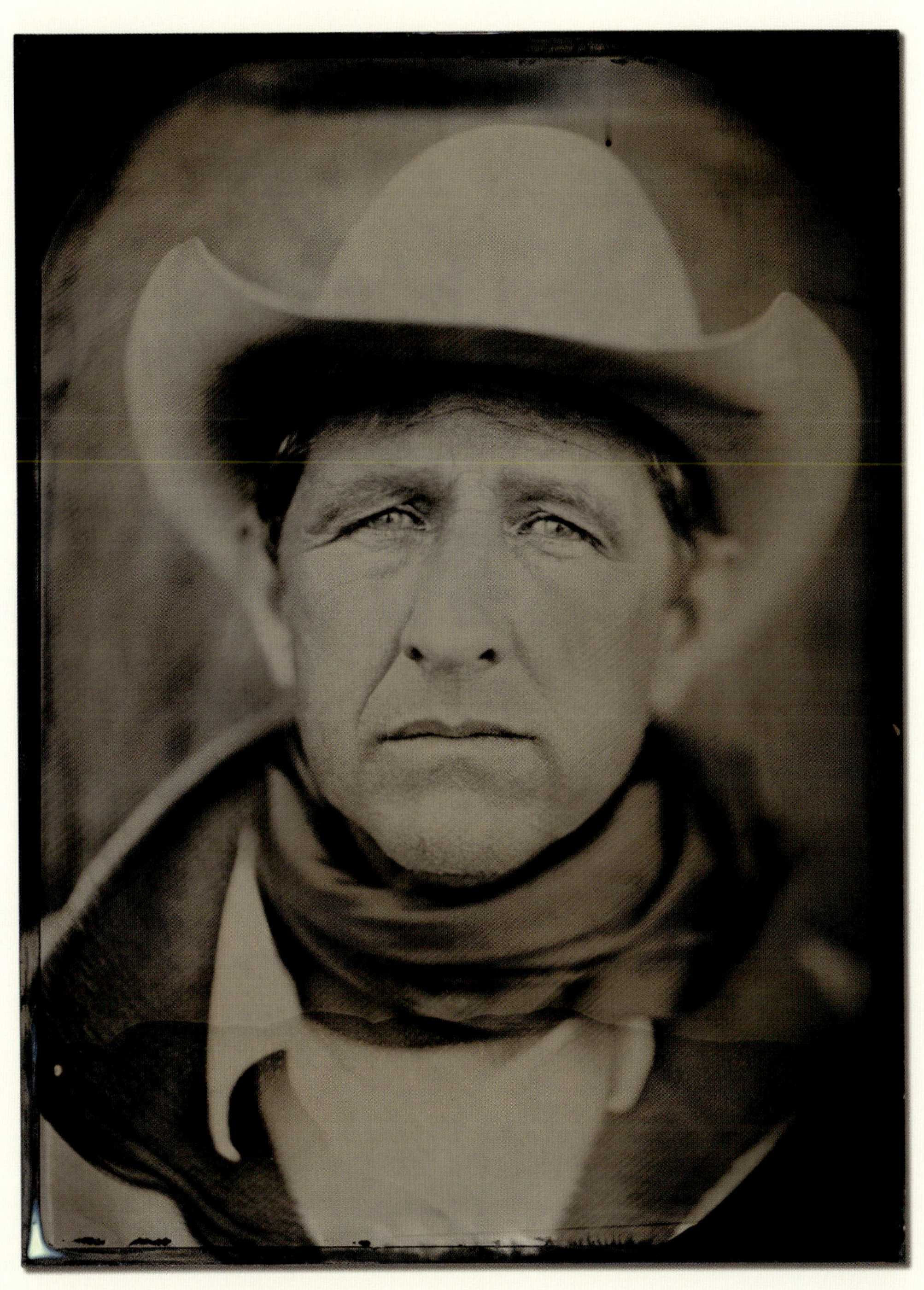

PLATE 07

JOHN FRAZIER

PITCHFORK RANCH

John looks for the good in a horse. "It makes the bad horses good, and the good horses better." He loves horses, and working with them always gives John a lot to think about. "I learn something from a horse every day. Just keep your mind open."

One thing he's learned is the value of hard work. "Hard work makes you a better person. Makes you think in a positive way and pays off in the long run, in obtaining goals you've set for yourself."

He says horses, just like cowboys, work hard. "They give you their all every day and expect little in return."

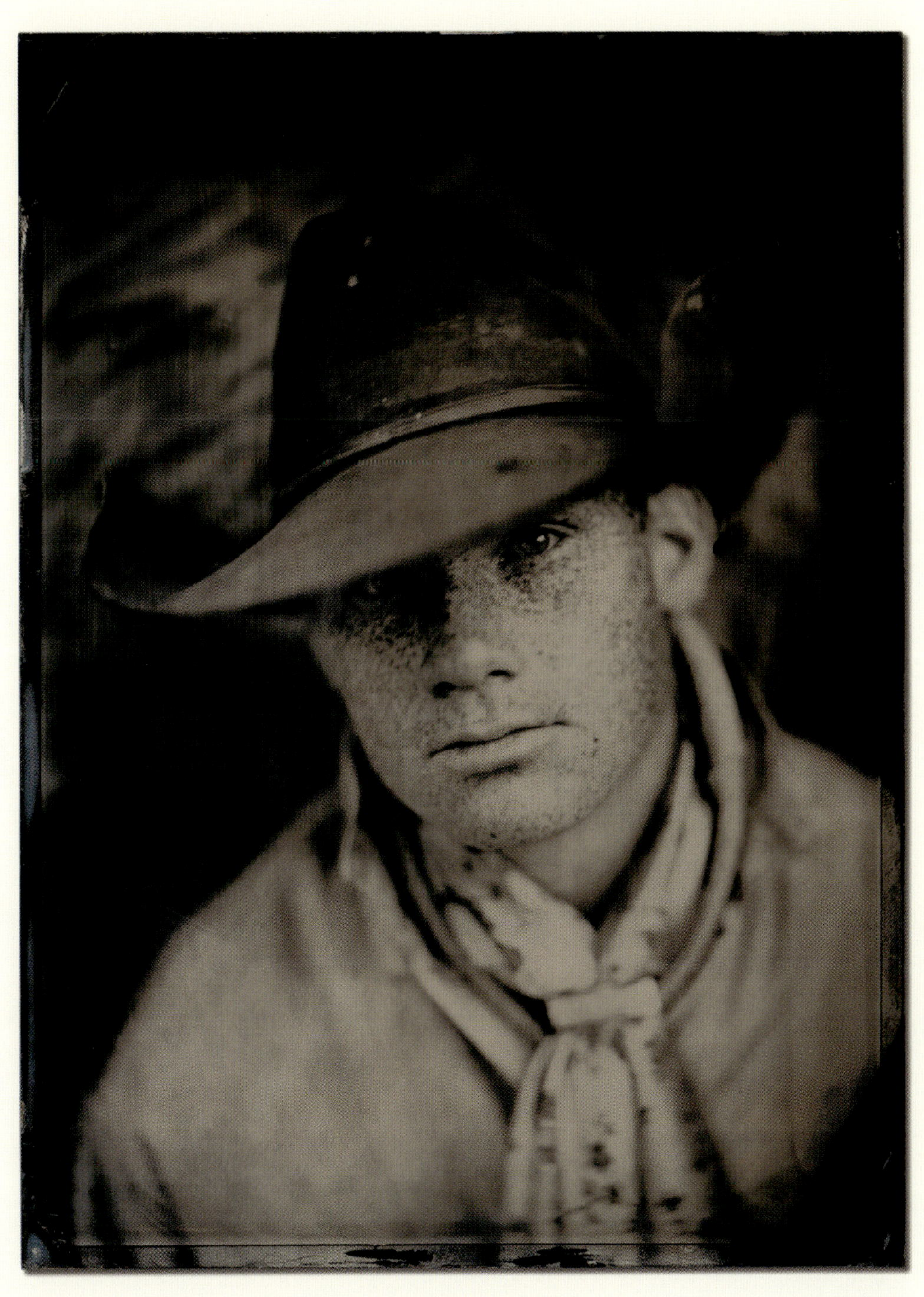

PLATE 08

R. D. HORN

JA RANCH

What does R. D. love the most about cowboying? "All the buckin' horse rides."

He has sustained a few minor scrapes, but he's okay. He was pawed by a horse while holstering up. After a day of driving cattle, a vet sewed him up; the next day he went out again on the drive. "To work with good men and riding good horses is not work. I hope the secret of cowpunching doesn't get out."

"Spent 90% of my adult life in a saddle, and in the process worn out a lot of jeans." Says he's at home in Texas.

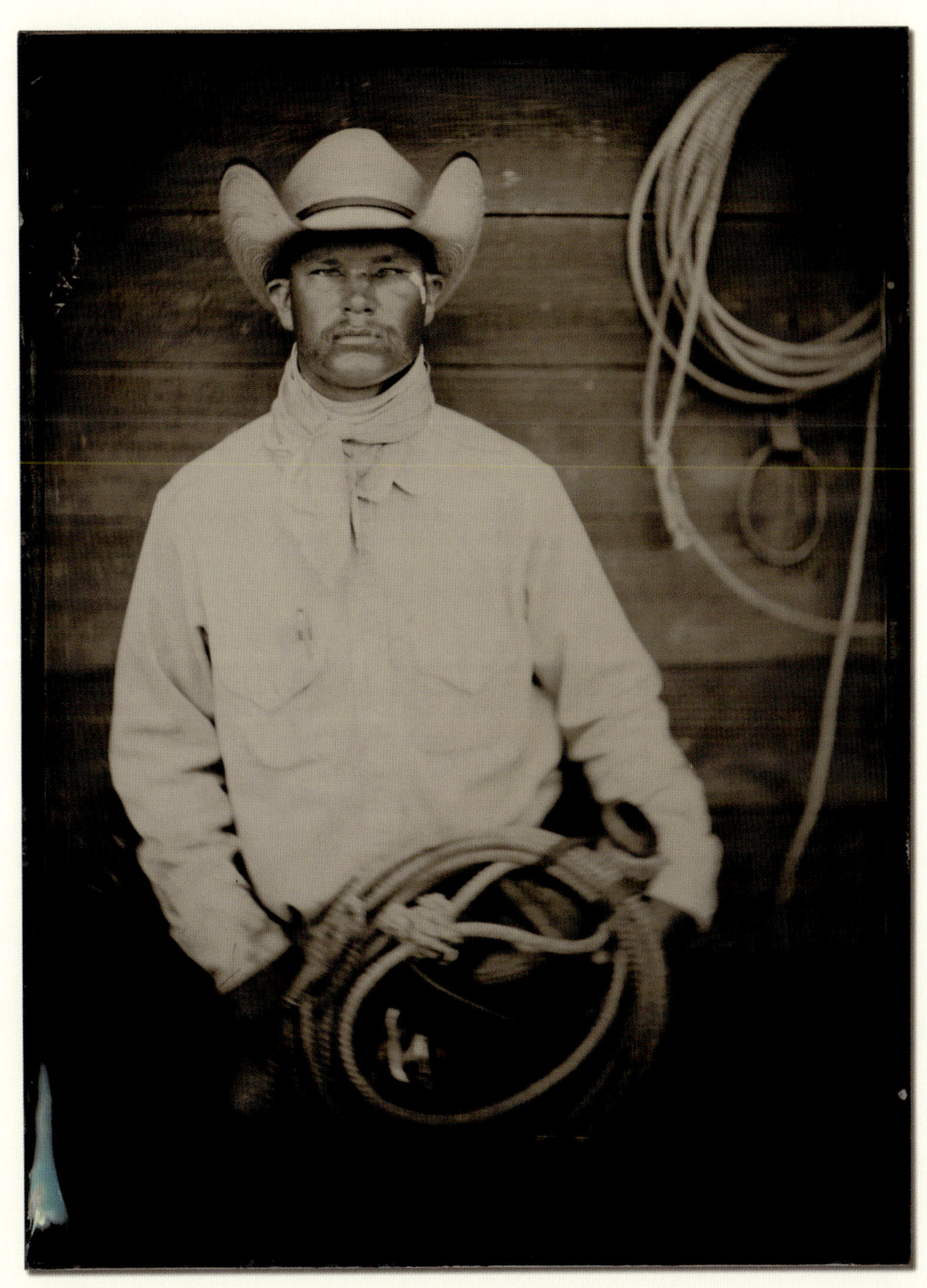

PLATE 09

BOOTS O'NEAL

6666 RANCH

Boots got his first job earning wages as a cowboy on the JA Ranch in 1949. "Back then we worked 360 days a year." He says some things about the job are easier now, but the traditions remain. "Gooseneck trailers and crew-cab trucks have changed the rhythm of working. With roads and such cut throughout much of the big cow outfits today, a job that might have taken three days now takes half a day. Cowboy crews are smaller because of this, but many things still have to be done the old way, which I enjoy."

He's 72, still working every day, riding, roping, and pulling his weight. "As long as I am a productive part of the crew, I want to stay. I don't hunt, fish, or play golf, so if I'm not working I don't know what I'd do." He's had other jobs.

"In my younger days I took a job as a brand inspector, kept it for three or four years. Pay was good, furnished nice clothes, a car, an expense account. But every time I finished work at one of the cow outfits and I saw the men ride off on their horses, I kept longing for the days I would have been right there with them. I had to get back in my car and drive off. One day I said, 'enough,' and went back cowpunching."

After 56 years, he still enjoys the life. "I go to bed looking forward to the next day's work."

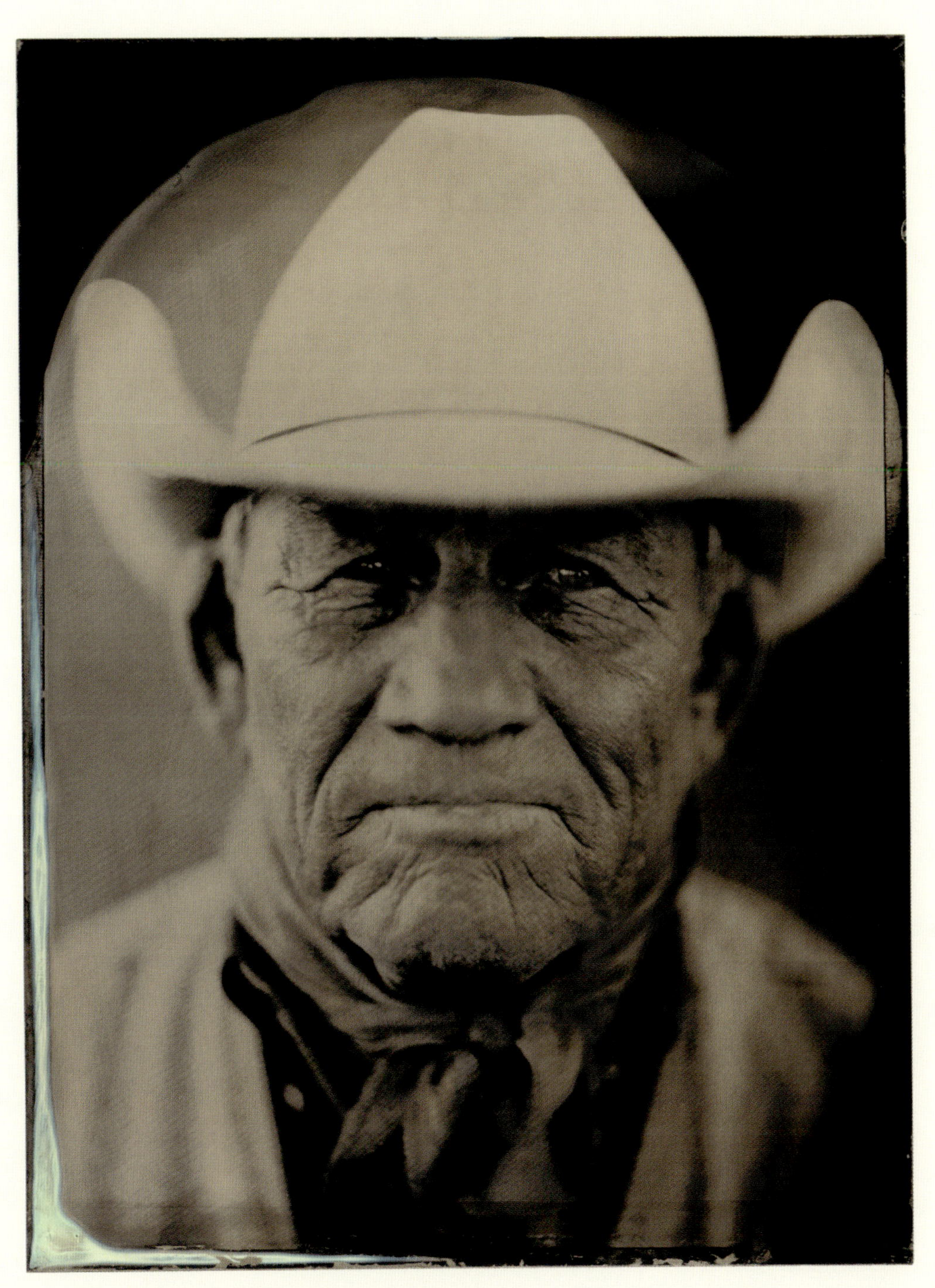

PLATE 10

ASHLEY DANIEL

6666 RANCH

Ashley was raised around ranch folks and credits her father with introducing her to the cowboy way of life. "I want to be like my dad. He passed away when I was 11. He was a hard-working man who let me work hard beside him and took me wherever he went. I want to do the same."

She says she wants to have a family, but she's not inclined to become a stay-at-home mom. "I want to have a family someday, but I want to work cattle and not be a cowboy's wife. I want to work with him."

"Hard work makes you feel good at the end of the day."

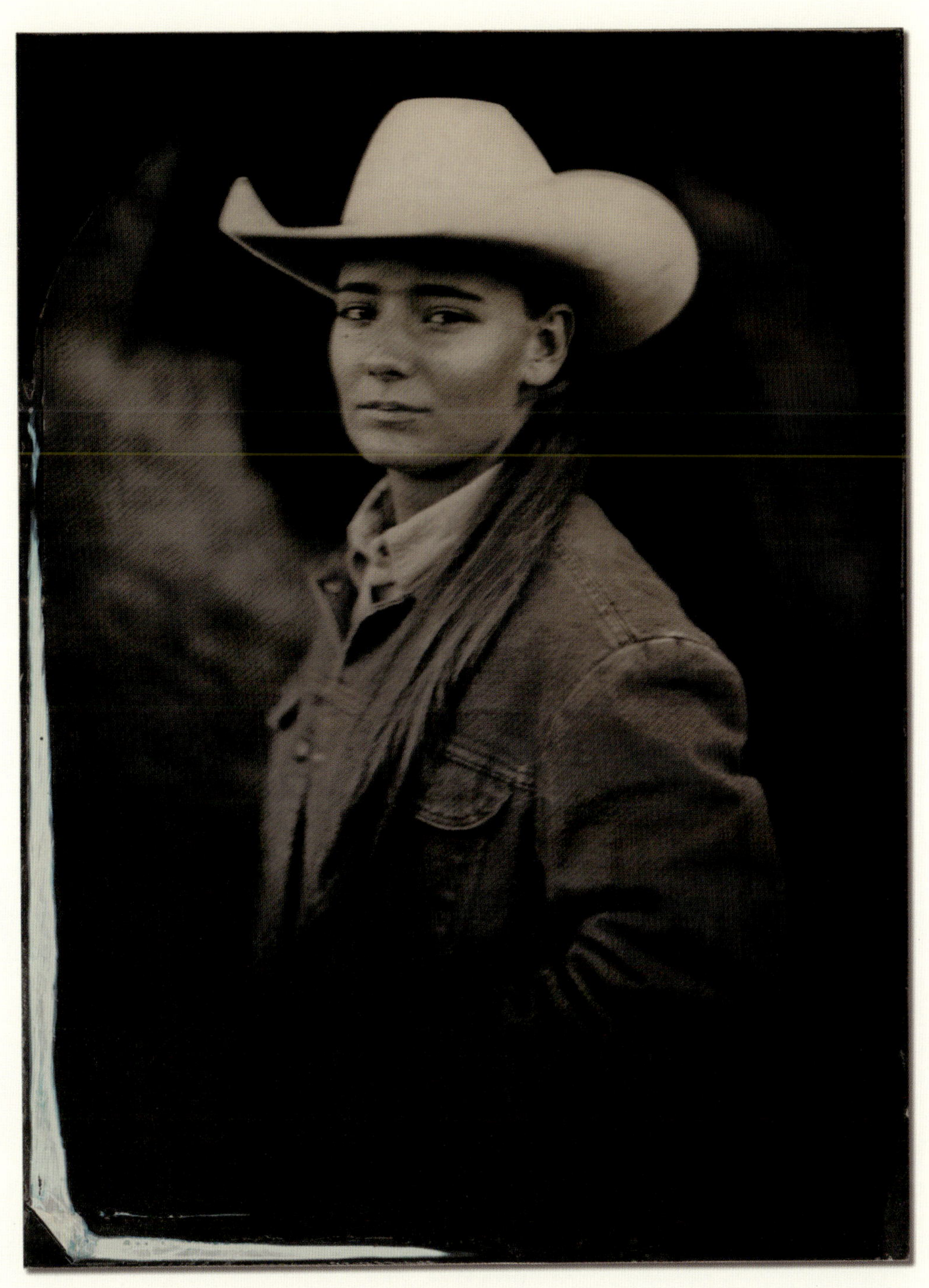

PLATE II

ELVAN GOODE

SILVERBROOK RANCH

Elvan enjoys being a cowboy. But his reason for doing it goes much deeper than personal enjoyment.

"I cowboy because it's a vanishing way of life."

Also, he says a ranch is just the greatest environment there is to bring up a family. "There's no better way to raise your kids than out here in the middle of God's creation. They learn to respect the land and the livestock, and I take great joy in that."

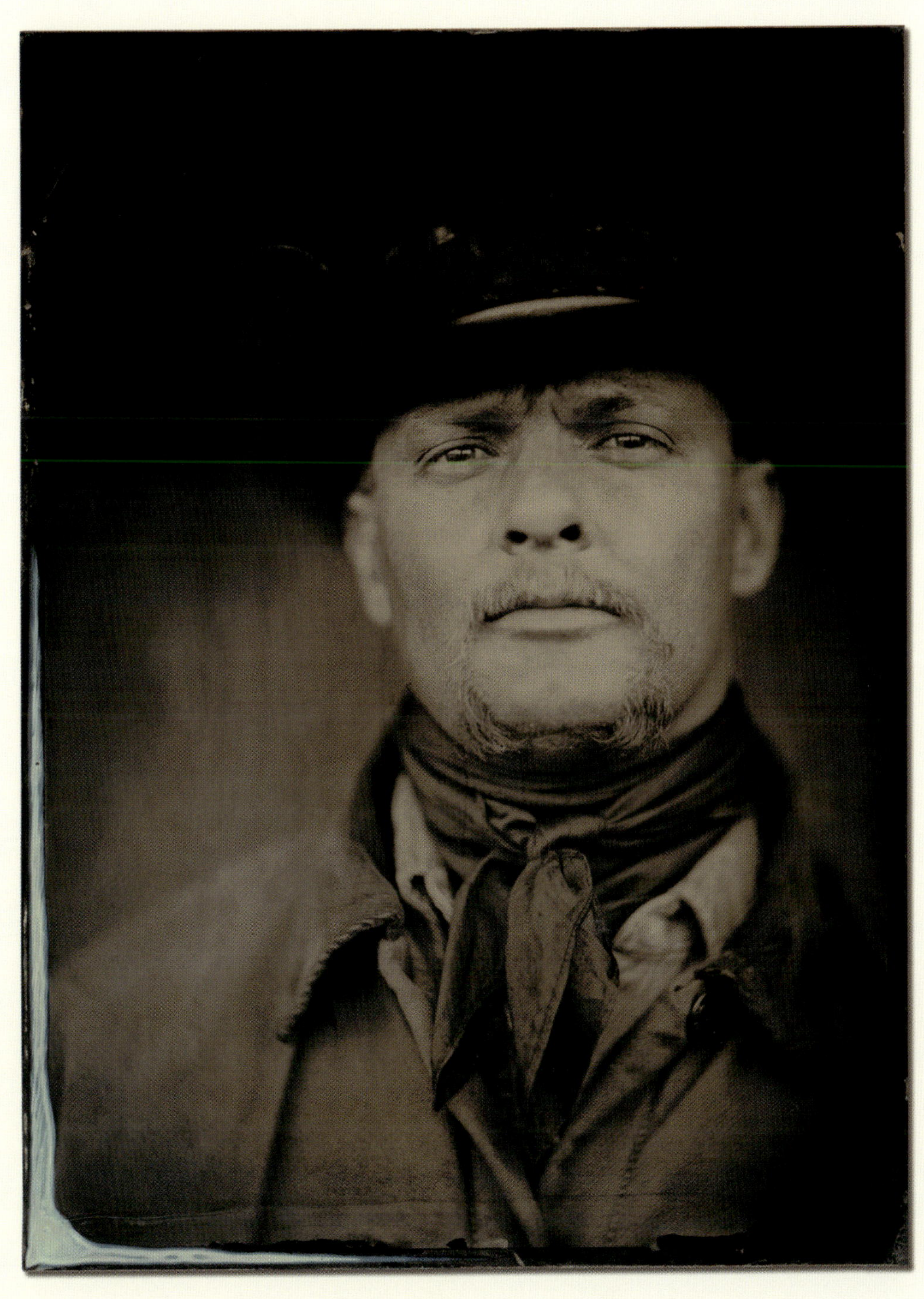

PLATE 12

JARED JEWKES

6666 RANCH DIXON CREEK

"I would have to say this is a great way to live a great life." For Jared, it really helps to have someone like his grandmother to look up to.

"My grandma runs a ranch in Dell City, Texas, where there just ain't much to grow but rocks, but she sure can keep her cows fed good. She can be rough and tough and sure let you know when you did wrong, but if it weren't for her I wouldn't be here today. I sure thank her for leading me into a great ranching lifestyle. If you ask me, there just ain't a better way of life."

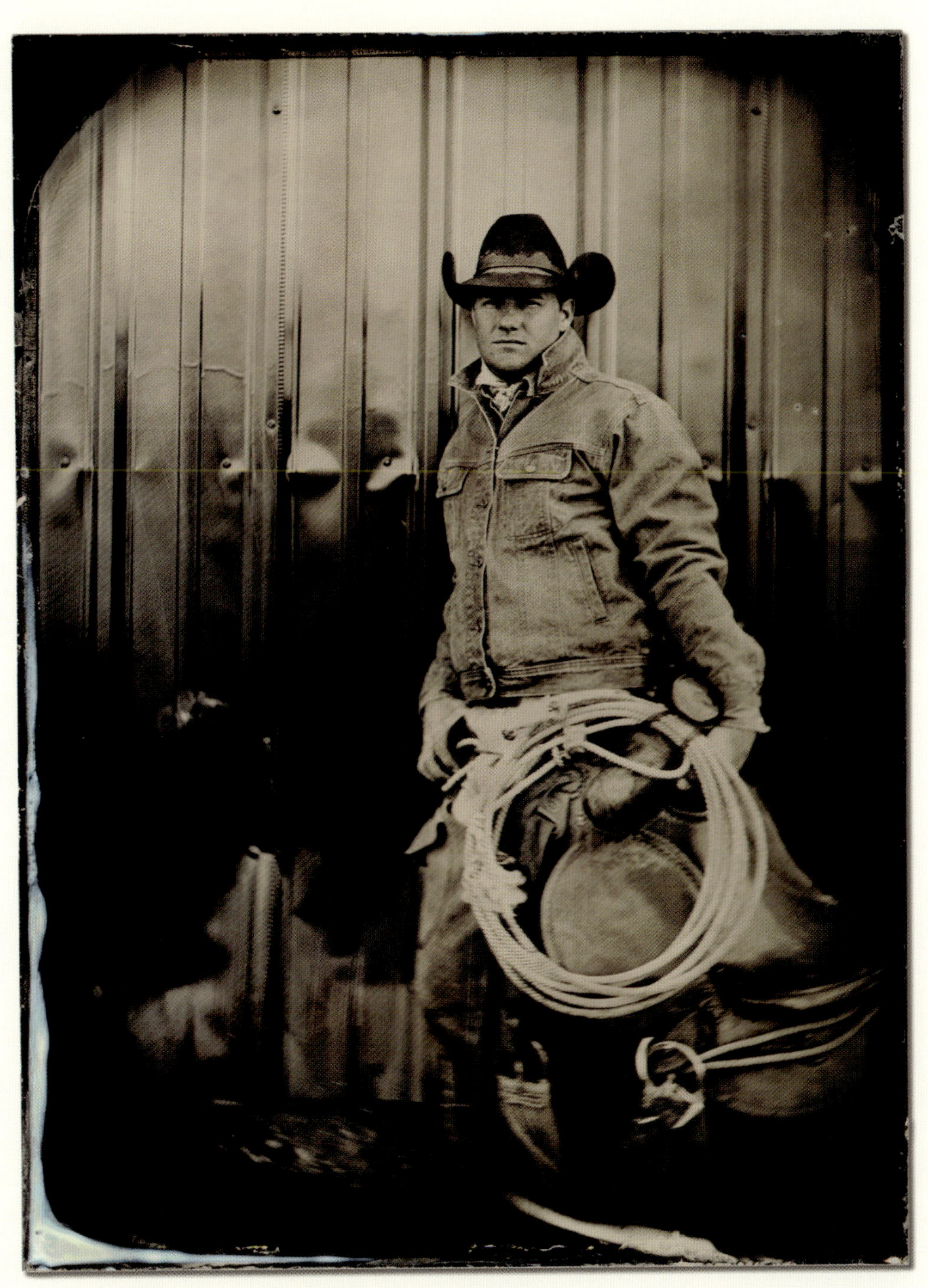

PLATE 13

ELIODORO PAZ

ARMSTRONG RANCH

Eliodoro says he decided to work on a ranch because he wanted to learn to ride a horse. "I've been here three years already and I love it. I enjoy rounding up cattle in the pastures because it is very challenging."

There are some downsides, though. "What I don't like is when the horse I am riding on gets spooked by a rattlesnake. That is very scary and dangerous."

To him, there's really no bad time to be on a ranch, but summer is not his favorite. "I prefer to work at the ranch during spring, fall, and winter months. During the summer it gets extremely hot."

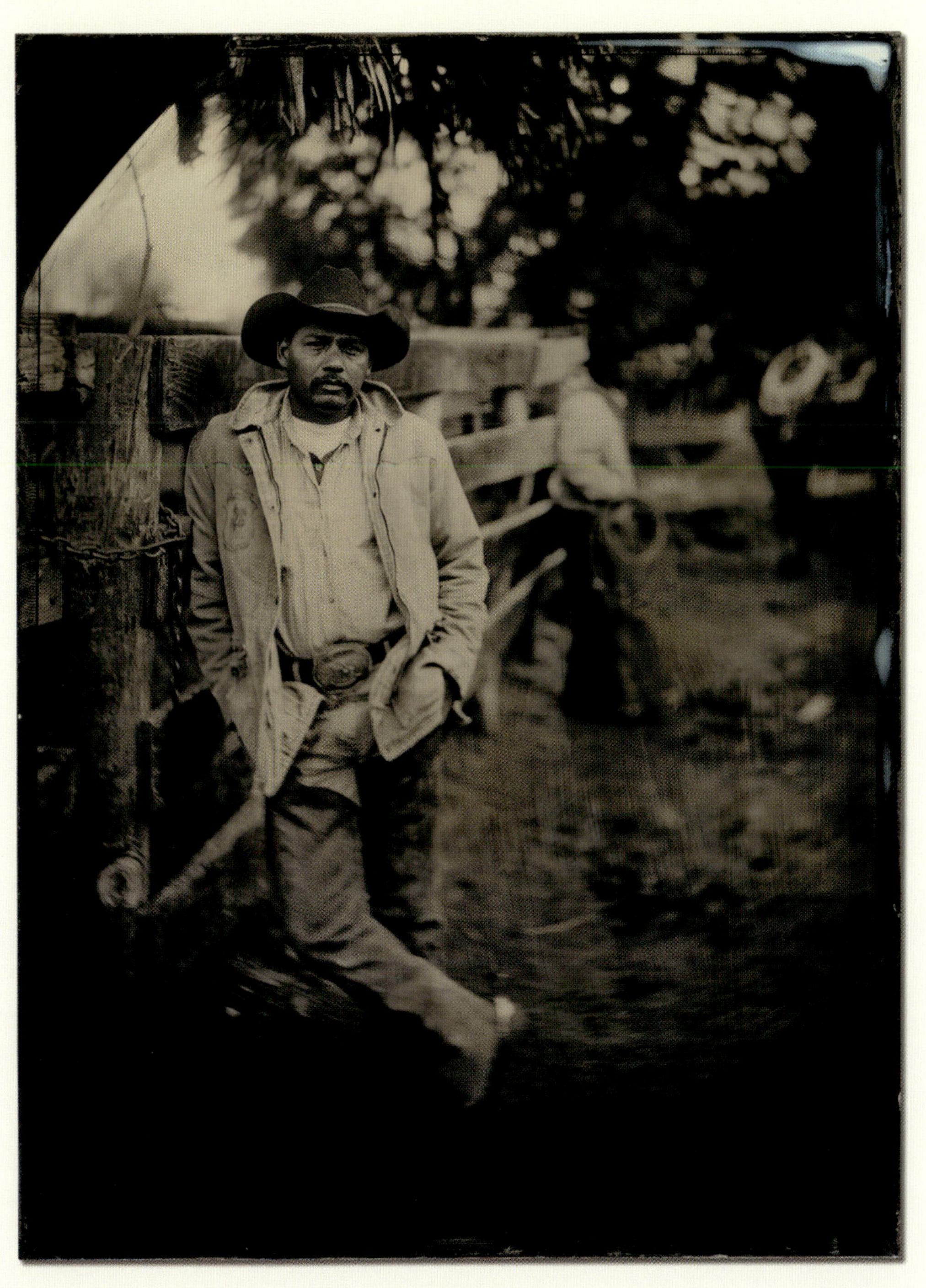

PLATE 14

ELMO ADAMS

PITCHFORK RANCH

Elmo's professional life has taken some twists and turns. He's worked on ranches, farmed, and even owned his own café. Now he's back at Pitchfork Ranch working as a cook on the wagon.

In hindsight, he says he should have just cowboyed all his life, instead of taking some of the career diversions he did. But those diversions are exactly what made him realize just what a special group of people cowboys are.

"I'm glad to be back."

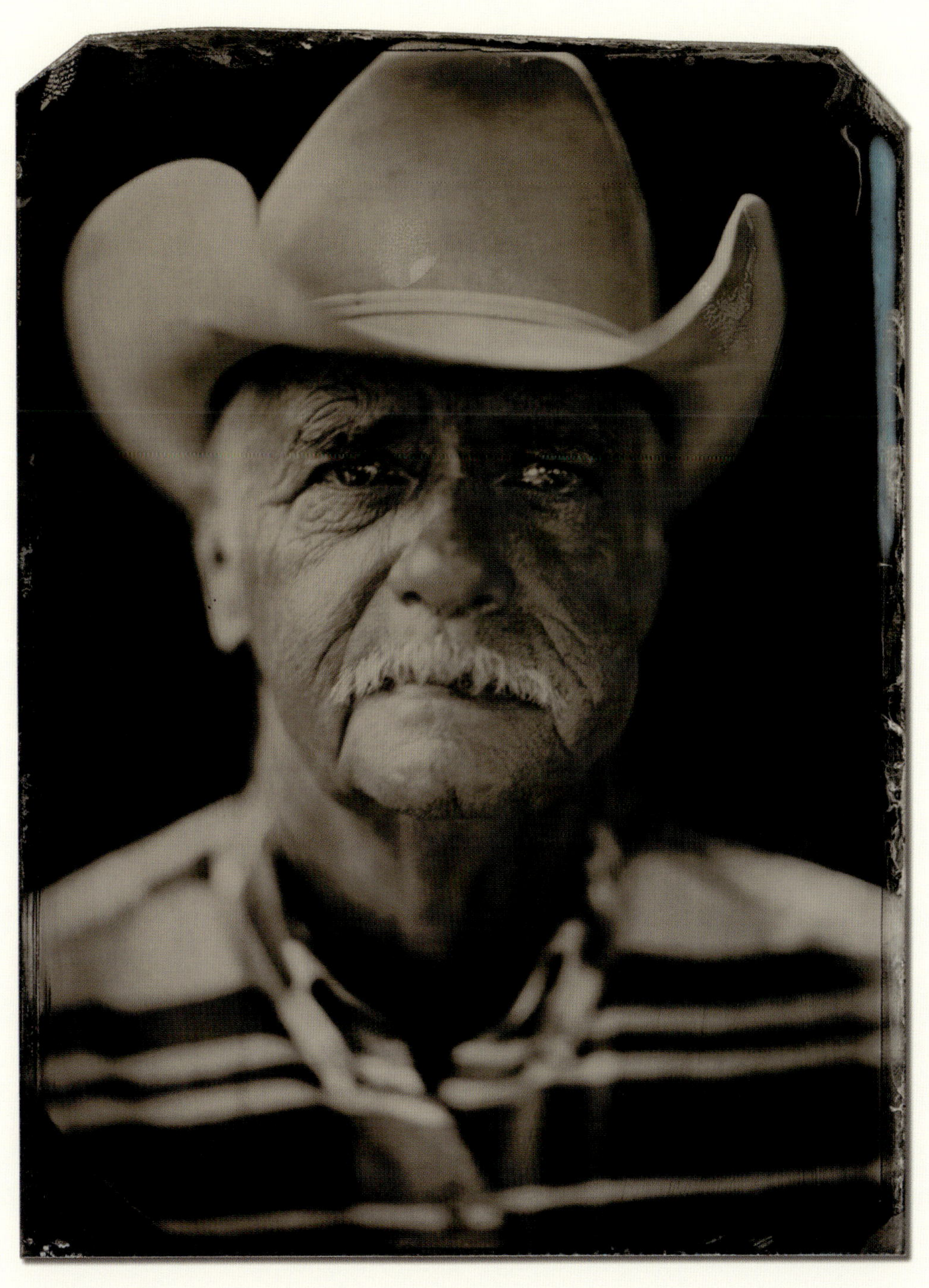

PLATE 15

CLINT JONES

DAYWORKER

Where Clint calls home, hard work and courtesy still go hand in hand. "Day-to-day responsibility and the manners used in this part of the country is what makes it so nice and easy raising a family."

Clint's way of living keeps him and his family a safe distance from the 21st century.

"Modern technology is taking from the world its hospitality, but it has not quite taken plumb over in this part of the world."

He doesn't need much to tell him who he is.

"It's the little things a man recognizes in a day that make him tick."

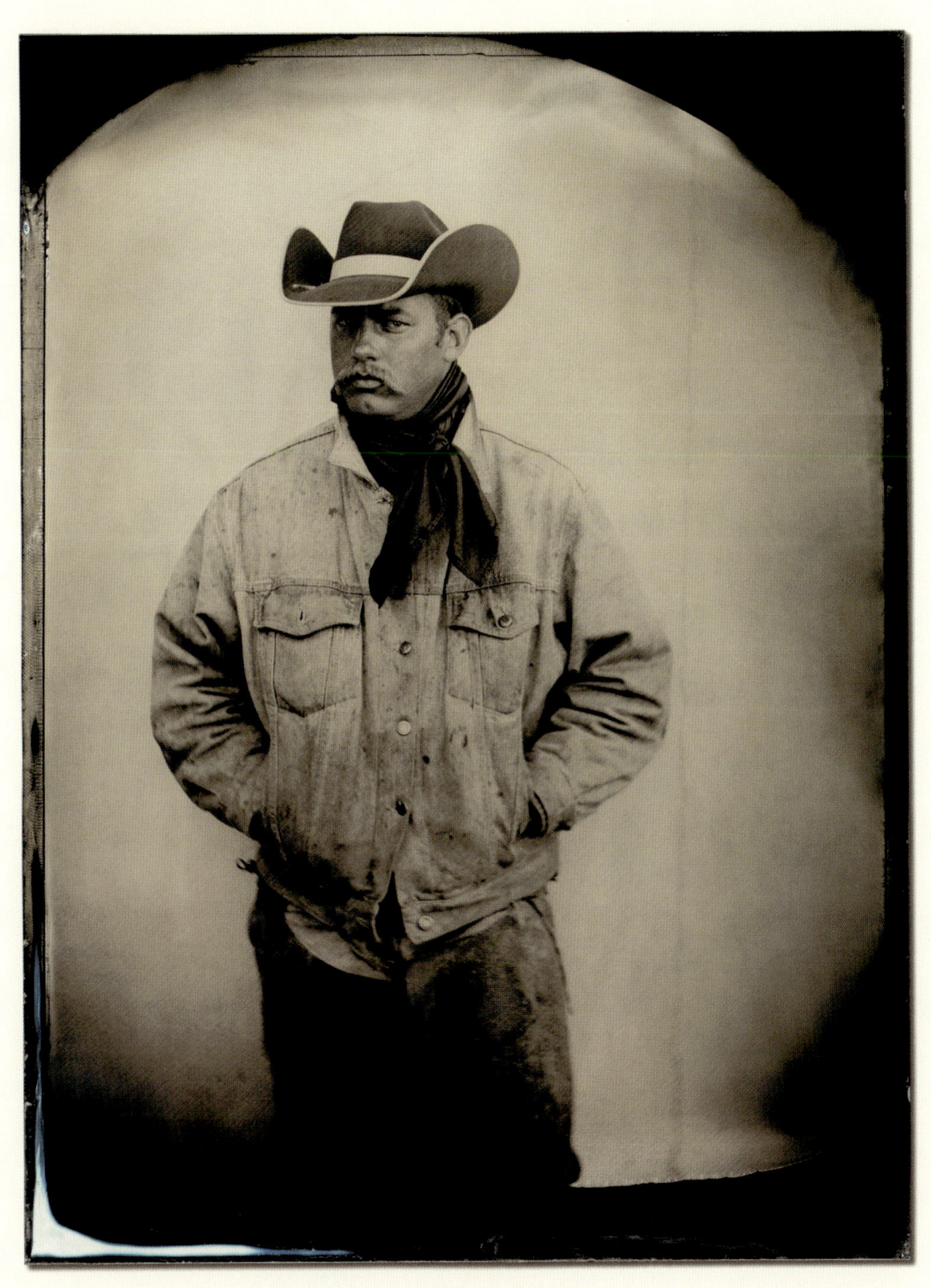

PLATE 16

JOEL NELSON

ALPINE, TEXAS

Joel is 59 years old and was exposed to ranching early on. He's worked on the Nail Ranch, the 06 Ranch, and the Parker Ranch in Hawaii.

He says what keeps him going is outdoor work and being horseback.

"I respect cattle and enjoying working cattle, and that's what gives us a reason to be horseback. It's about working as a partner with your horse, trying to work as one. The ultimate relationship with your horse is to become of one mind."

In 1991, he moved to starting horses. Says it's a great way for a man to learn about himself. "It taught me faith, that in time, if I persevere and don't demand too much too quickly, I will be a lot more successful in making good horses."

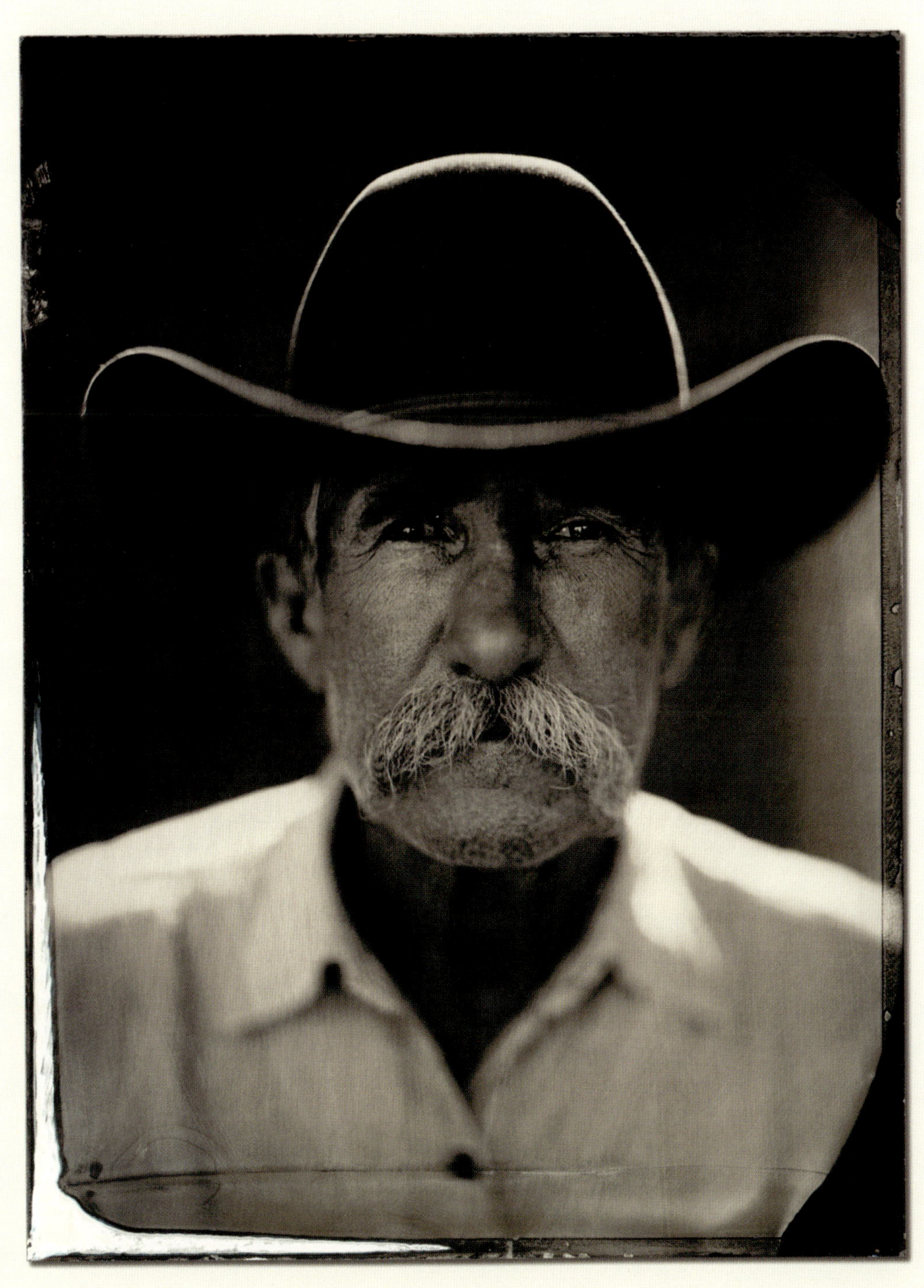

PLATE 17

DUSTIN HANEY

PITCHFORK RANCH

Dustin is 23 years old and has been cowboying around for six years. Did leatherwork from age 14 to 18, but then figured he wanted to be in the chaps he made for others.

"A clean, honest living keeps you pure. I won't get rich, but too much money can make a man compromise his values."

He says that no matter what you're doing, put someone else ahead of yourself. "With that mentality your back is covered."

"Scars and bruises are part of the paycheck."

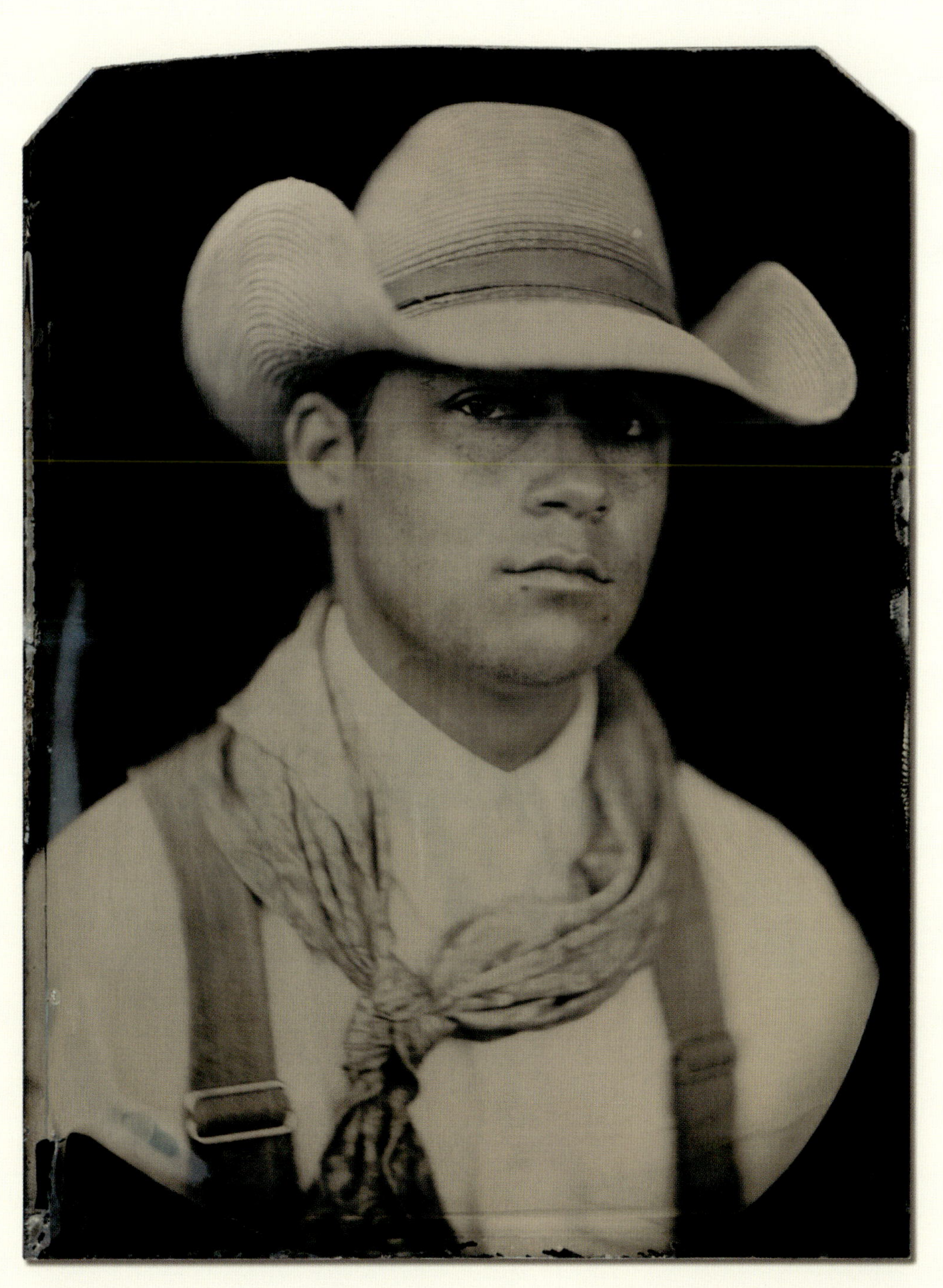

PLATE 18

NICK AUKER

I BAR RANCH

When you're born and raised on a dairy farm and ranch in South Dakota, chances are pretty good you're gonna grow up cowboy. "My uncles were cowboys in South Dakota. Ever since I was a button of a kid, I remember their stories of bunkhouse life, big pastures, and roping horses. From those days on, I was hooked."

For Nick, this way of life gives him the chance few people get. "It's not a job. It's who I am and others wish they were." When it comes to the long days, he says, "If you don't think about it as work or a job, the things that need to get done don't bother you." And at the end of every day is a well-deserved rest.

"Never have trouble getting to sleep after a day of cowboying."

Just as Nick learned to respect the cowboy way of life as a child, he's now teaching his own children."Ranch kids learn responsibility the city kids can't experience. They see the cycle of life and seasons. The freedom and life experiences my kids have growing up on a ranch can't happen anywhere else."

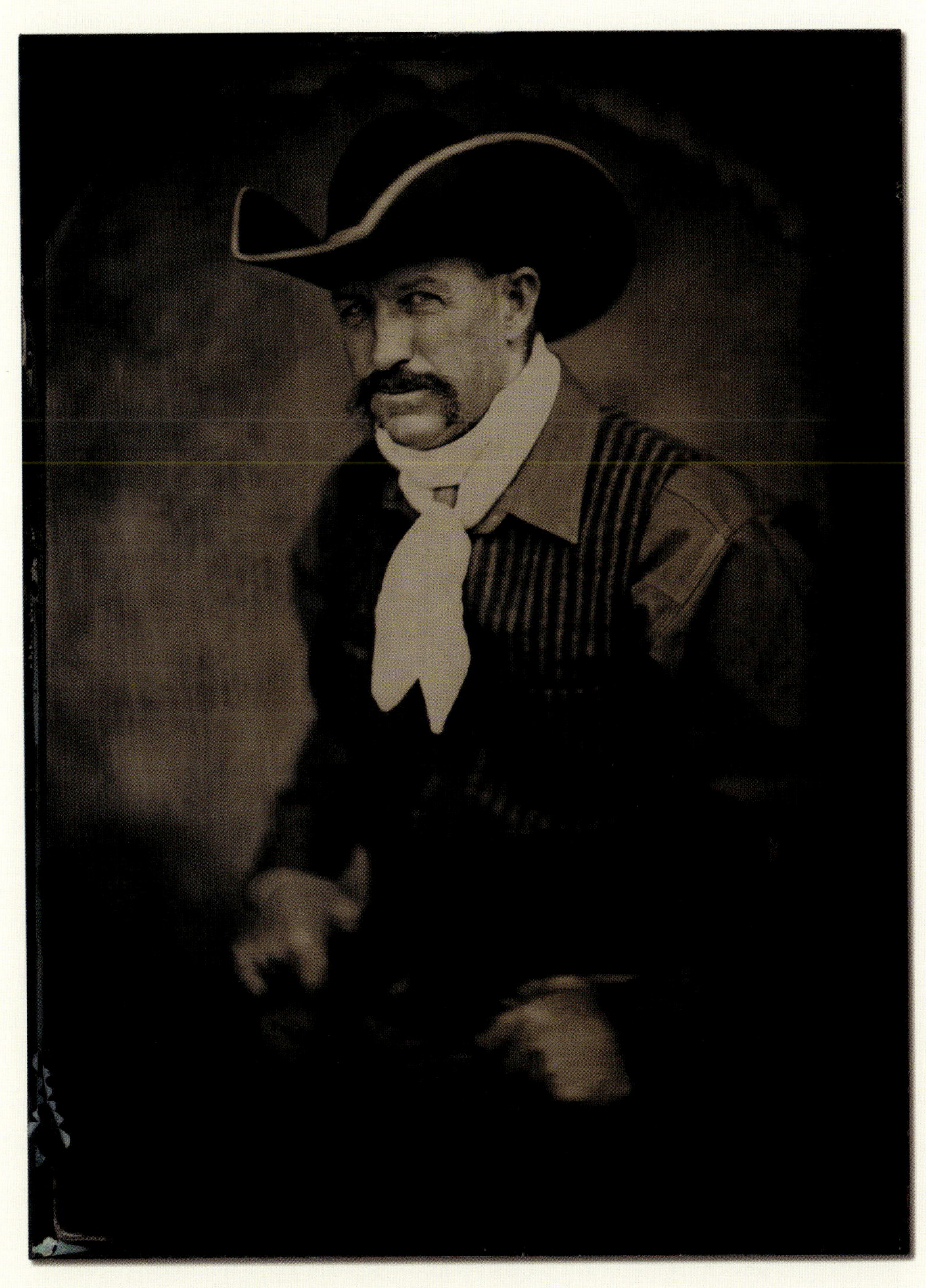

PLATE 19

GAGE MOORHOUSE

MOORHOUSE RANCH

Gage is 14 years old and is the fourth generation on his family's ranch. Says there's no doubt in his mind that he will be a cowboy once he gets done with school and out of college. "Everything I love in life is tied up in this way of life."

Says the Moorhouse Ranch is very traditional. "We don't use computers, we don't have oil. We have land and cows and hard work." He wants to continue that kind of ranching and even preserve it for future generations of his family.

The ranch offers plenty of things for a 14-year-old to do. "On weekends my friends and I go horseback and live off the land using packsaddles. We leave on Friday afternoons and go on four-day trips on our own."

"Cowboys are hard-working, honest people. I want to pull my weight."

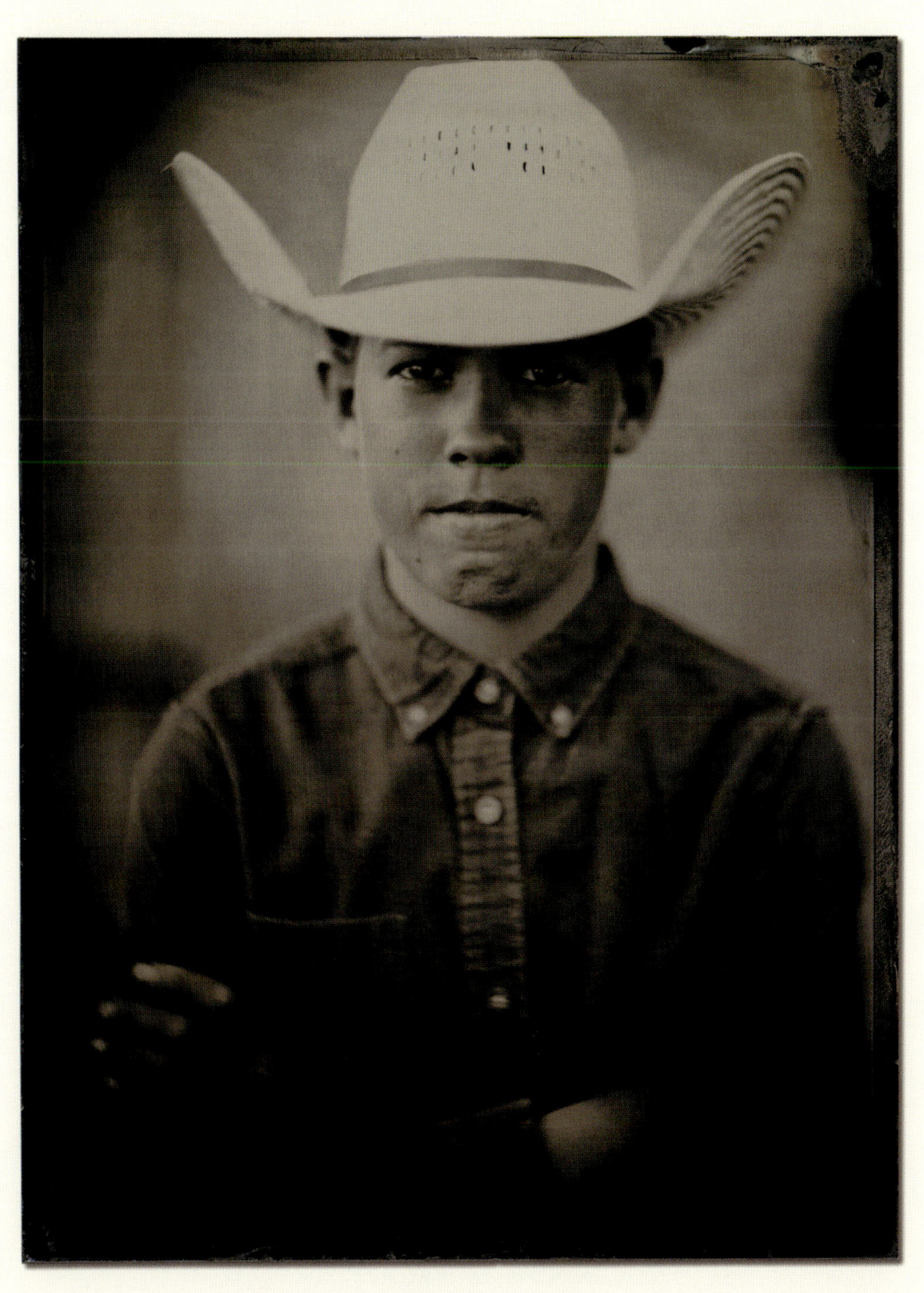

PLATE 20

BRENT CHARLESWORTH

PAISANO RANCH

Brent grew up on a 600,000-acre ranch in New Mexico. Started drawing a check at age 10. He says growing up and working on a large ranch make a person feel small.

"When it's 300 square miles and three cowboys working it, you begin to realize how immense the world is."

He is continuing the cowboy tradition in his family. "If I can be half the cowboy my dad was, I'd feel like an accomplished man. I really admired him. Seeing my dad cemented my ambition to do this."

"We don't do it for the money. Quality of life is very rich, and that's part of my pay."

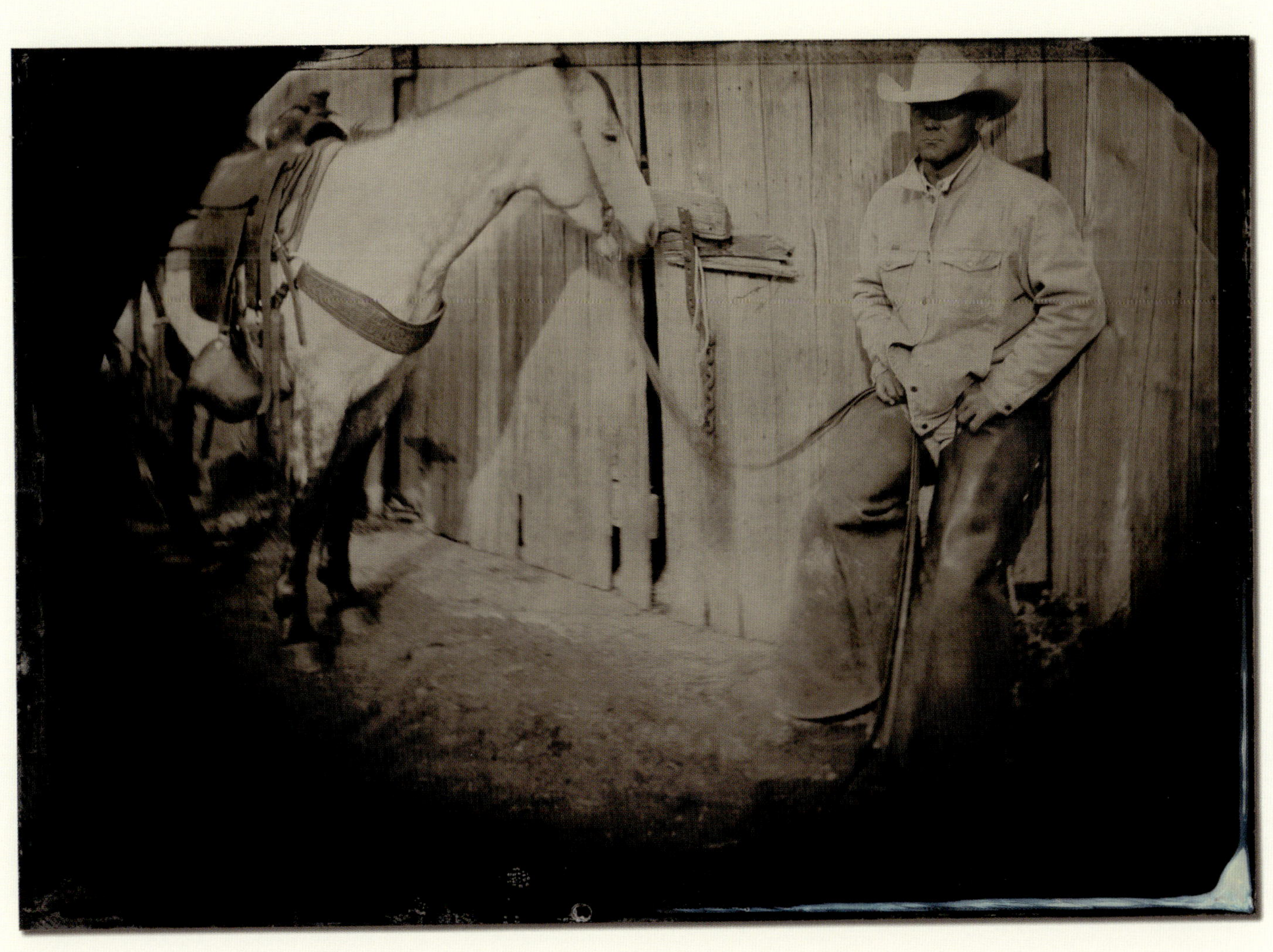

PLATE 21

BUSTER McLAURY

PADUCAH, TEXAS

Buster's been a paid cowpuncher for 36 years, starting with his first wages at age 11. He likes the independence, the right to roll up your bed and quit if you need to or feel like it.

"My first cattle drive was at age 5. I was hooked. 'Swarthy' was the horse I was on, and I thought I was a cowpuncher from that day on."

Raised on the 6666 Ranch, Buster says that responsibility and the consequences of not doing your work are learned early, as are life lessons.

"Seeing life and death as part of life at an early age teaches kids how fragile and valuable life is."

Buster reflects on his way of life from time to time and shares those thoughts in poetry and prose. See the "Afterword" in this book for a glimpse of his earned wisdom.

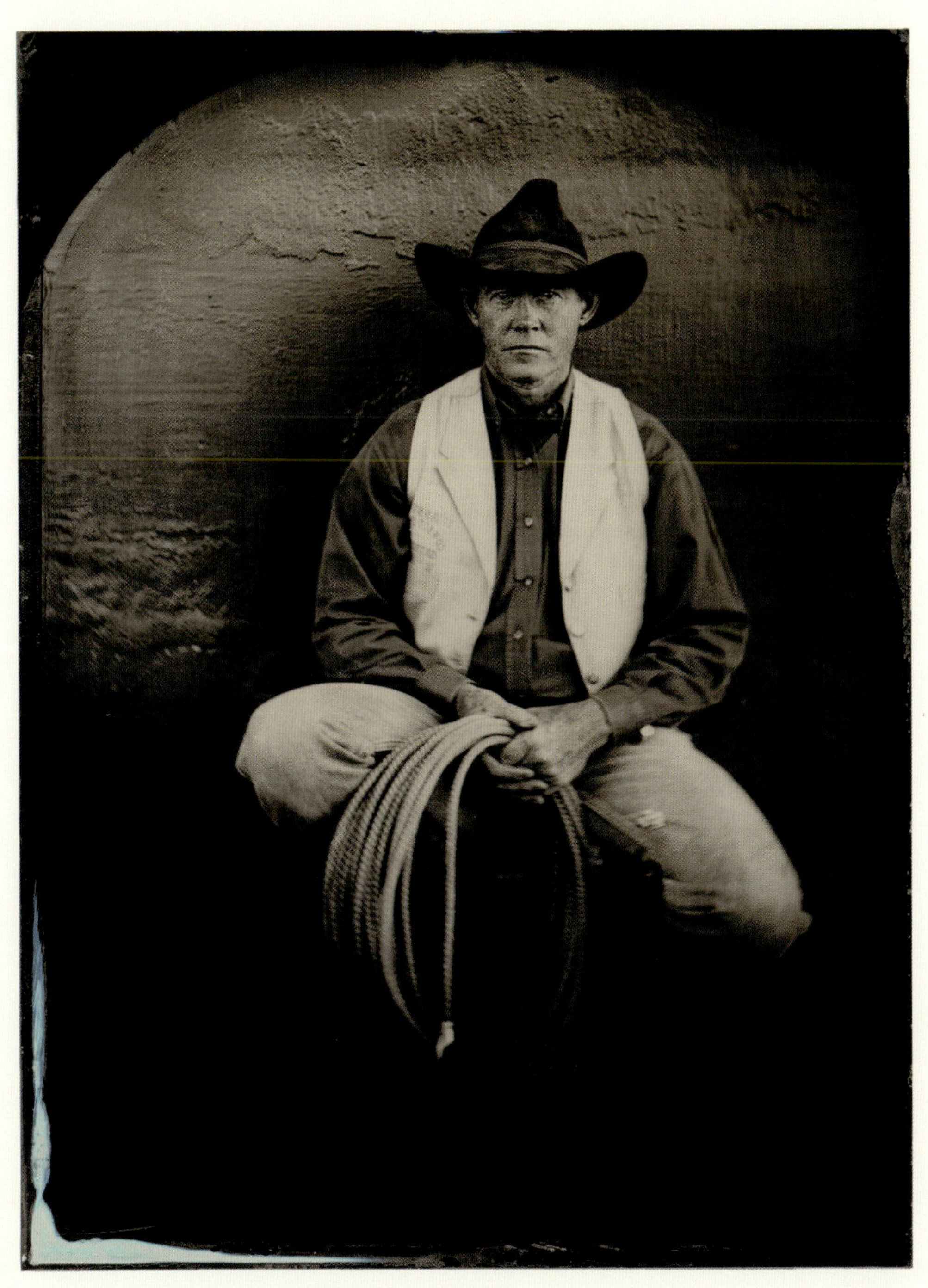

PLATE 22

DUSTIN PARSONS

EASY LAND & CATTLE

"Ever since I was born I've wanted to be a cowboy, for the adventure of the cowboy life, and to be the best hand I could be."

Dustin, 25, has worked on several ranches through the years, including W. H. Green, J. R. Green, W. T. Waggoner, Cowen Ranch, and 6666 Ranch. Now he runs his own cattle company, Easy Land & Cattle, which originated with his great-grandfather, Easy Parsons.

"He was the person who put me on my first horse, which put me in the direction I am today."

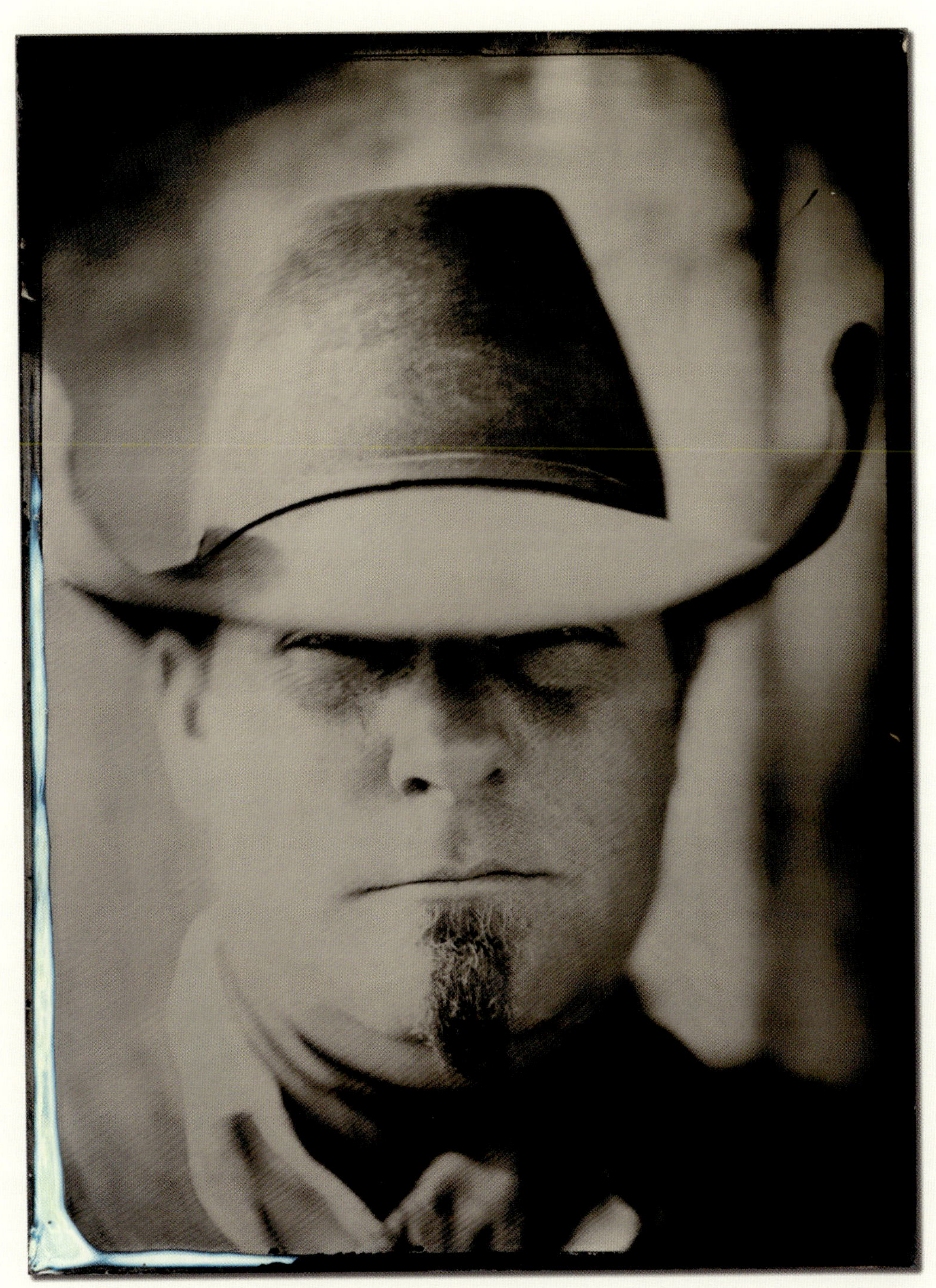

PLATE 23

RODE LEWIS

PAISANO RANCH

Rode is a fourth-generation cowboy. Grew up on a ranch helping his dad. "He taught me how to be a good hand."

In April of 2003, Rode had a kidney transplant. It nearly ended his days as a cowboy. "Doctors said no more saddle-bronc riding. Doctors also said it would be best to find another job that wasn't so hard on my body."

But for Rode, cowboying isn't his job. It's his life. And you can't quit that.

"The docs don't know about it. Punching cows, being on horseback, working with good hands, and being outside all combine to make it a great way of life."

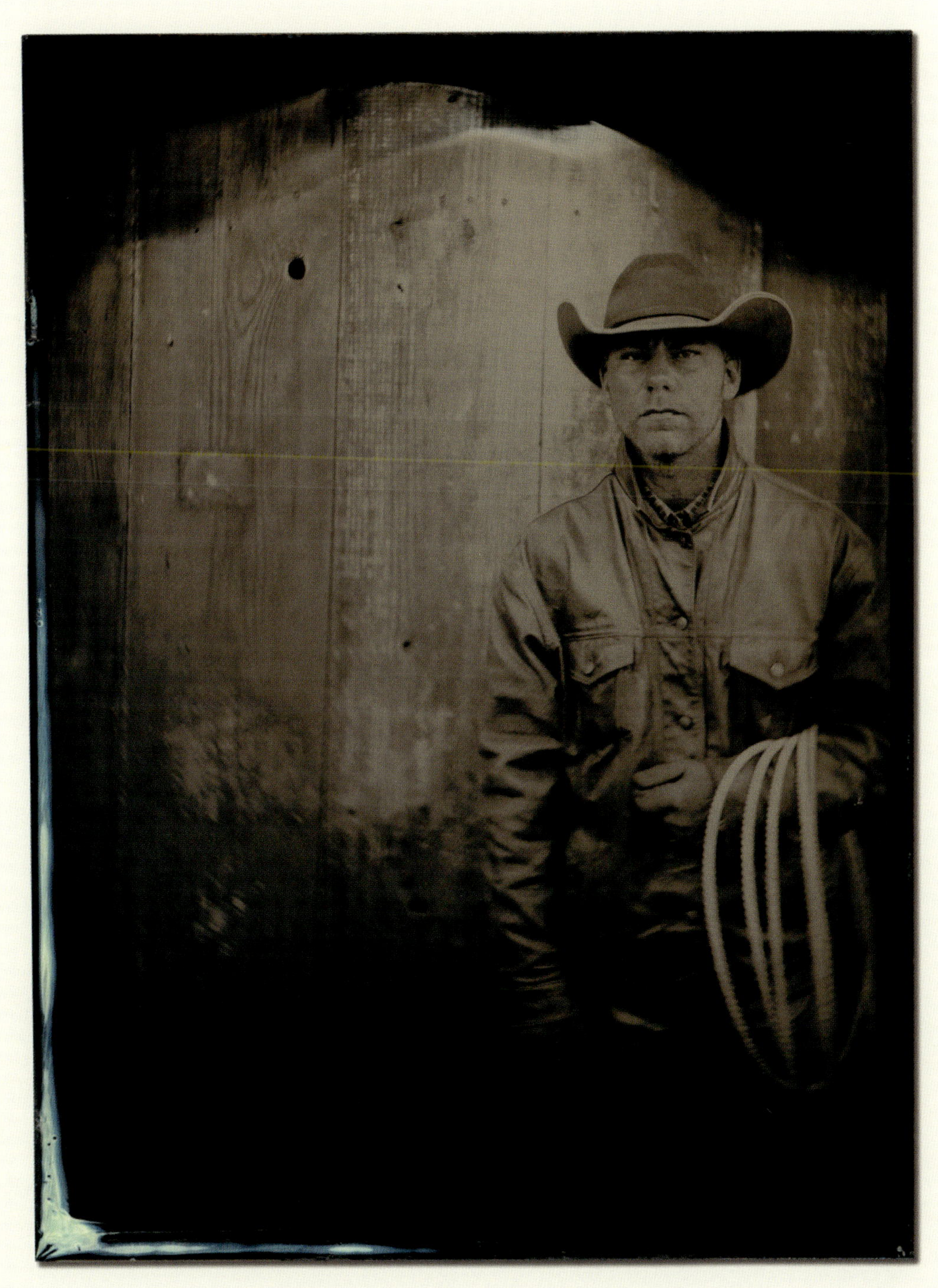

PLATE 24

ANGEL ROSALES

LAMBSHEAD RANCH

Cowboying is in Angel's blood. He grew up on a ranch in Mexico, the third generation of his family to work as a vaquero. When he was 25 years old, he came to the United States, and he's been working at Lambshead ever since.

He appreciates the necessity of hard work in ranching and knows the importance of working with good men and good horses. But the thing about being a cowboy that Angel loves the most is simply getting to work outdoors.

"Fresh air, being out in the elements makes you feel alive."

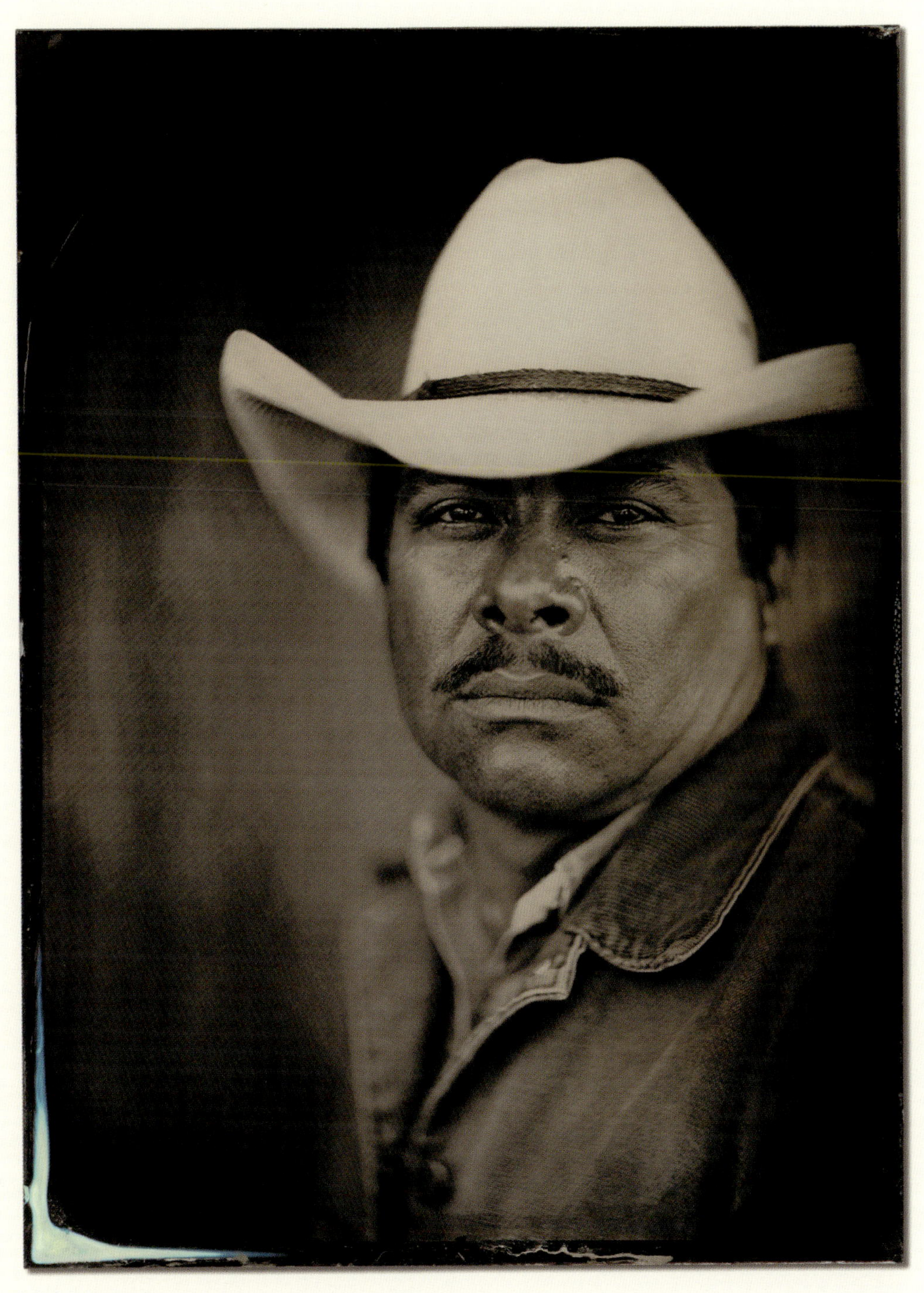

PLATE 25

BRAD WILLIAMS

KING RANCH

Brad is 37 years old. Grew up on a ranch in Colorado. Rodeoed for 12 years and trained horses.

"I love the cowboy life. Spending time with the other hands, taking care of horses and cattle. Living the free life."

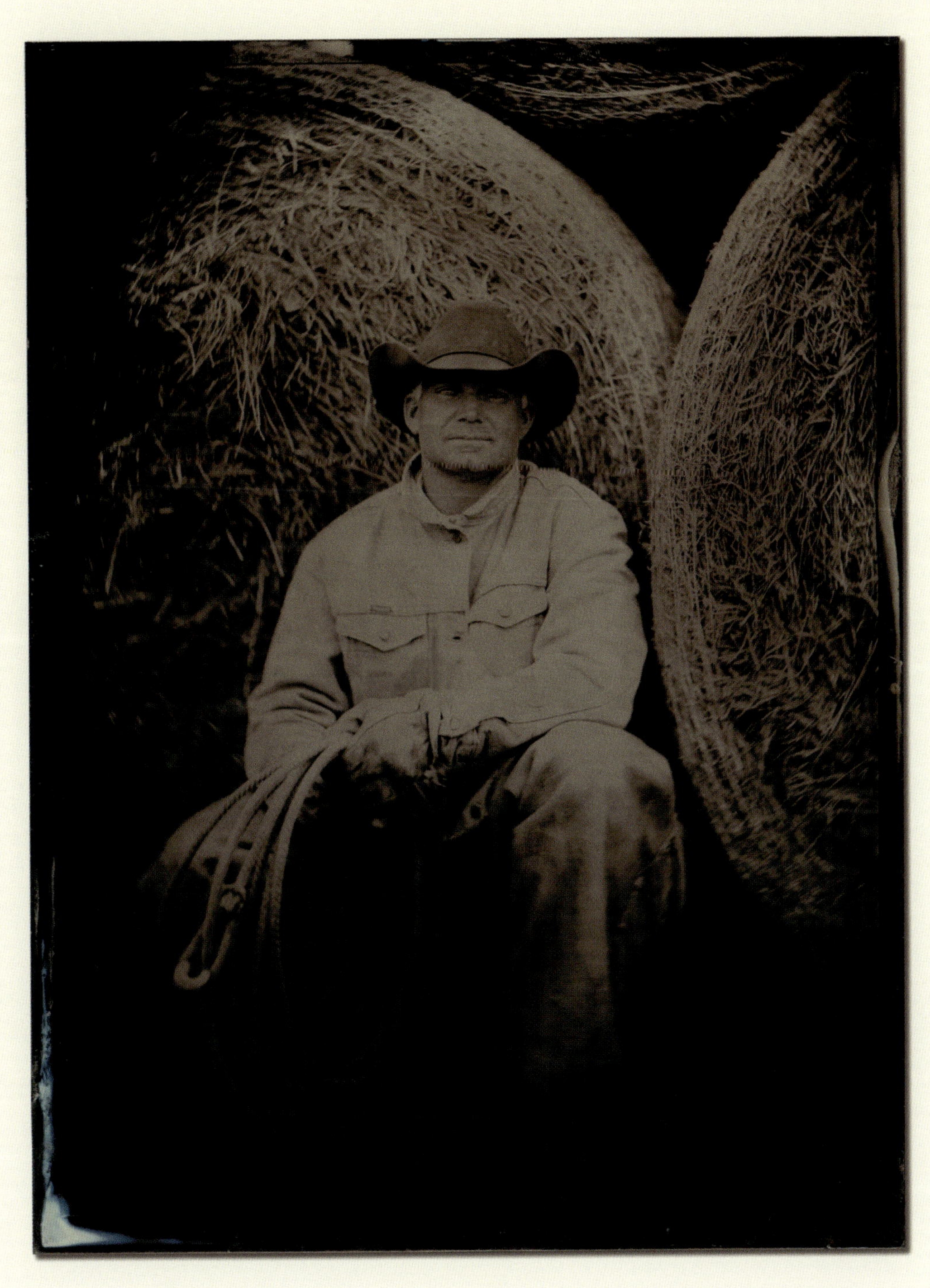

PLATE 26

TOM "STRETCH" BOWERMAN

XI RANCH

Stretch was born in Nocona, Texas, and raised in Hamlin, Texas. Picked up cowboying at age 17.

"I had a guy take a chance on me, and that is all I needed."

He says in cowboying, everything is your responsibility. "You're not pampered. You're self-reliant. If you make it, you did it on your own. Make your opportunities, because no one gives you a handout."

The job doesn't pay well, but money isn't his focus. "It's more than enough if it's really in your heart to do this work."

For him, a lot of what it takes to cowboy happens from the neck up. "Even though you work 12 to 16 hours a day, your mind is engaged, you're challenged. It stimulates you and makes you think. When you're away from the distractions, you learn the basics of life."

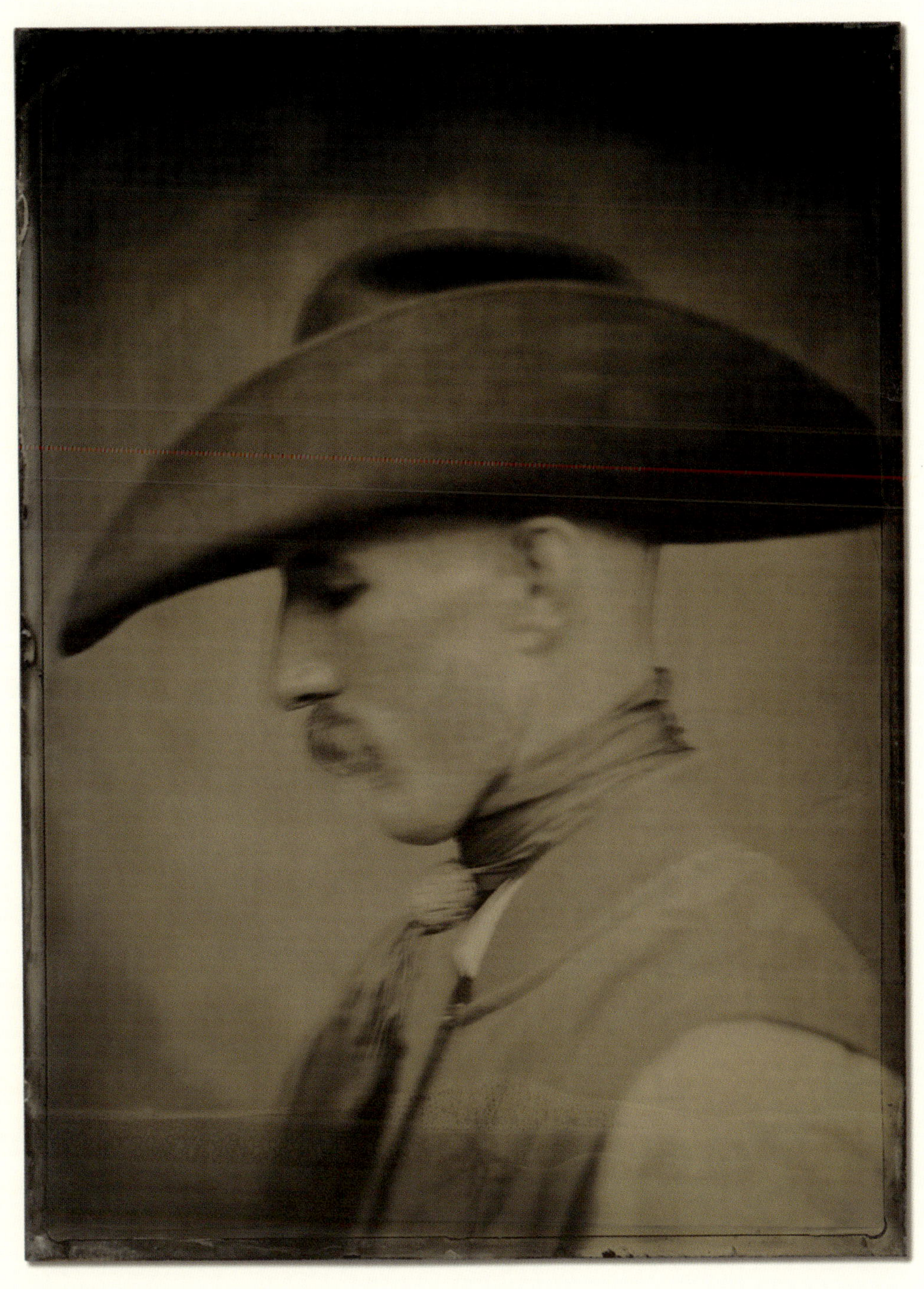

PLATE 27

G. L. PROCTOR

WAGGONER RANCH

It may be some kind of record. G. L. is the foreman at Waggoner Ranch, where he's worked for 53 years.

"I've ridden every inch of Waggoner's. At 553,000 acres, it's the largest ranch under one fence in Texas. I've ridden horseback around the earth twice and never left that ranch."

He says, at age 80, that there are two things that have given him a full life. Enjoying his work. And riding horses. Although he didn't specify any particular order.

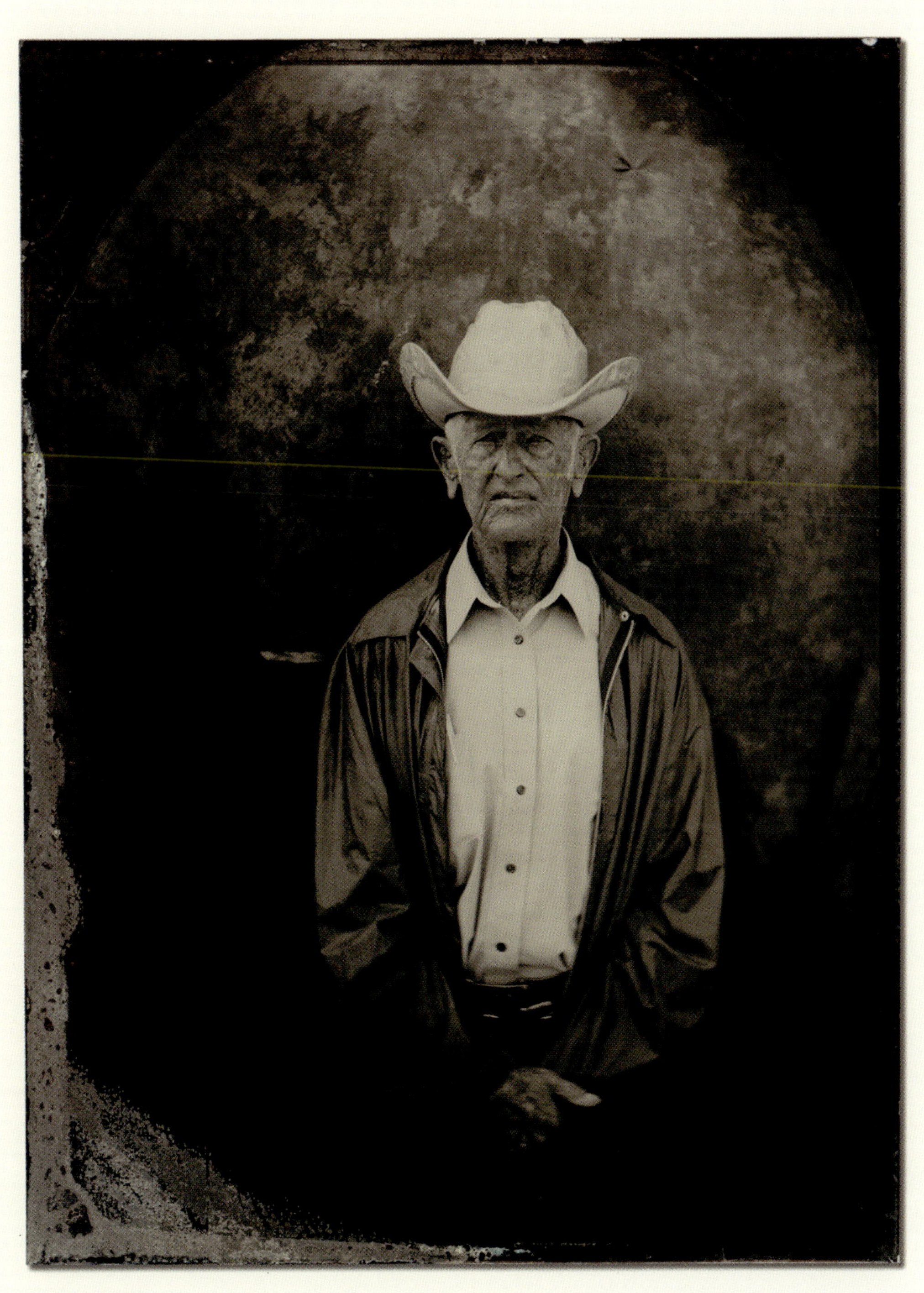

PLATE 28

DAVID ROSS

PITCHFORK RANCH

Ross, as he's known on the ranch, likes the solitude cowboying offers. "You, your horse, and a lot of open country with cattle to work. Nothing better."

Ross winters five months out of the year, mid-October through mid-March, at a remote part of the ranch where he keeps geese off the winter wheat. He stays in a 10′x 10′ range teepee. No running water, electricity, or heat. For him, it's a great time and place to relax, read, and get some peace of mind.

"Cowboying is hard work that is good for the soul."

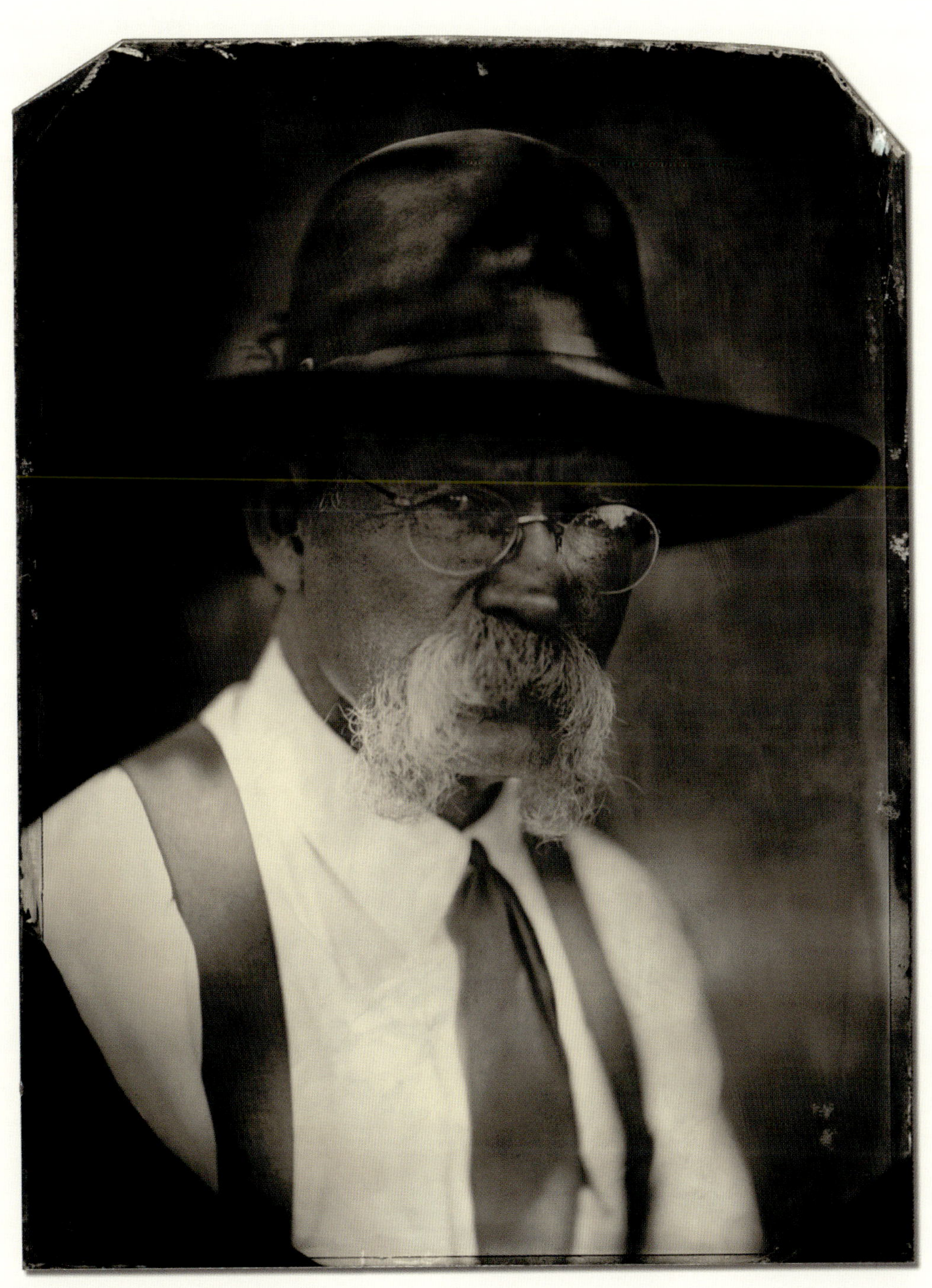

PLATE 29

ROBERT CAUBLE & HENRY GREEN

W. H. GREEN RANCH

Robert and Henry work side-by-side on land Henry's great-grandfather settled in the 1880s.

Robert says his life is never compromising and never boring. "It's a good honest living. Never do the same thing, and every day is an adventure."

And as far as the folks he gets to meet, he says you'd be hard pressed to find better. "The people you work with are the best bunch of people a person could have to call his friends."

Henry's been riding horses and working cattle ever since he can remember. "I like the traditions and physical nature of the work."

He's quick to remind people how important cowboys have always been to America, today included. "Cowboys are still a vital part of keeping our nation fed. Without them, there wouldn't be anyone to care for the cattle that eventually end up at Morton's, Arby's, or the supermarkets."

And like a true cowboy, Henry says the best cure for anything that ails you is a good horse.

"Riding good horses makes the long, hard, dusty days all worth it."

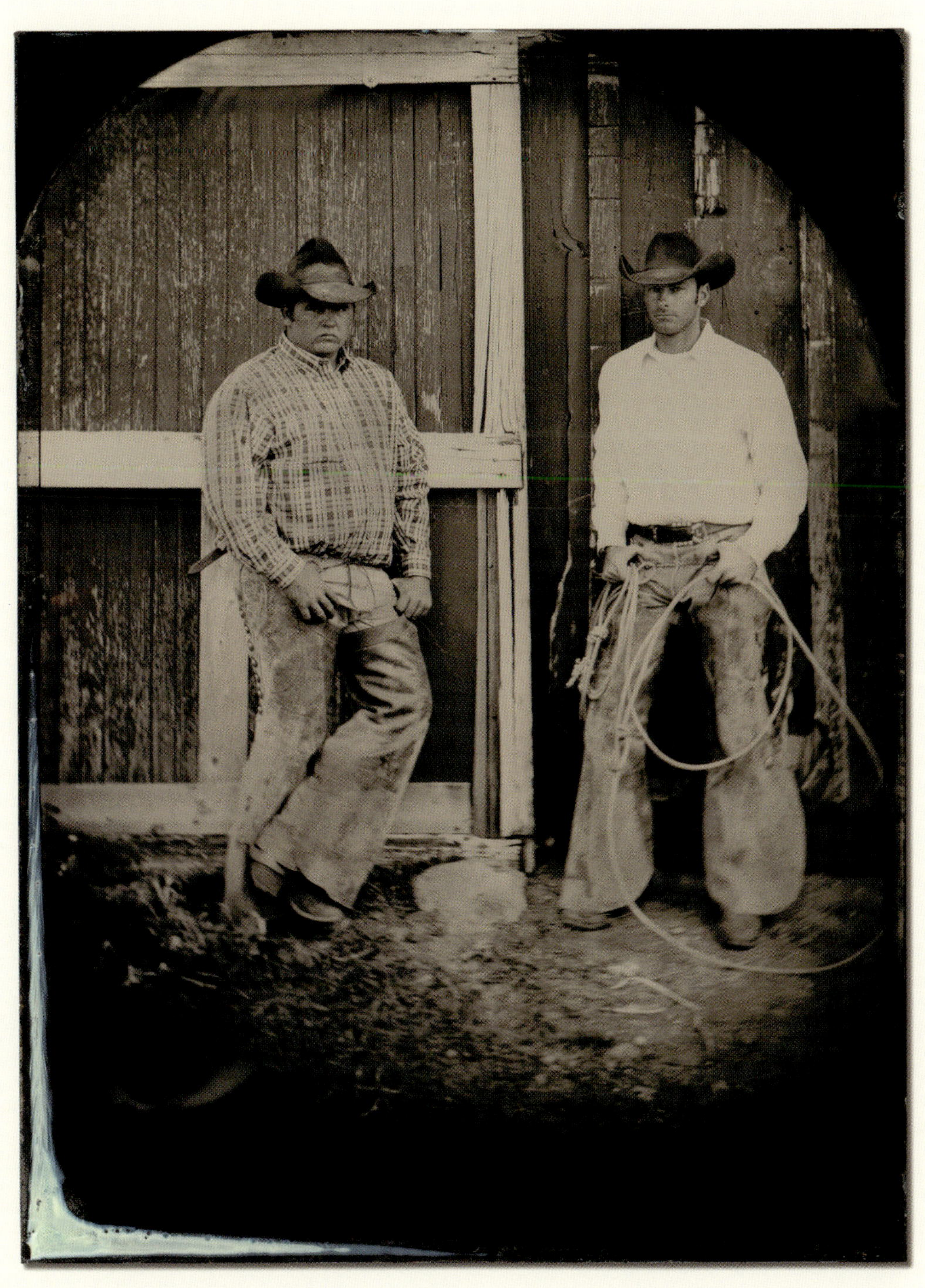

PLATE 30

JOSH ALLEN

DOUBLE HORN RANCH

Two things, Josh says, makes cowboying just about the best thing in the world: tradition and way of life. It's not an 8-to-5 job. It's a calling, unlike any other. Nobody watches you. Nobody supervises you. Nature sets your schedule. And you depend on yourself to do your work the best you can.

"I live the life that people dream about. I don't take any day for granted. I know at the end of the day what I've done and if I've done right."

For him, there's nothing more enjoyable than riding. He can be having the absolute worst day, but once he throws a leg over, everything changes. "Horses are calming. No matter what you do to a horse, they always forgive. Horses teach you more about patience and how to deal with people, especially women."

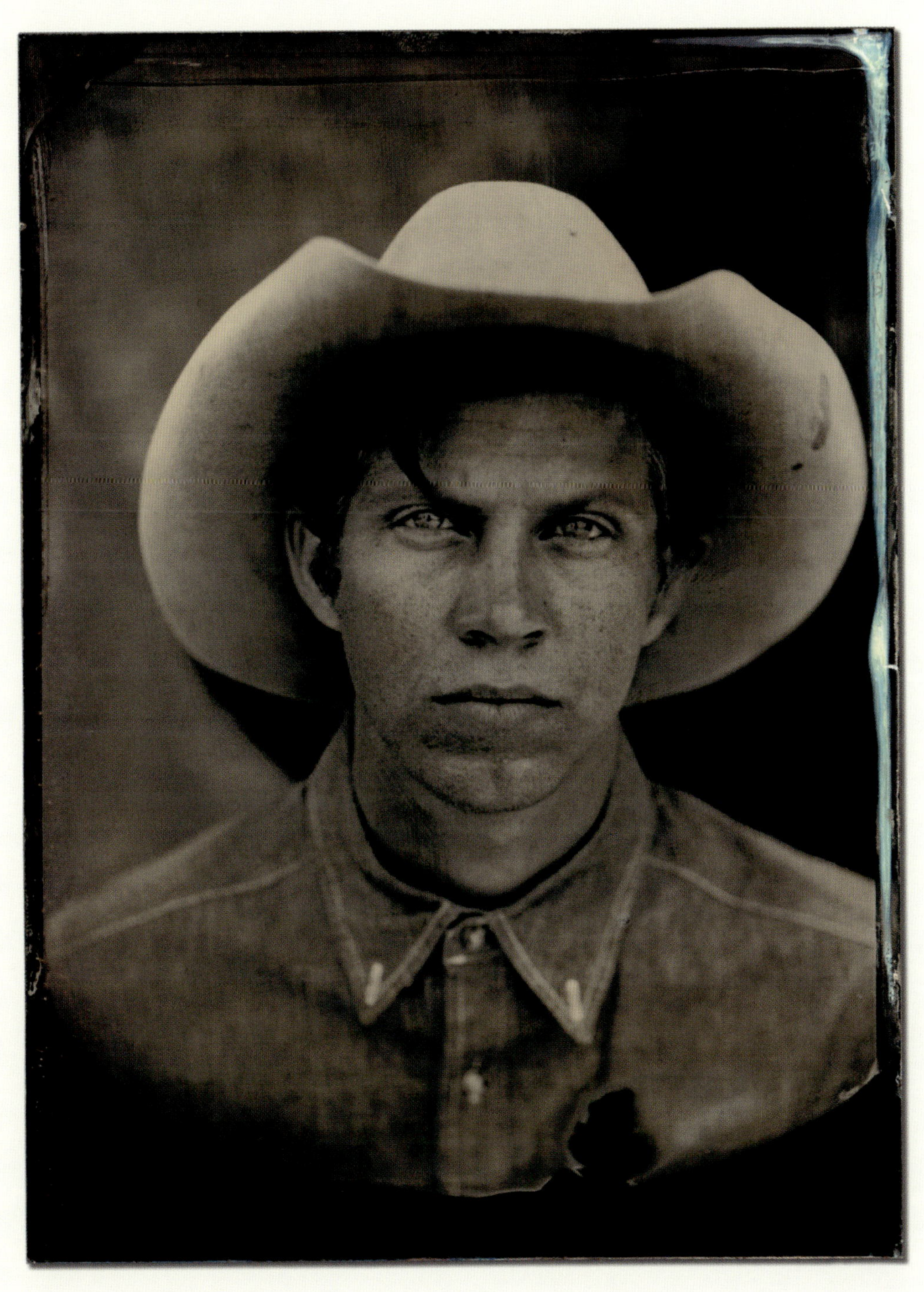

PLATE 31

SUSAN STEPHENS

QUIEN SABE RANCH

Tradition runs deep in Susan's family. She says it is impossible to replace the cowboy ways that have been around for more than a century. Like being on horseback.

"There is no feeling like the motion of a horse under you, and how you just fit there. It's also amazing that this powerful animal will trust its rider, and, when you're working together, what the two of you can accomplish."

For her, ranch life is peaceful, yet at times lonely. "You have to be comfortable with yourself or otherwise the quiet solitude ways of ranch life could push you over the edge."

Her comfort comes from the people and places closest to her.

"Relationship with God, good husband, good horse, good grass, good rain, my home, my garden, my quiet, and my space are some of the most important things in life. Simple, but never easy."

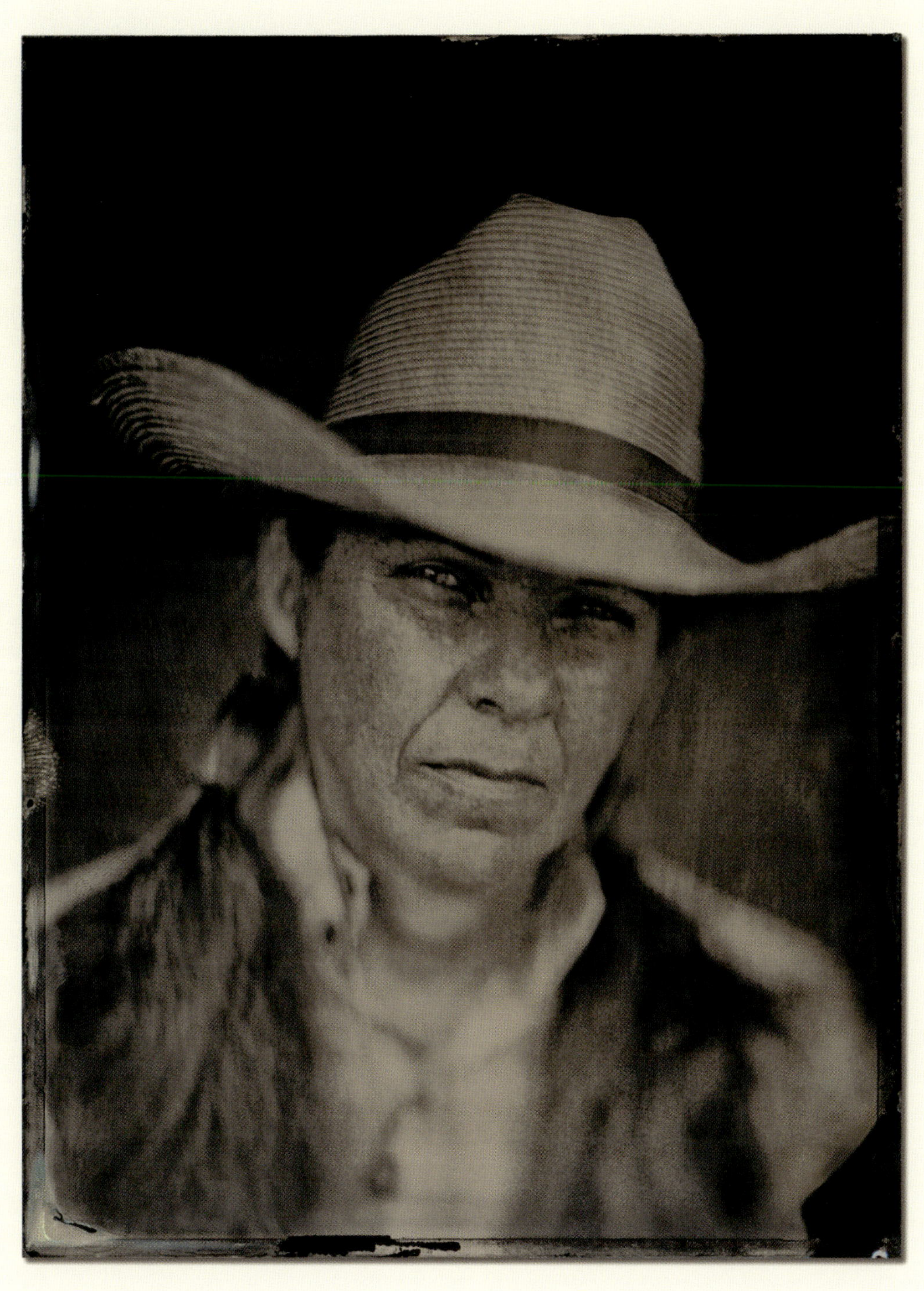

PLATE 32

DEWEY HILL

SAUNDERS RANCH

Dewey didn't become a cowboy to have a career.

"To me, being a cowboy is not a job. I believe if a man goes to work for a paycheck, his heart can't be in it."

"I like to ride good horses, gather big country, and be around good cowboys. Things like that are just some of the reasons I do what I do for a living."

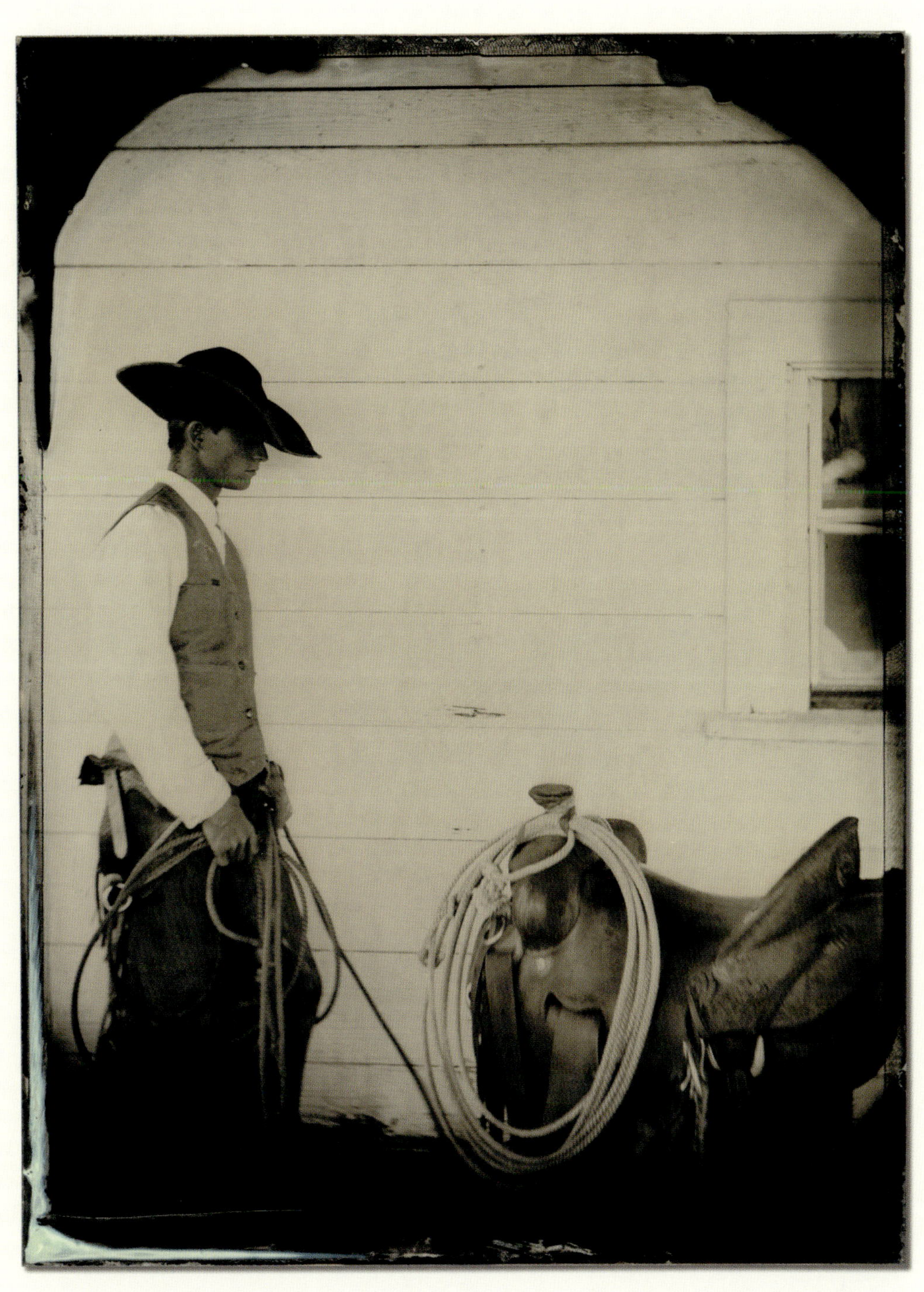

PLATE 33

CHARLES ELLIS

ELLIS CATTLE CO.

Charles grew up in Odem, Texas, the fourth generation in 100 years in the same place. "No regrets about my way of life. Enjoyment of my life is important. Don't make a lot of money doing it, but you can't buy personal fulfillment."

He says ranching life makes a family strong. Gives you the time to spend with your family. And in that time, your kids experience life. They live it. "Before my kids started school they'd seen the beauty of life and the reality of death. Pulling calves does that."

"Proud to say my son will be the fifth generation to live on our family's place."

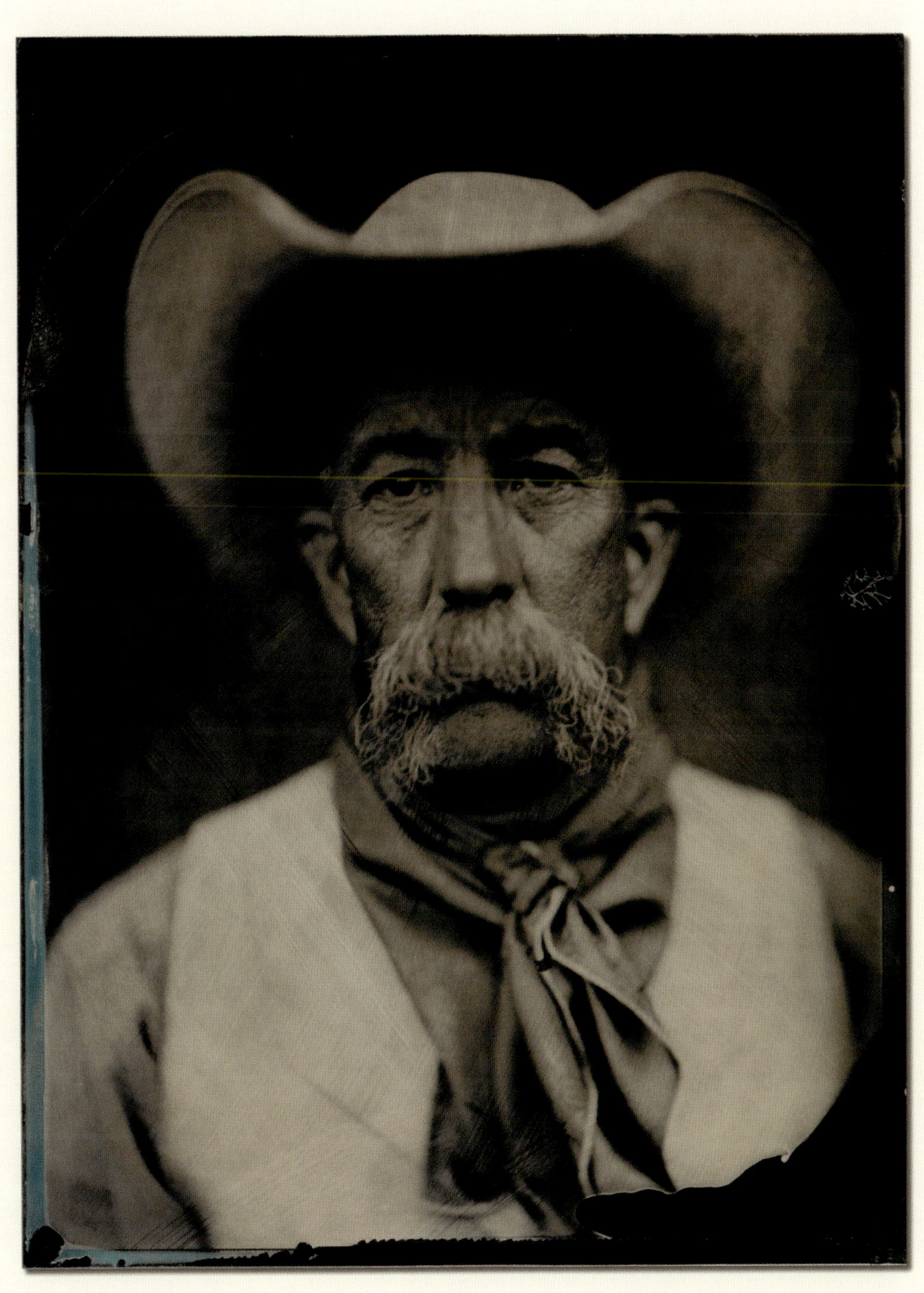

PLATE 34

JASON PELHAM

SPADE RANCH

Jason says that, regardless of what you see in movies or read in books, "there's not a lot of romance in the reality of cowboying. Most of the time you are alone. You get praised about twice a year. You got to live in the past but remember the future."

But he likes where he works. Thinks the Spade Ranch is a great outfit, run by good people. "You get respect, you can bring up some ideas, and they'll let you try it."

Says being patient when working cattle is important. "Time doesn't mean anything to a cow."

"The thing about cowboying is, if you want to do it, you can do it."

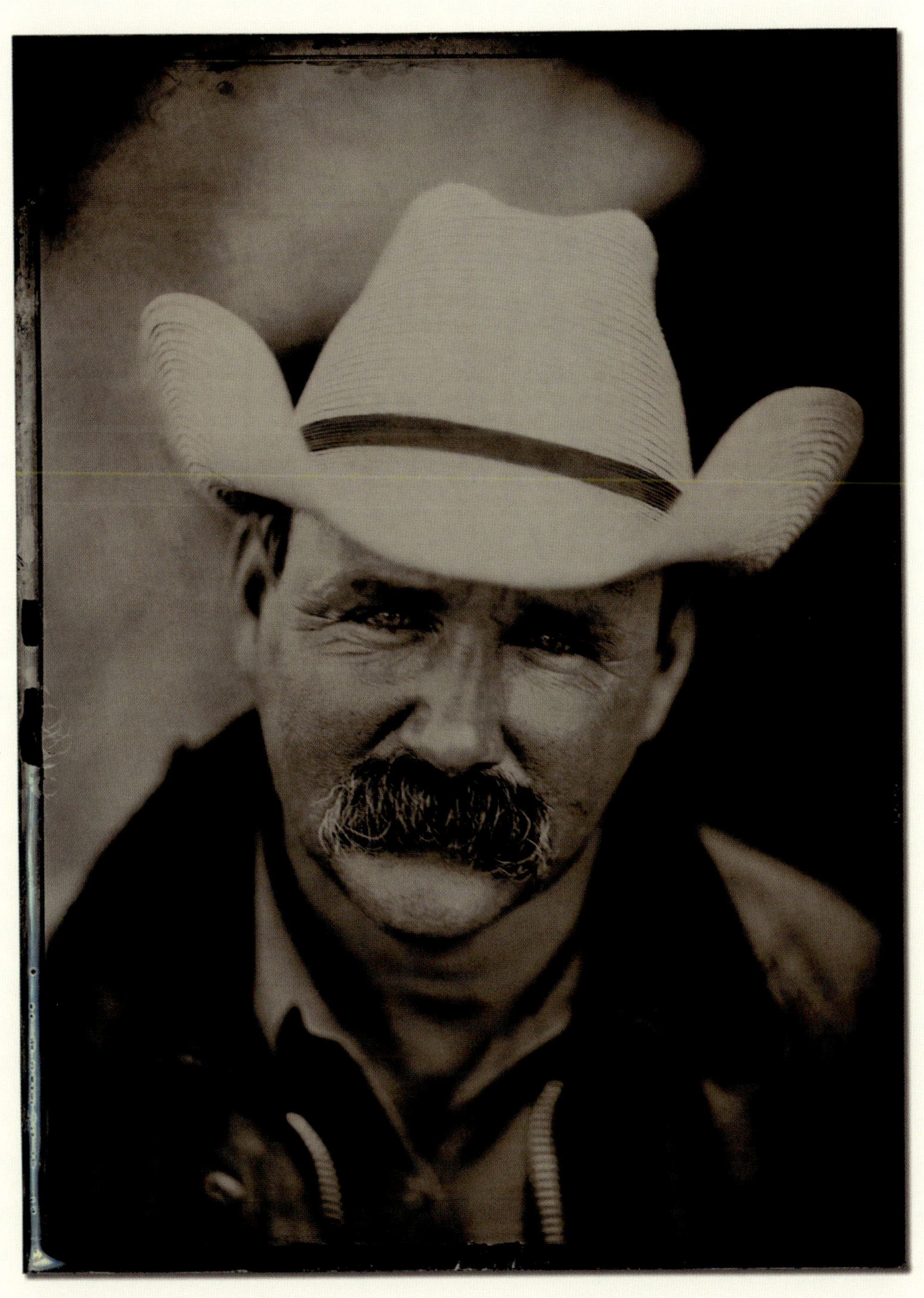

PLATE 35

RON REDFORD

MOORHOUSE RANCH

Ron is grateful to have grown up on a ranch.

"I went everywhere with my dad. Great memories. At age four, I was a regular fixture on a horse."

For him, cowboying gives him exactly the kind of freedom he's looking for.

"Every day is a new adventure. You're outside and not chained to a desk."

And even though the work is tough and the hours are long, Ron says that as long as you give it your all, "there's no problems."

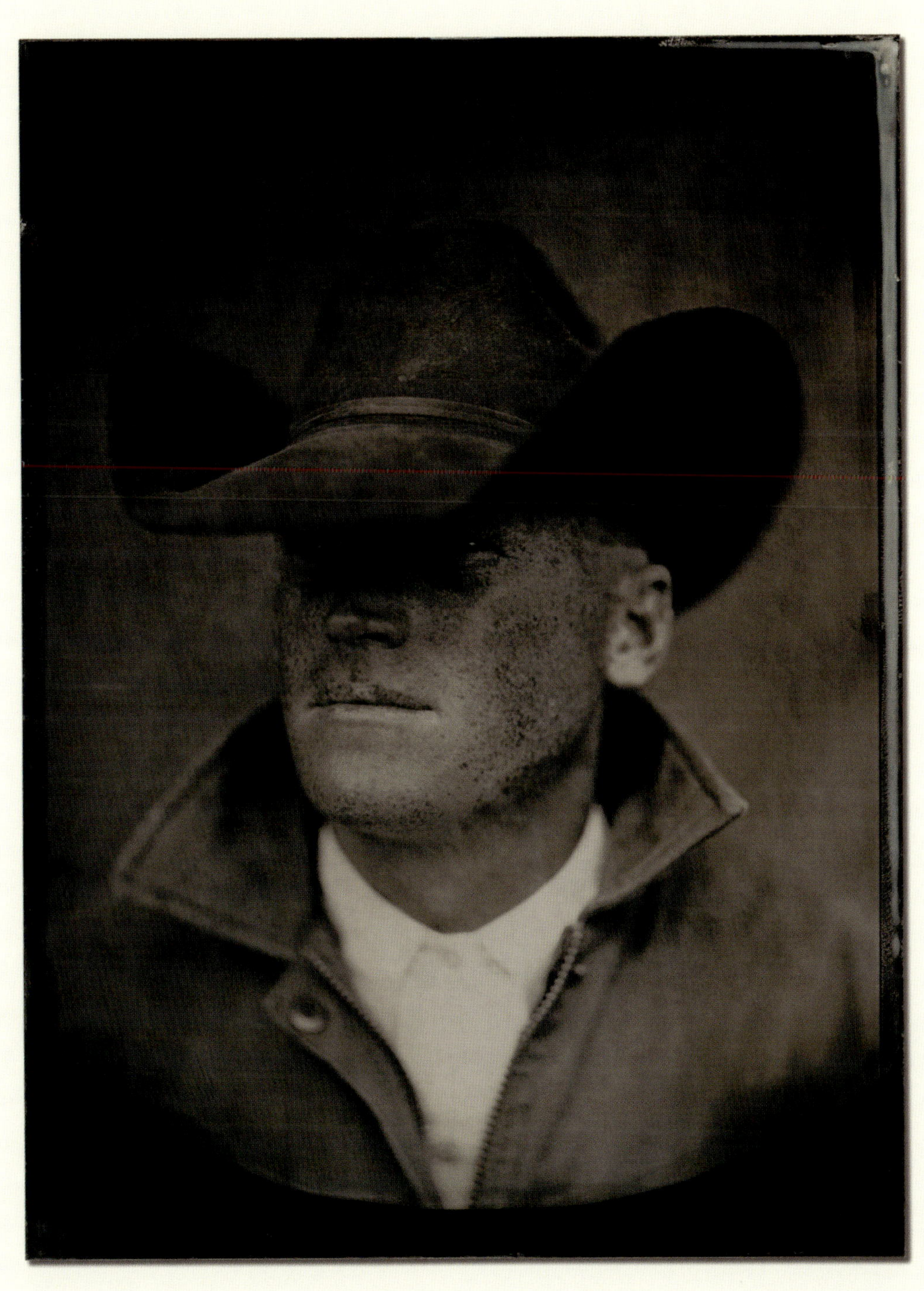

PLATE 36

EFRAIN CORRALES

SANDHILL CATTLE CO.

Efrain loves riding horses. "It's in my blood." He also enjoys the camaraderie he shares with the other men he works with on the ranch.

He doesn't complain about the work. "I chose my life, and you just get it done when the weather's tough."

He says that living on a ranch teaches his children responsibility, and also gives them something else that means a great deal. "Freedom."

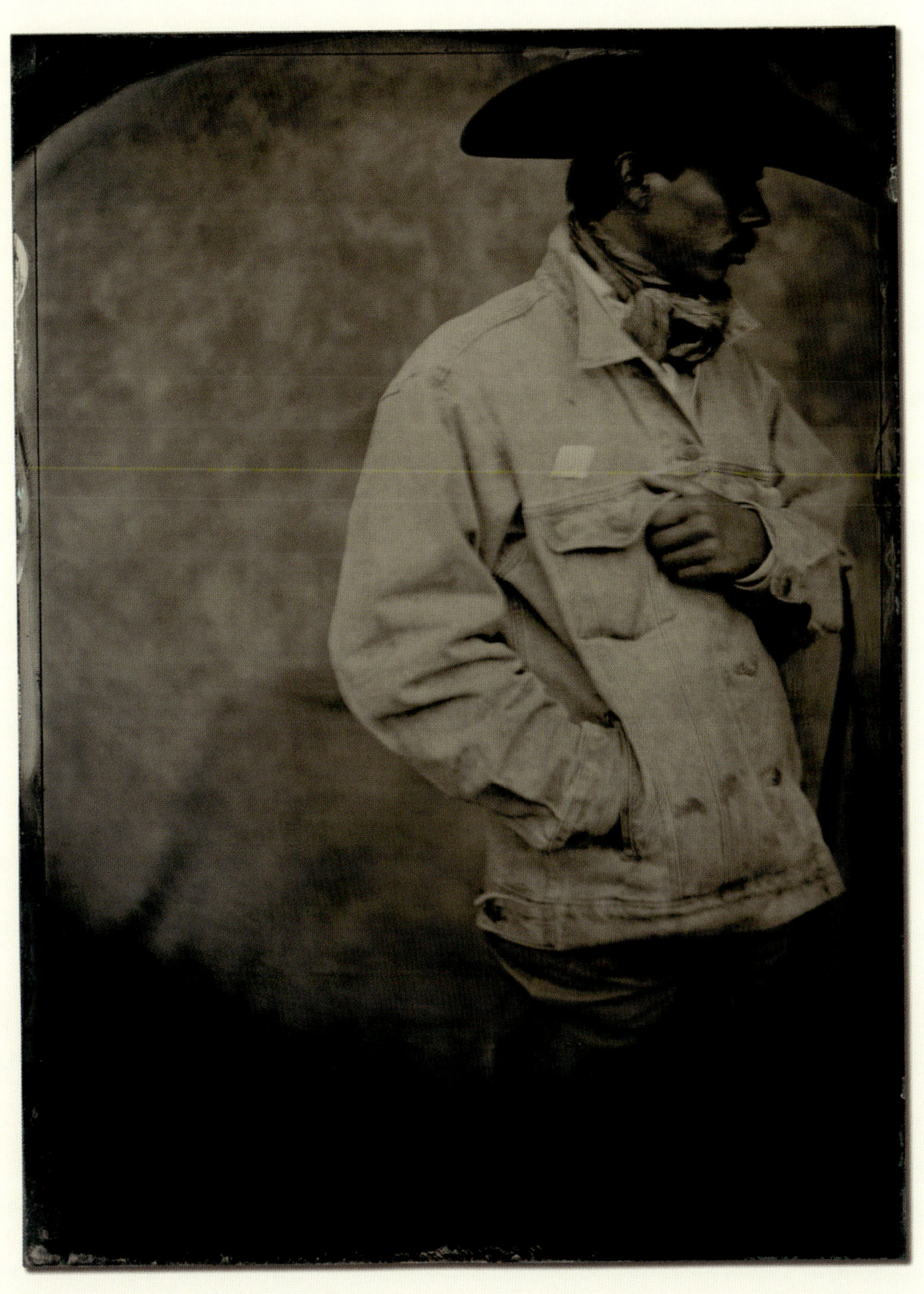

PLATE 37

JASON "SHAG" BOWMAN & JAY HART

HART RANCH

Shag and Jay share a love of the cowboy life. But both say neither one does it for the money.

Jay is a fourth-generation cowboy. He's tried other jobs. But nothing ever worked for him like cowboying. "It's a way of life I can't replace. Once you're hooked, you're hooked."

He says the trick in working with cows is to quit thinking like a man and start acting like them. "It's a challenge to think like a cow, but it's fun and I love it."

This work keeps Jay around good people and lets him live a life true to his values. "Honesty is a quality among cowboys I know and respect. You can do this work and still serve the Lord."

A man of few words, Shag adds, "Cowboying—it's not the best way to make a livin', but there is no better way of life."

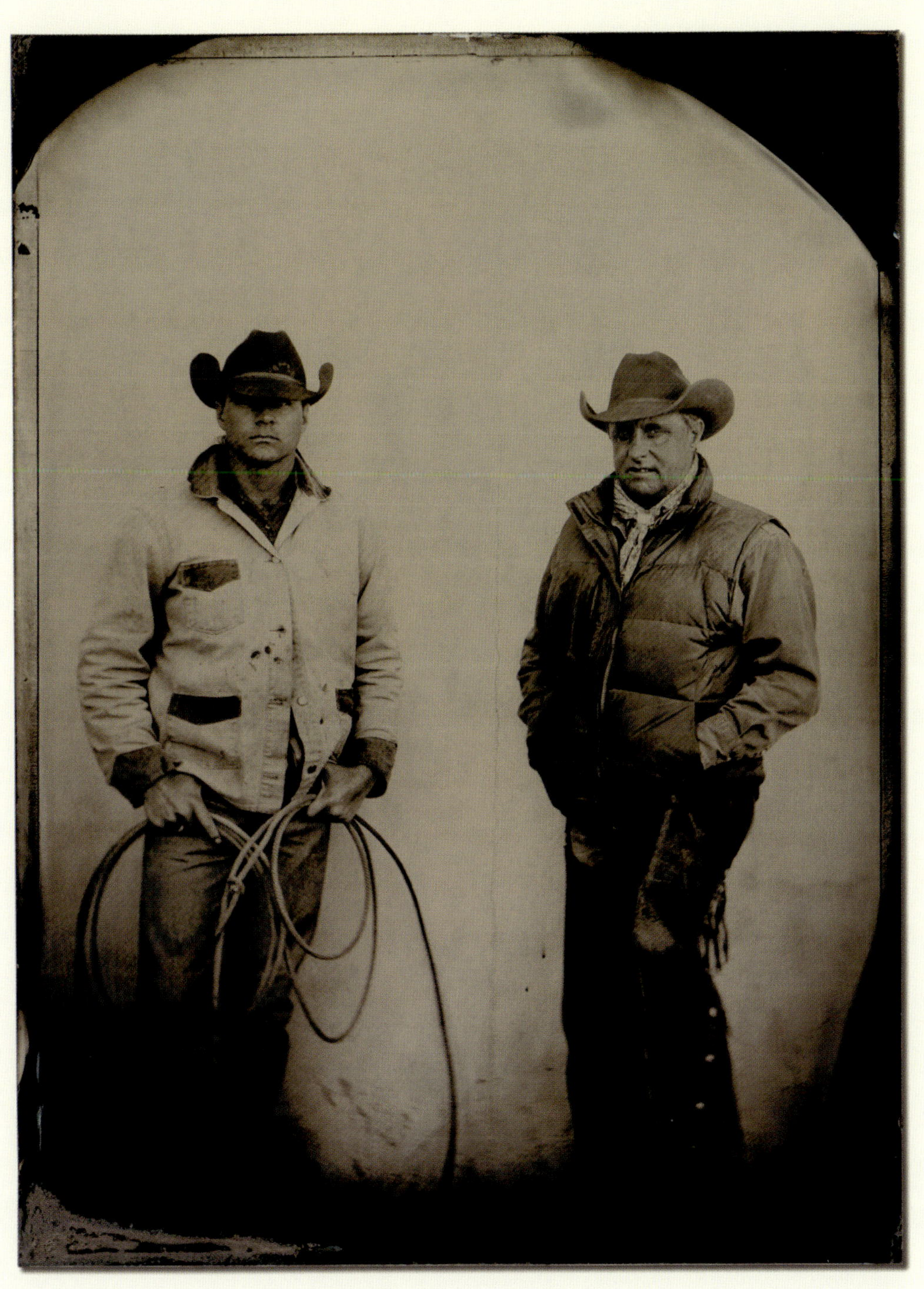

PLATE 38

DICK SAYERS

PITCHFORK RANCH

At age 16, Dick got invited to go work on a ranch in New Mexico. That was 31 years ago.

"Learned a couple journeyman skills along the way, but cowboying is what's in my heart."

At Pitchfork Ranch, Dick owns the responsibility of running 1,000 head of cows on 4,000 acres—by himself. "That's really satisfying. I'm my own boss in many ways." He says that the land he lives and works on is so rough that you have to stay sharp. "The cows may not show up when you feed, so you have to run this camp on good sense and good instinct."

He acknowledges that the hours are hard, but there are too many positives to do any complaining. "Starting horses, working cattle, and being in the wide-open country makes the long days worthwhile."

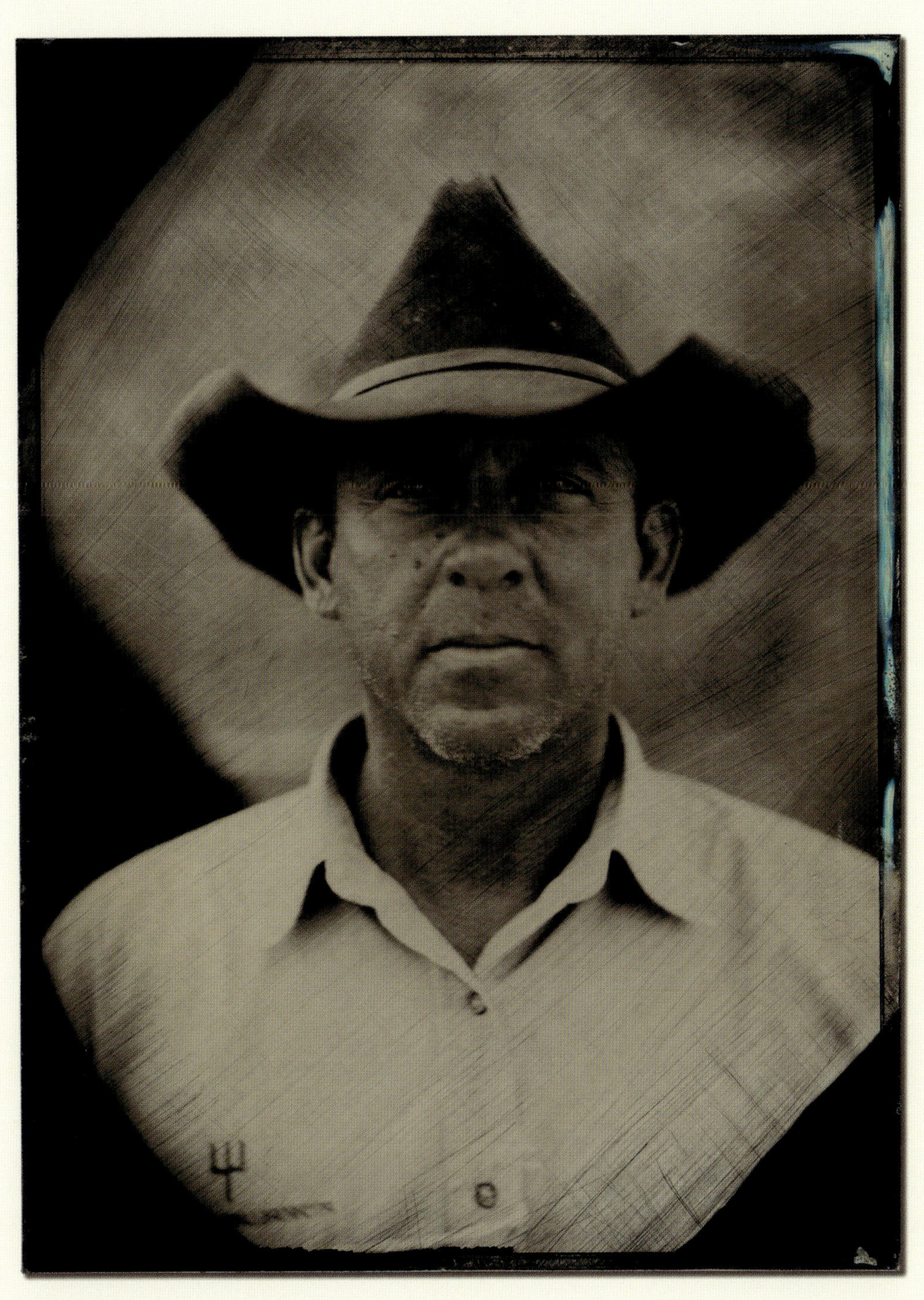

PLATE 39

ALF MEANS

Y-SIX RANCH

Alf was raised on the ranch that has been in his family since 1892. He says after high school, his father sent him to the best school he could. "New Mexico Military Institute. Took Ag Science. I haven't tried anything else and have never wanted to."

To Alf, principles are a foundation of a ranch upbringing. "You learn respect and how to treat ladies." And out here, people have a mindset of community and love of the land.

"Ranch people will die for each other."

Alf is 85 years old.

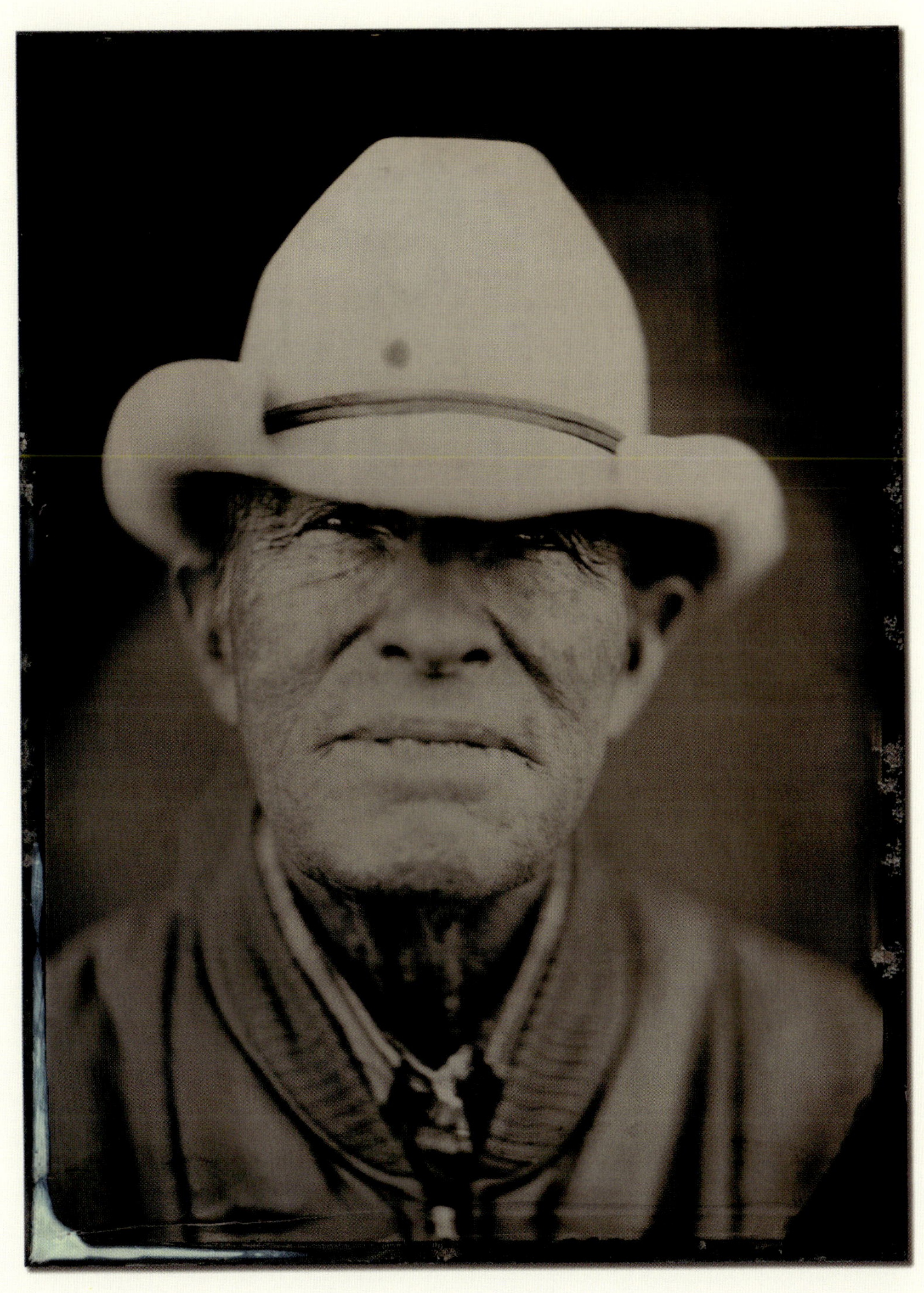

PLATE 40

CHRIS SPENCER

LONG X RANCH

"Lean times fall on most cowboys, but we come back to it 'cause we love it," says Chris, who drew his first paycheck at 14. Chris has been around ranching all his life.

He says good families come out of ranch life. "Family members get close, living out here." Being out and working with animals gives his children a lot of responsibility. Including his four-year-old. "Everyone has to pull their own weight." Chris says his kids are always anxious to get involved with the work, and that helps them stay close. "As a family we try to do as much as possible together."

"Hard work is easier when you work with your hands."

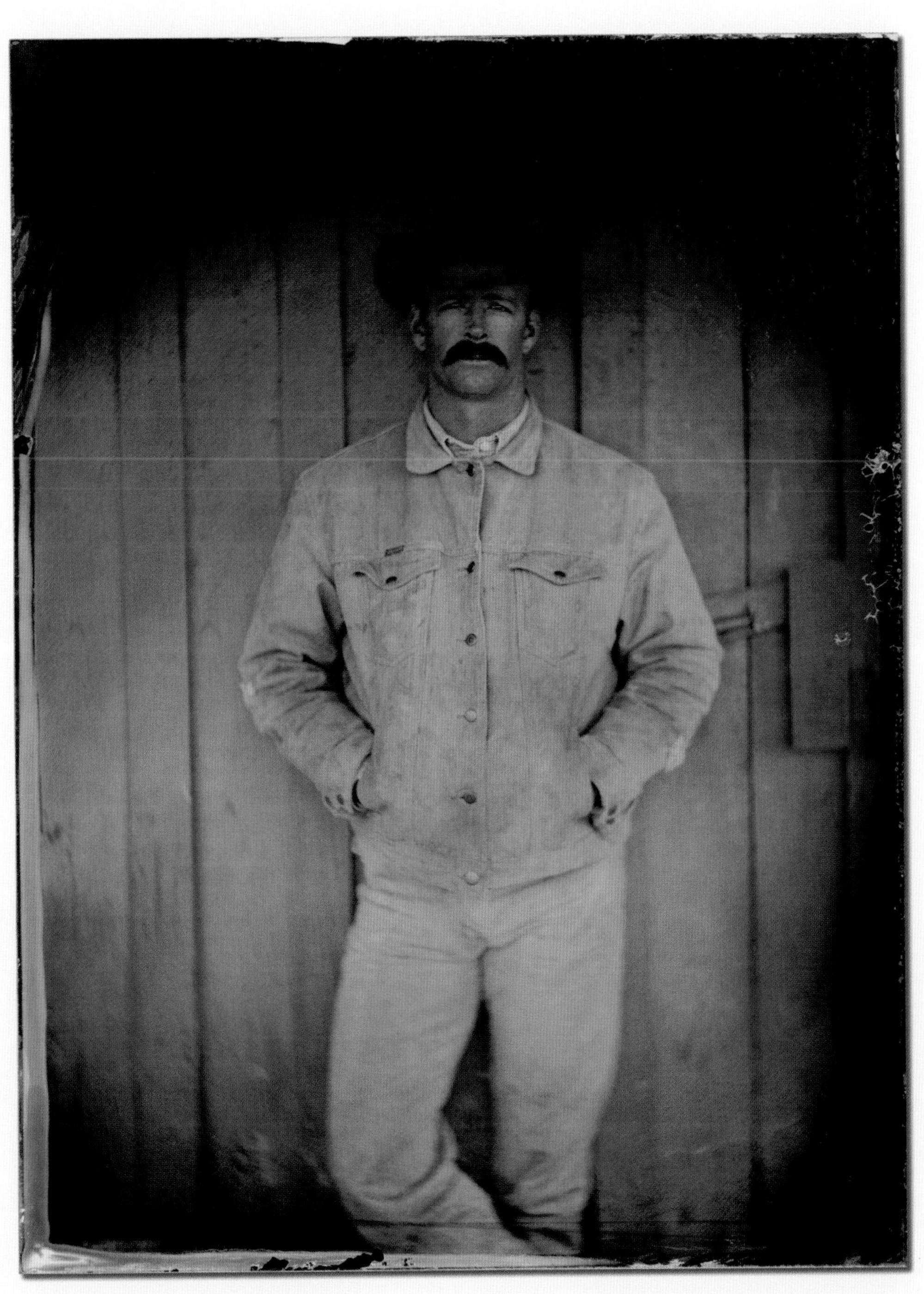

PLATE 41

JULIO SOLANO

HASKELL FARMS RANCH

Julio is 41 years old and inherited cowboying from his dad. "My father was a vaquero and I loved growing up alongside my father and helping out."

He likes being horseback, working cattle, and getting paid to do it. "Not many people draw a check for a job they love. I'm fortunate to live this life."

"Rain, snow, hot, or cold—if I'm on a horse I am happy."

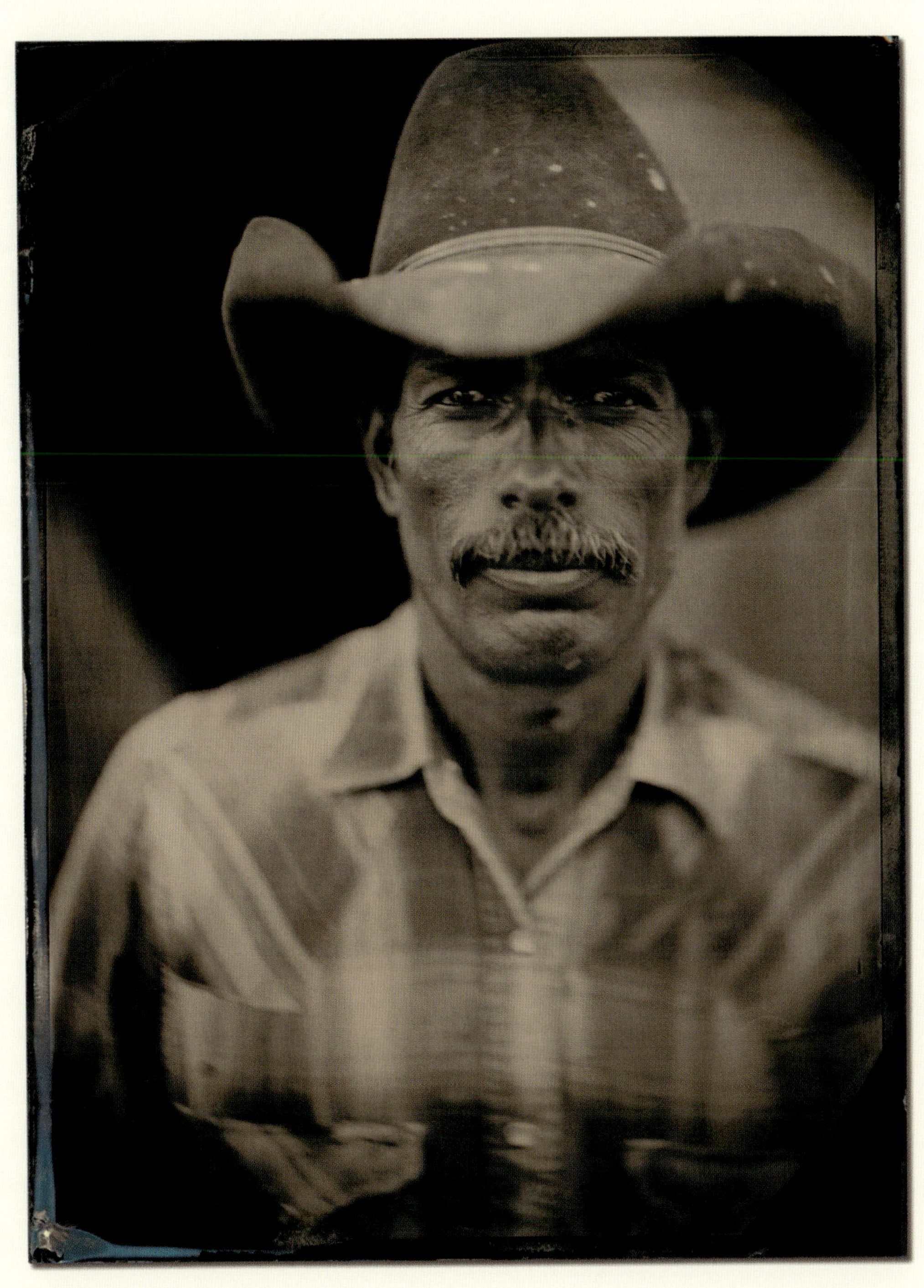

PLATE 42

TOM MOORHOUSE

MOORHOUSE RANCH

"I was raised on a ranch, and it's all I've ever done." Tom was born, raised, is living now, and says he will die in the same house. Raising his own family in this house, he says a ranch is a good place to teach your kids value.

"I have no ideas of doing anything else, and I've never had a mid-life crisis. The weather is real tough, but I'm proud to be able to get through it." Seeing things come together—the smells, textures, visuals of it all—is what's worthwhile to him.

Says that when you work together with other men, you build bonds that are hard to forge any other way.

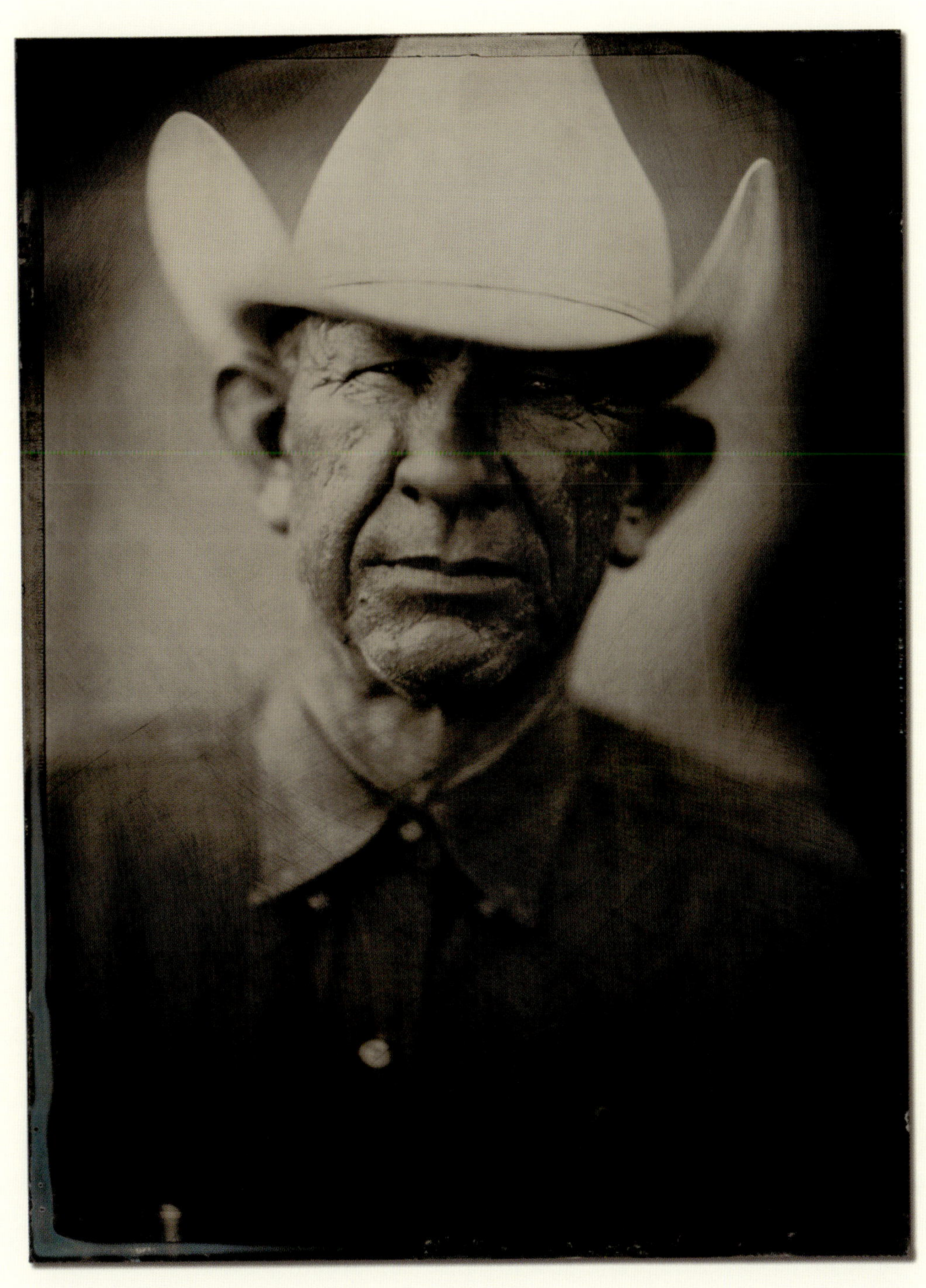

PLATE 43

PAUL IVY

COLLINS CREEK RANCH

Paul says ranching is more a lifestyle than an occupation. "You have the biggest office in the world—no walls."

"The best thing about ranching is the people—some great characters."

Says he couldn't imagine raising a family anywhere else but here. "I hope my son gets to experience everything I did. Without the ranching way of life, we might forget where we came from."

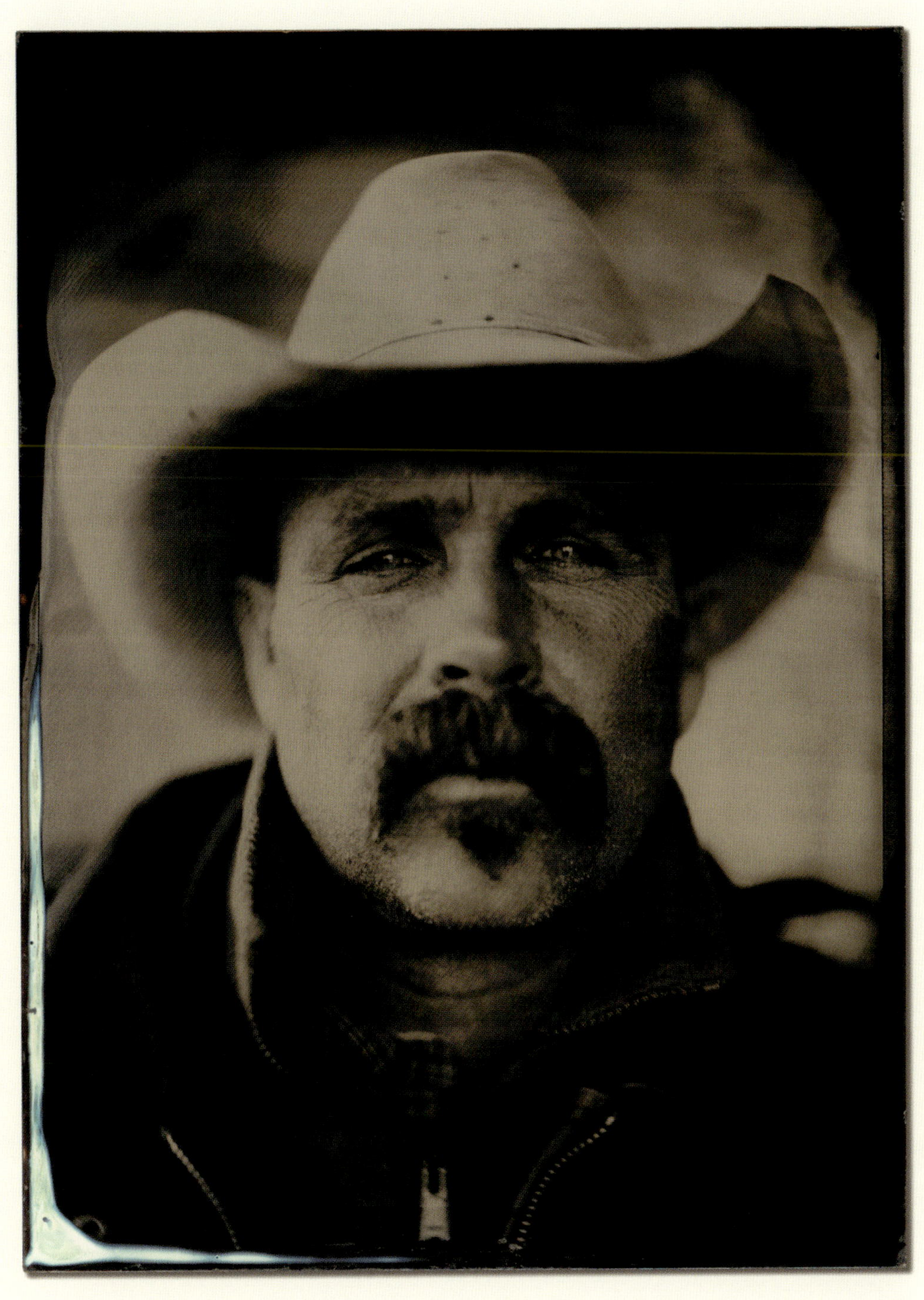

PLATE 44

ROBERT CHAISON

CINCH RING RANCH

Growing up around the stockyards of Fort Worth during the mid-'50s, Robert says his childhood heroes were cowboys. "I met Roy Rogers when I was six—had my hat, chaps, and gun on my tricycle. He shook my hand and said, 'What's up, pardner?' I didn't wash that hand for a long time."

Says living out here helps teach kids responsibilities, and adults patience. "A ranch life for a family becomes a real team effort. When everyone takes care of the small details, seems like the big details take care of themselves. There's a forced self-sufficiency for ranch kids."

To him, being horseback is a great privilege. "Every time I get a horse between my legs I feel fortunate. Makes a bad day go away real quick. The outlook on the world changes when you see it between a horse's ears."

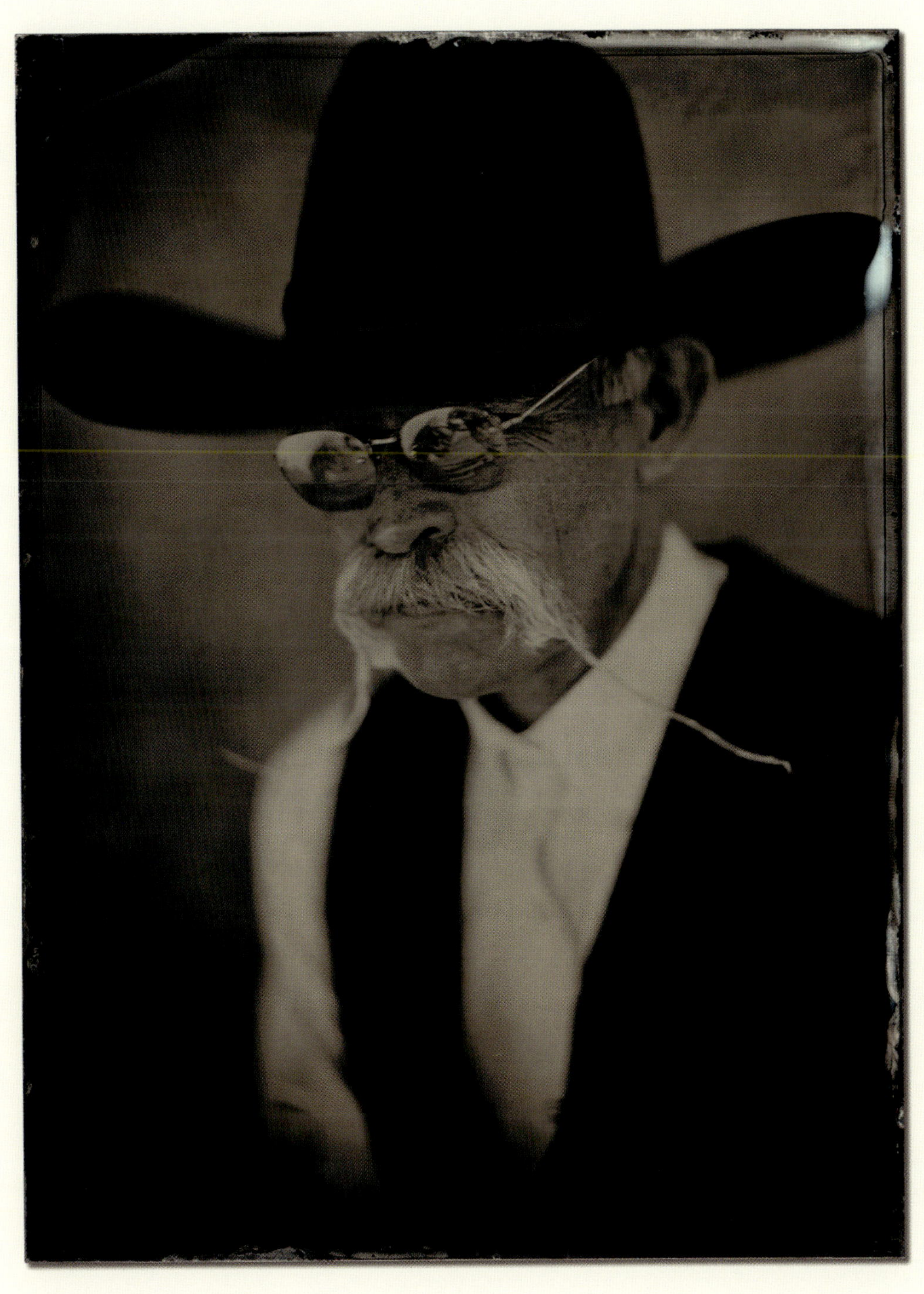

PLATE 45

BRENT BROWNLEE

TRIANGLE RANCH

"Ranching and cowboying have been a part of my family's history for many generations, and I hope they will be for many to come."

Brent likes this life for the freedom. "We have an independence that few can get from a job. Most of the jobs we accomplish are most often done on our own, and there is a great sense of accomplishment in that." He also says that when you work with a crew it takes teamwork to achieve your goals. "This makes for good friends and co-workers."

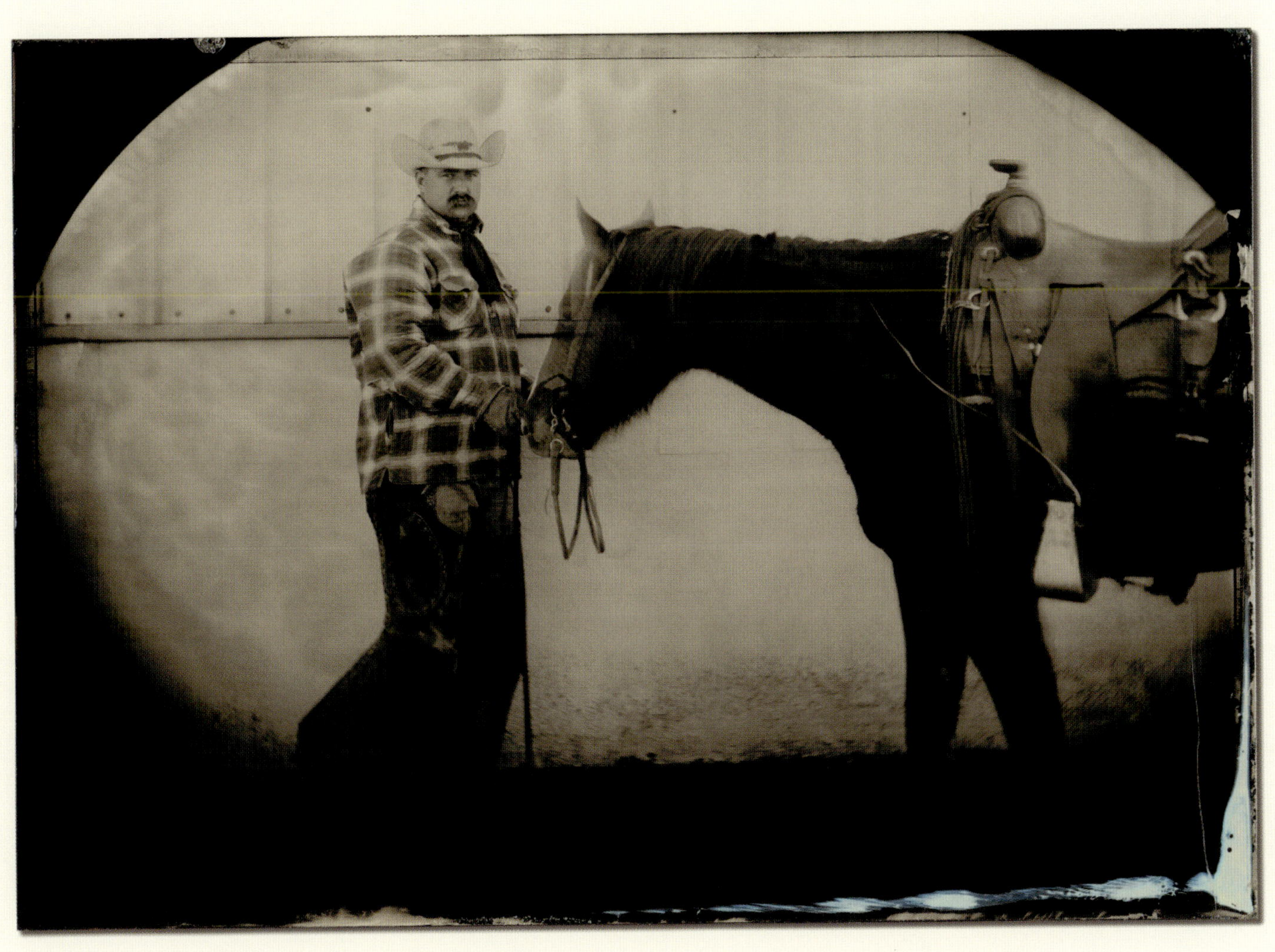

PLATE 46

FRO WALDEN

MOORHOUSE RANCH

Fro spent his early years on a ranch up in Nevada. At 13 he started drawing a check as a cowboy. Now, 41 years later, he looks after 700 cows and 22,000 acres on the Moorhouse Ranch.

"Tom Moorhouse either trusts me or doesn't like me, 'cause he doesn't tell me what to do."

Fro says hard work and good hands coming together are what help get a big job done. "Going to the wagon to brand 2,000 cows over four weeks in the spring and six weeks in the fall is the highlight of cowboying. We still use range teepees and it's the old way. Which I love."

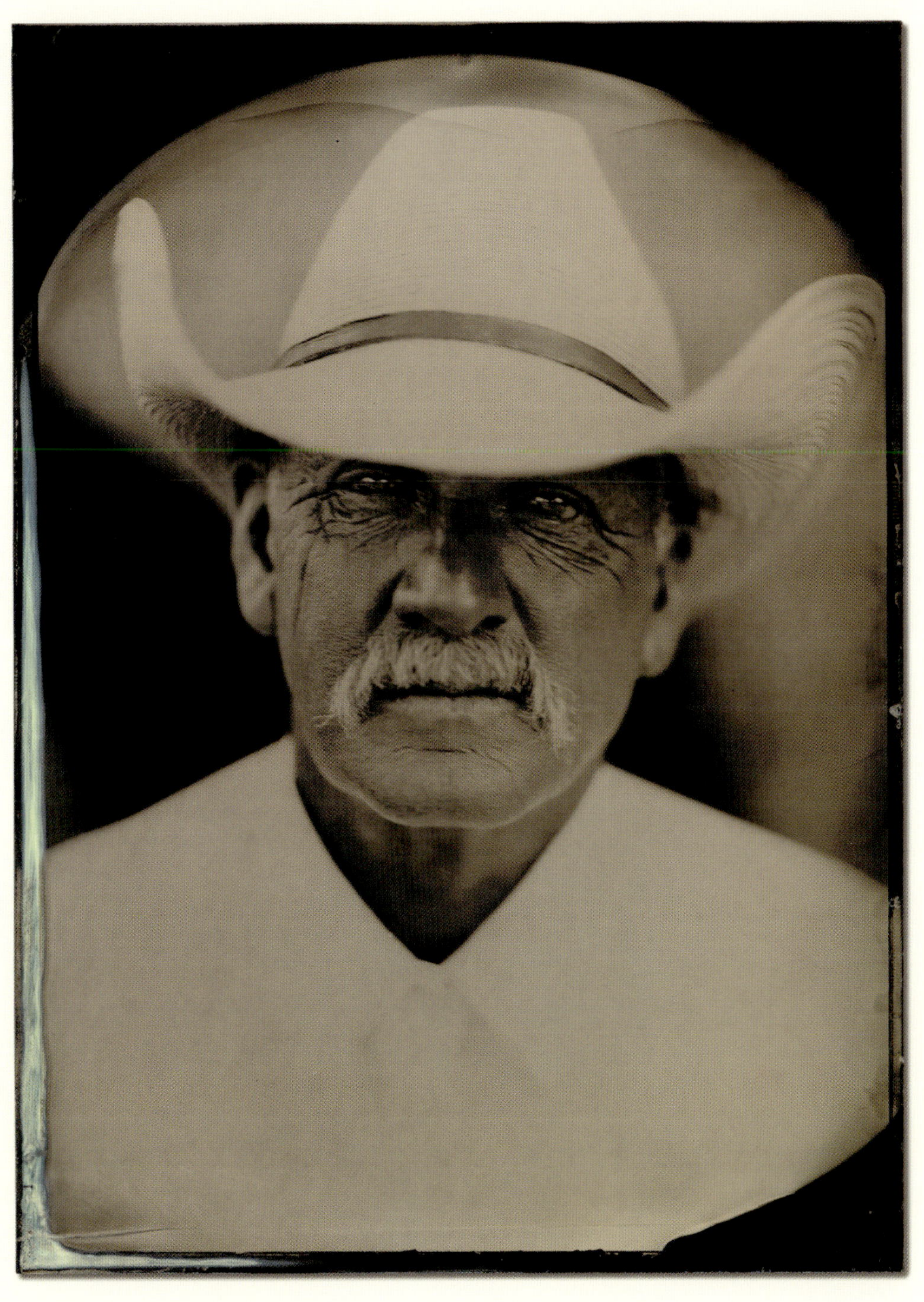

PLATE 47

JIM DACUS

DACUS LIVESTOCK

Being raised around ranching, Jim learned early on to keep his eyes and mind wide open. "Living close to nature, living outback, making a life out of ordinary days taught me to be mindful of my life."

In the 21st century, Jim is quite pleased to live this life he's chosen. "Cowboying teaches you what you're in control of and what you're not. It's about how you live life—with a good work ethic, perseverance. I feel blessed I get to do it my way."

It gives him all the time he needs to raise a family right, to spend time together. The kids get involved in the work. Start early and stay late. That, Jim feels, helps them learn to be adults.

He says ranching teaches you lessons, if you're open to learning them, but that you'll never learn all of it. "You'll never say you did it all, but it teaches you about yourself—who you are. You can reflect on what you're about. That's important to me."

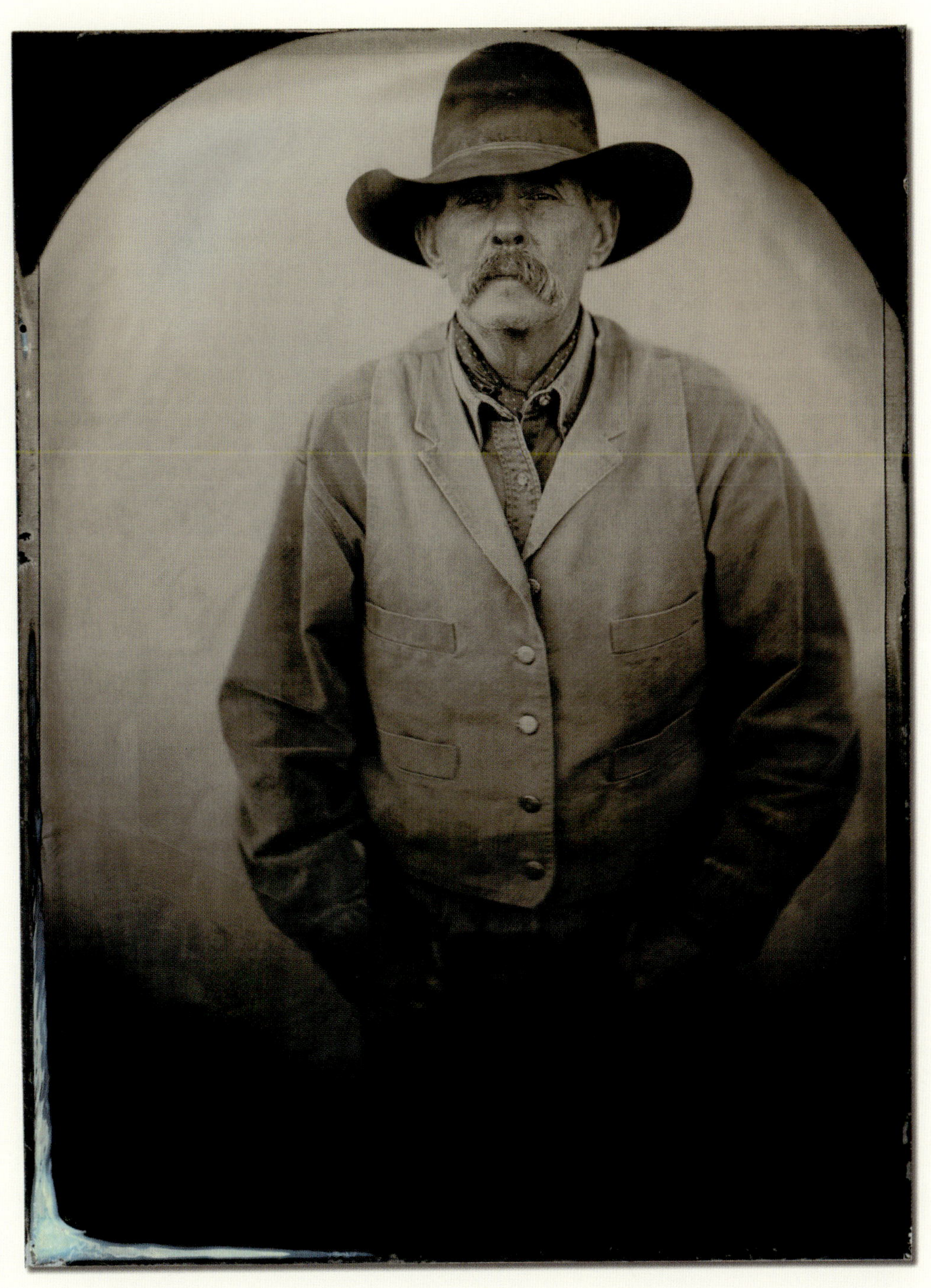

PLATE 48

J. D. HENRY

WAGGONER RANCH

There are ranches to work at outside Texas, and J. D.'s tried some. But he found his way back home soon enough. "I've tried going to Arizona, but love Texas."

He says the advice and the stories you get from people working out on the range are the best.

"Learning from older fellers. You can't get that education in college."

And as far as what he wants out of life, it's pretty simple. "Enough money to survive and have some occasional fun. If you gotta work with guys, better make it fun."

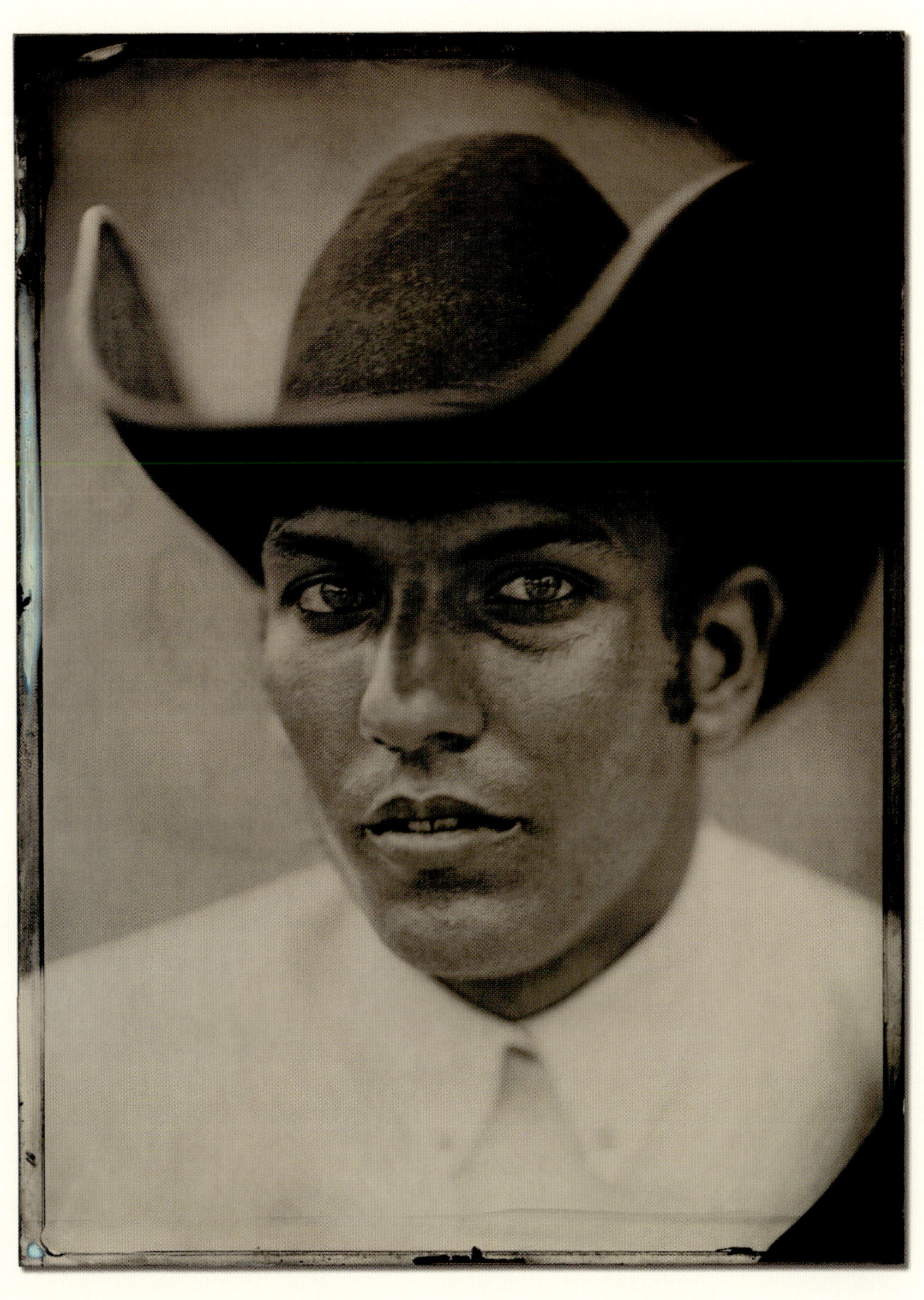

PLATE 49

PATE MEINZER

TONGUE RIVER RANCH

At age 20, Pate glories in the outdoor life. Can't imagine being tied to a desk or a vehicle.

"I think the main reason why I love what I do is because I'm always outside and always seeing different country and wildlife."

Don't try to fence him in.

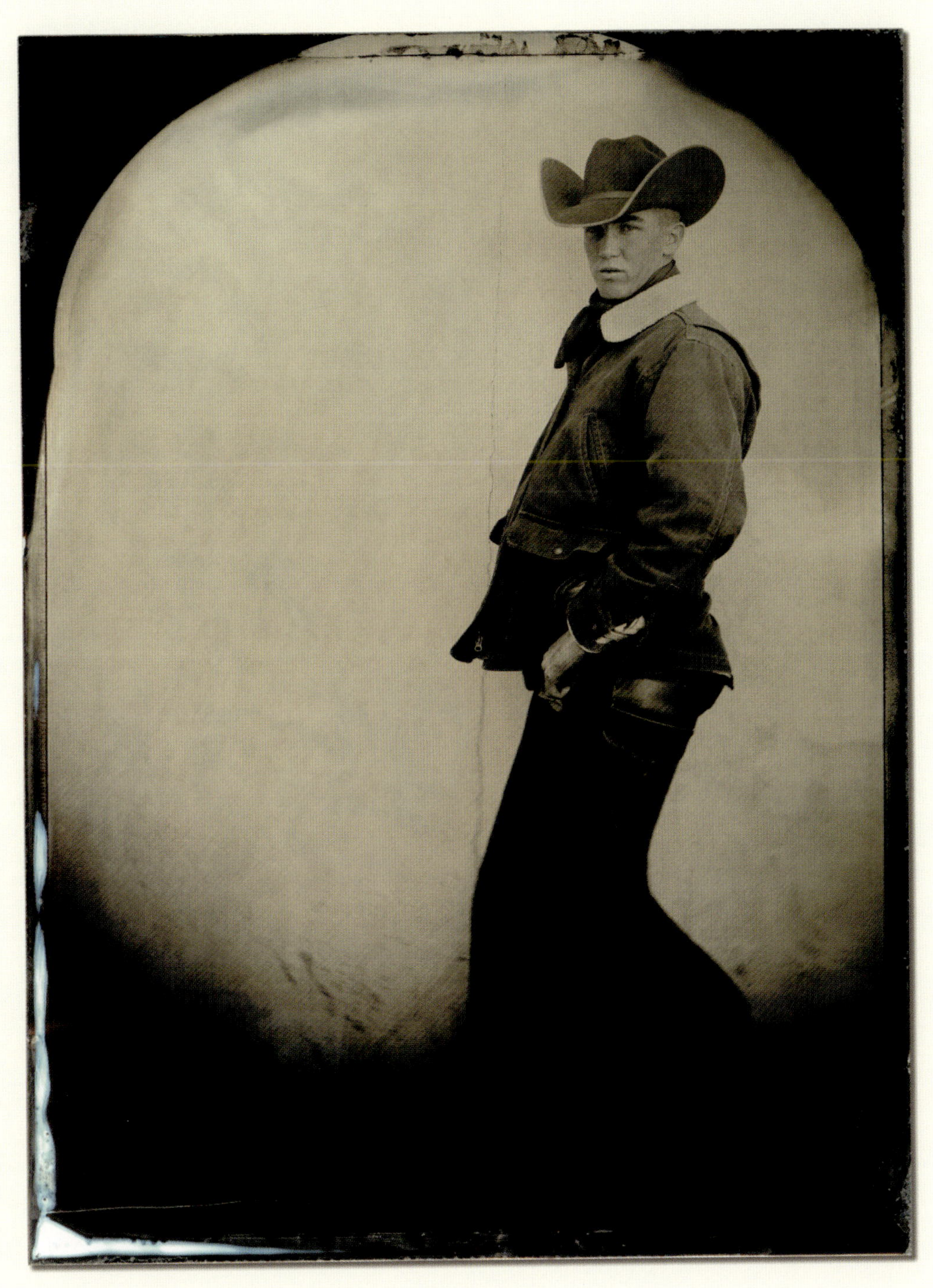

PLATE 50

TIM STOUT

QUIEN SABE RANCH

Tim is 31 years old and has held two occupations in his life: serving his country and cowpunching. "Cowboying was a passion of mine since the day I threw a leg over a horse."

"I'd rather take less money for a riding job than to have a big paycheck and not have my feet dangling every day."

He says there is an etiquette that forms a bond among cowboys, where you depend on each other to watch out for the other man. "Mutual respect and the honesty of the hands you work with cannot be traded for any other job out there."

"God gives this life to only one kind of feller."

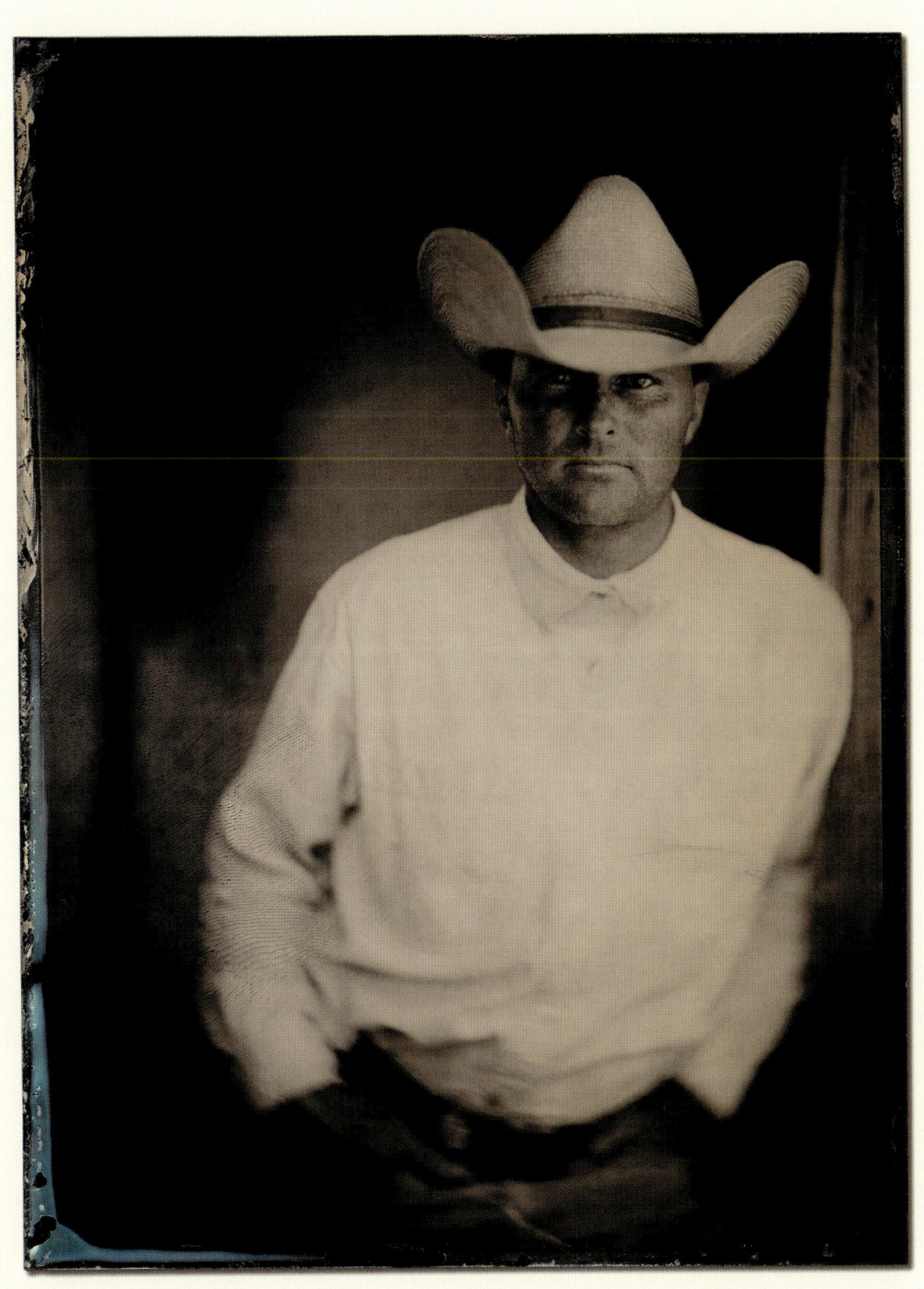

PLATE 51

BOB HOLLOWELL

6666 RANCH DIXON CREEK

Bob says life out here is real living. And the work is just the kind that suits him. "I like cowboying because I get to ride good horses, and work cattle, and live in the country, and don't have to punch a clock."

Nearing 70 years of age, he doesn't think of doing anything else.

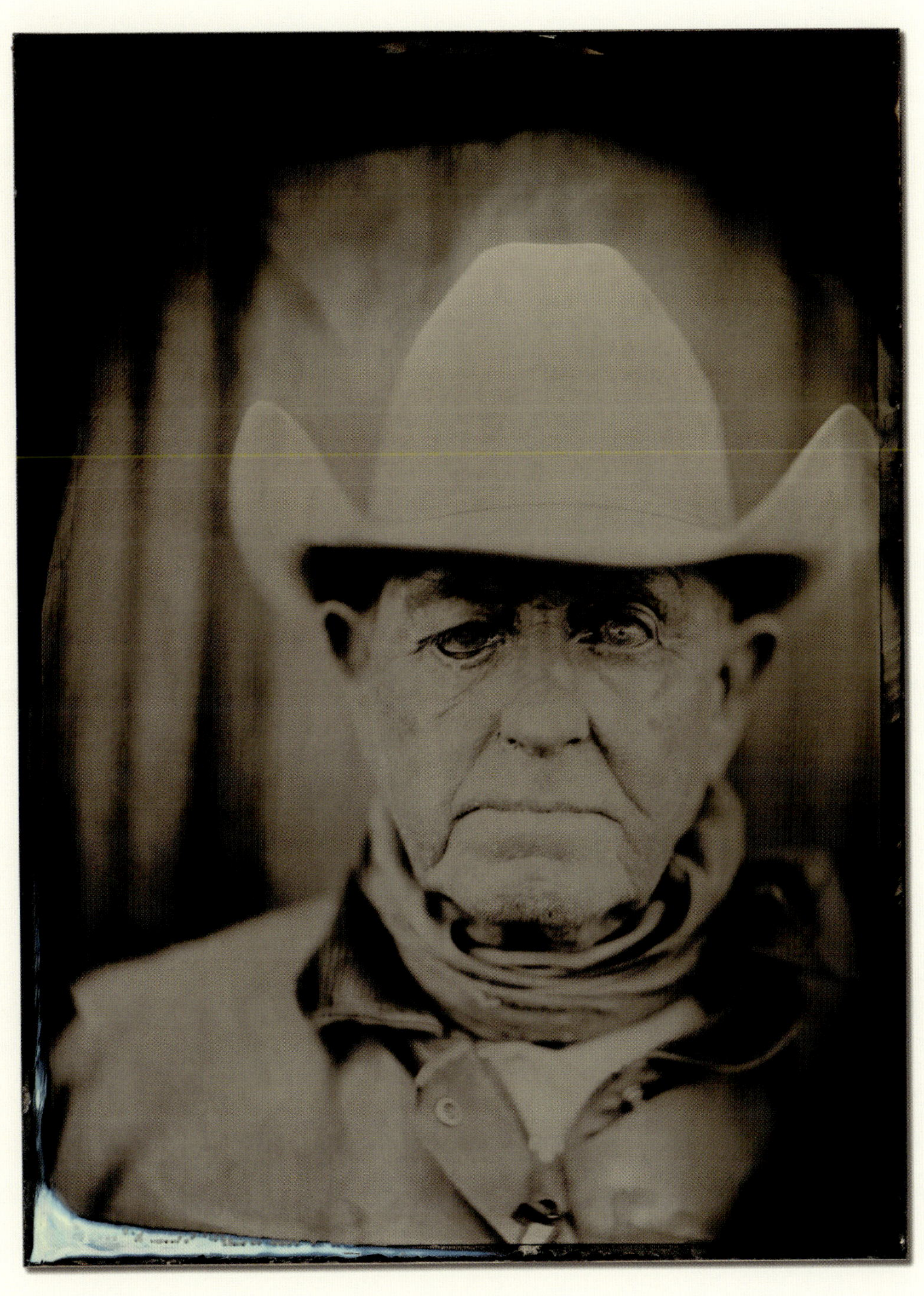

PLATE 52

CHANCE STOUT

QUIEN SABE RANCH

Getting up before sunup and being on a horse, watching as the sun's coming up, "That's one of the best feelings," thinks Chance. He loves living in open spaces. Having lots of animals.

Another plus is being with his father. "During branding season I get to work with my dad finding cattle that are hiding down in the canyons."

"I'm considering being a cowboy when I'm older, but I want to keep my options open." Mostly, he says he just wants to enjoy his time on the ranch as he's growing up.

"As a kid, the older cowboys help keep you on the straight and narrow. They care about me and want to keep me pointed in the right direction."

"It's a good life with few worries."

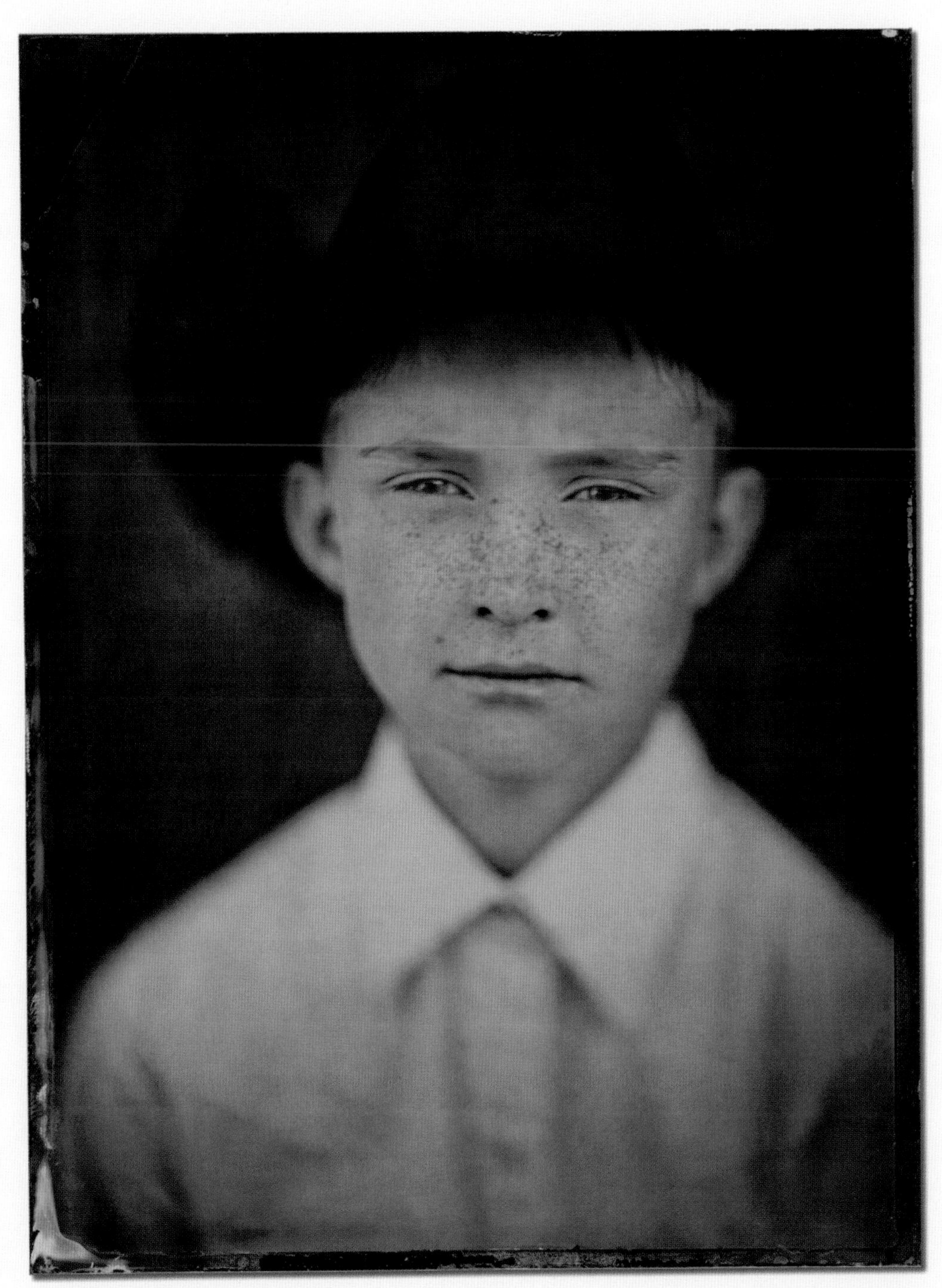

PLATE 53

GARY MATHIEWS

RA BROWN RANCH

Gary is 32 years old. Grew up on a small family farming and ranching operation, went to college, and on to graduate school in animal breeding and animal genetics. Now he puts all that book learning to good use.

"I have been extremely fortunate to have found a job that allows me to use these technical skills in the field of animal breeding and genetics to improve livestock, while at the same time using the time-honored traditions of the American cowboy to accomplish these tasks."

"I have a job that I enjoy doing every day, and one I would consider to be my hobby. There are not many people who are fortunate enough to say that about their profession."

But most important, he says, there is no better place to raise a family, and teach your children important life skills, than on a ranch.

"I have been truly blessed with a great family and way of life."

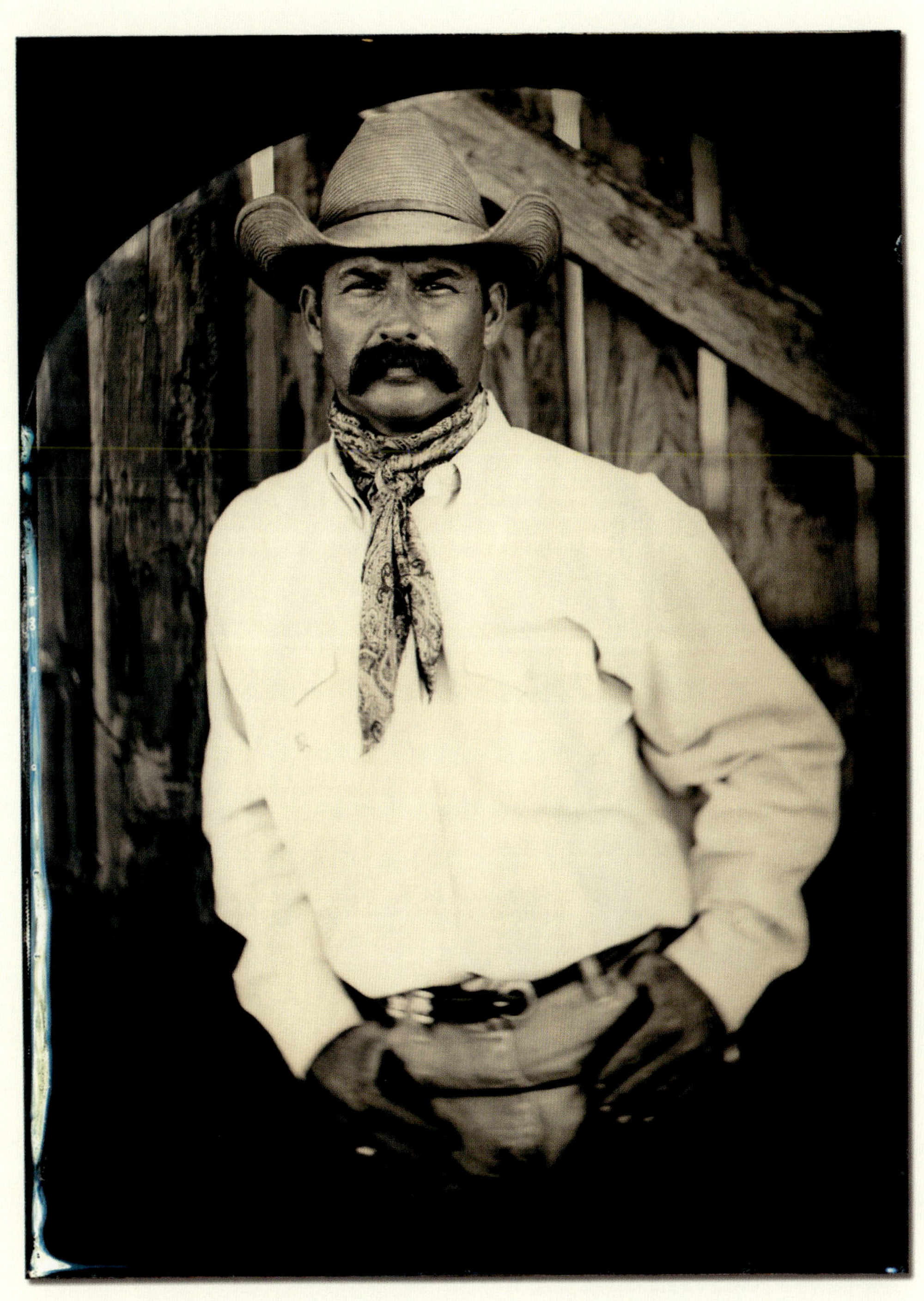

PLATE 54

CHRIS ROACH

LA ESCALERA RANCH

Chris was born in Alpine and works in the neighborhood. But what a neighborhood—no asphalt, plenty of stars overhead, and lots of space in which to roam.

"Worked here a little over a year," says Chris, who isn't moving anytime soon.

His job description may give him leeway to move over the plains, but he won't be likely to roam into the city to look for work.

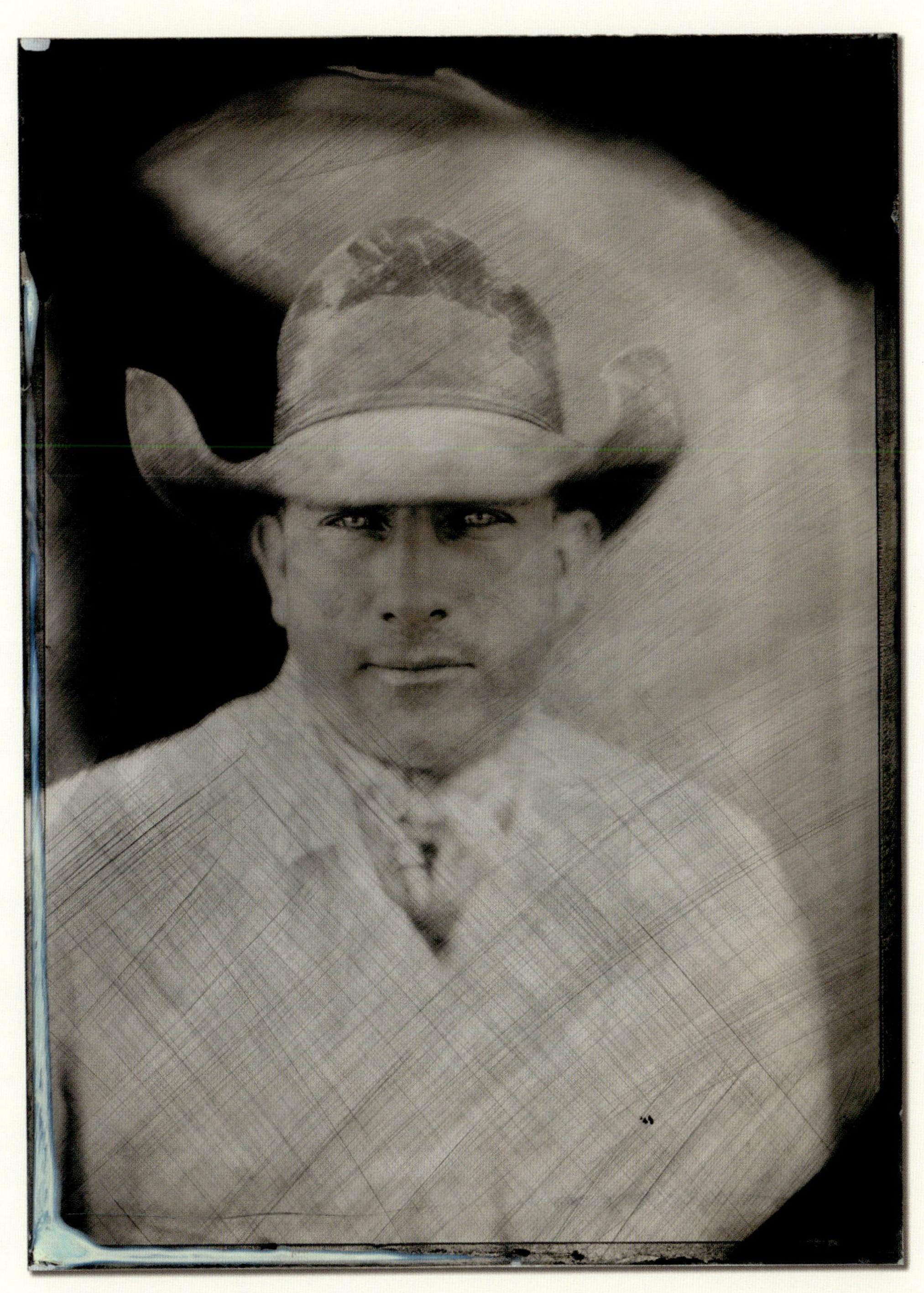

PLATE 55

ROBERTO FERNANDEZ

ARMSTRONG RANCH

"When I was a very young kid, like eight years old, I would go and watch the old cowboys break horses at the King Ranch. Now it's me doing that."

To Roberto, working with cattle is challenging, dangerous, and fun. "I love rounding up cattle out of big pastures. I love to rope cattle of all sizes. I enjoy everything involved in working cattle...branding, vaccinating, and separating the mama cows from their calves."

There's only one thing about his work he doesn't like: the weather. "I don't enjoy working cattle during the cold winter season because your hands and feet get numb, and it's very hard to handle a rope if you have to rope a cow or bull. Other than that, I love working for the Armstrong Ranch."

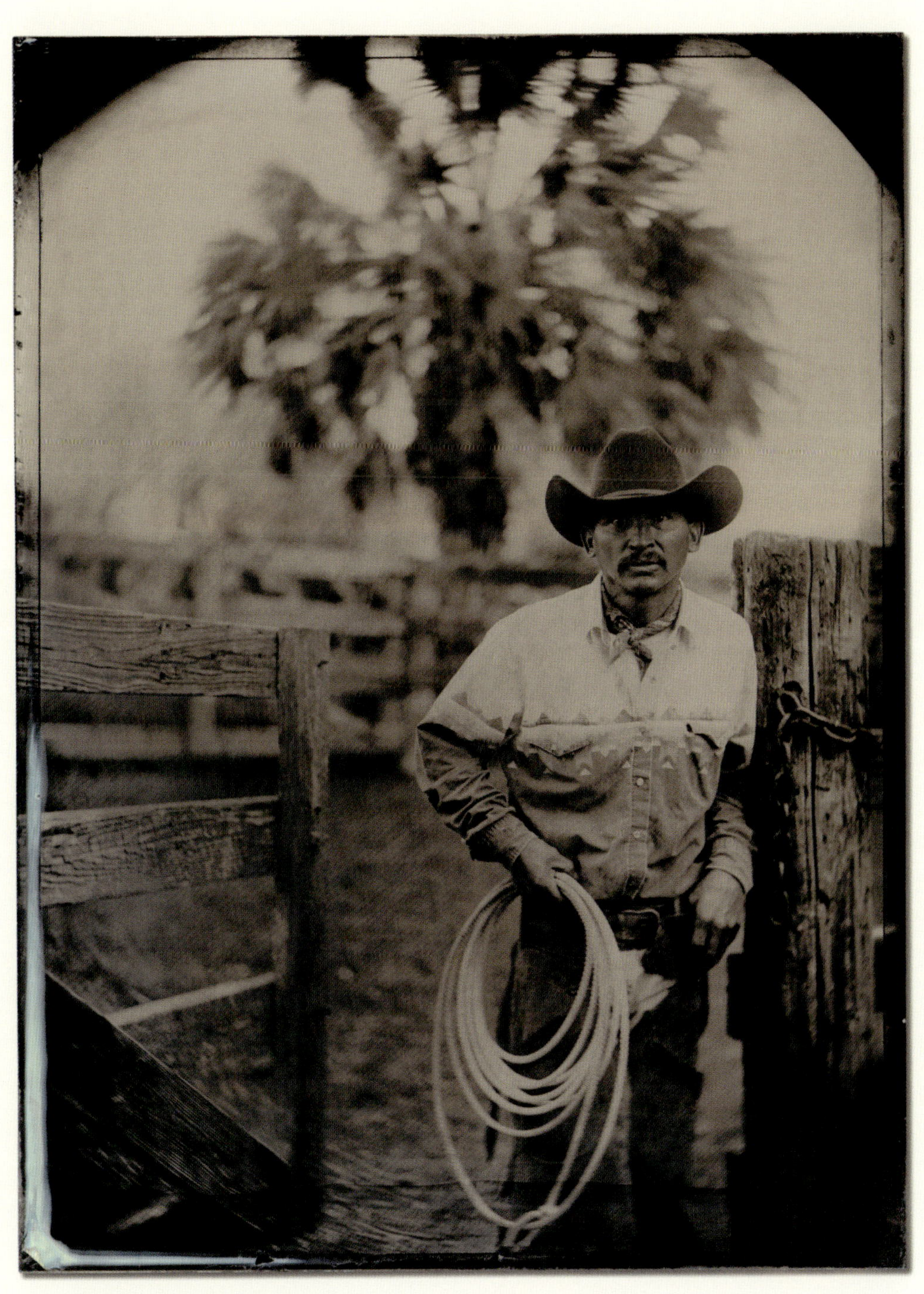

PLATE 56

JULIE KING

ALPINE, TEXAS

Julie grew up on a ranch that's 500 sections. "It's nice to get out on a horse at age seven and be on your own. Riding open country and taking responsibility for yourself. It's a sense of freedom that's rare."

She rides colts and has been starting colts and working problem horses since she was 14. "By working hard I was able to build a name and respect for working horses."

She says all aspects of ranching are mainly seen as men's work. "It's hard for women to be involved in the cattle part especially." But even so, she can't see herself doing anything else but living on a ranch, working leather and starting more colts.

"Once you show you can pull your weight, you've got their respect. It builds character."

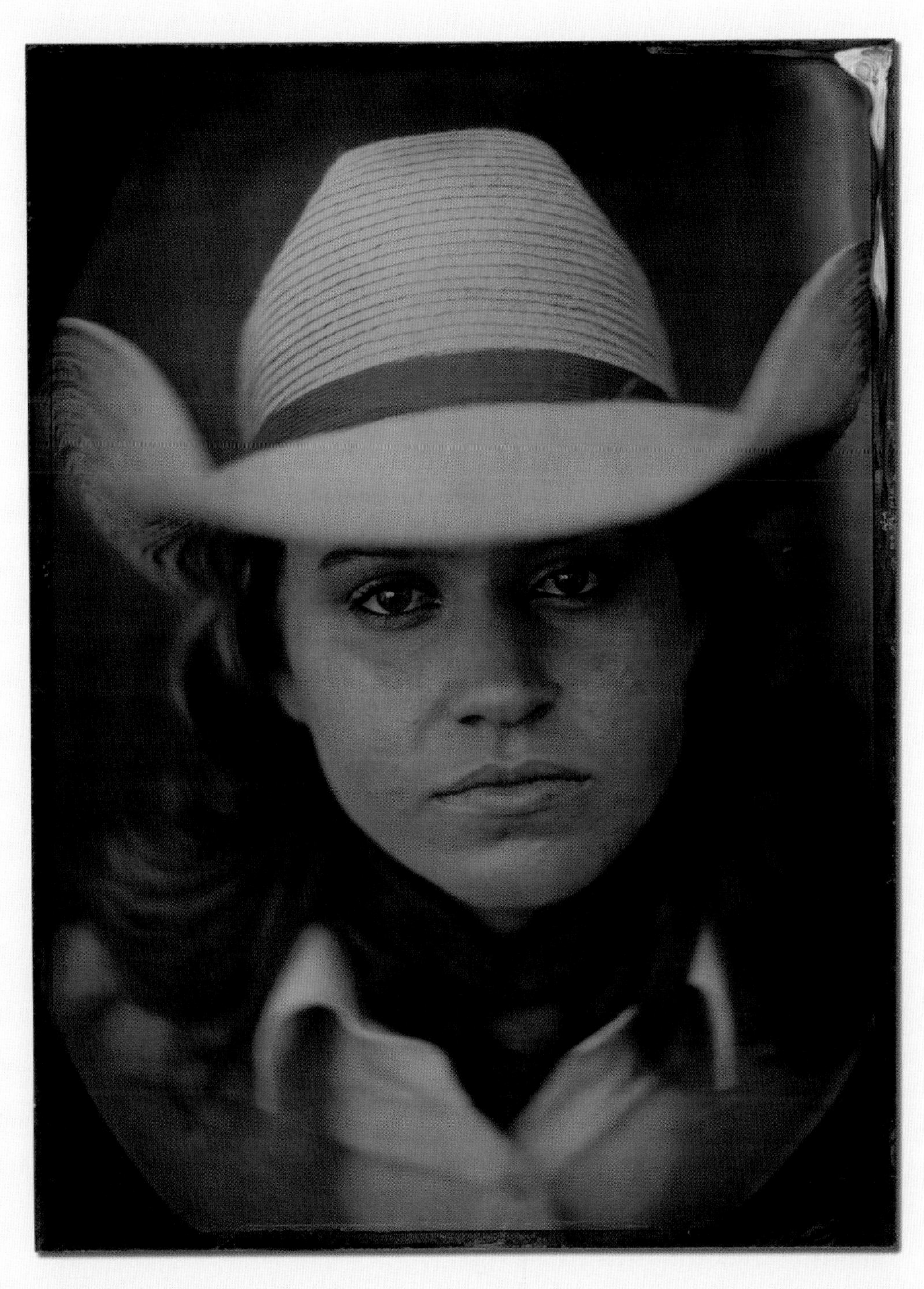

PLATE 57

ROSS BULLINGER

DAYWORKER

When he was 15, he started riding colts for people and day working.

"When I was little, we had horses. I loved being around them. We rode them and then we sold them. When we sold them, I really felt empty. That is when I knew I wanted to pursue working with horses."

Make no mistake, Ross wants to be a cowboy. But he recognizes the need to know the business side of things too. "I'm pursuing a degree in Animal Production, so I can pursue cowboying in a way that would allow a ranch to run traditionally but use science to make the business have a higher value."

Ross grew up in Haskell, Texas. He is 19 years old.

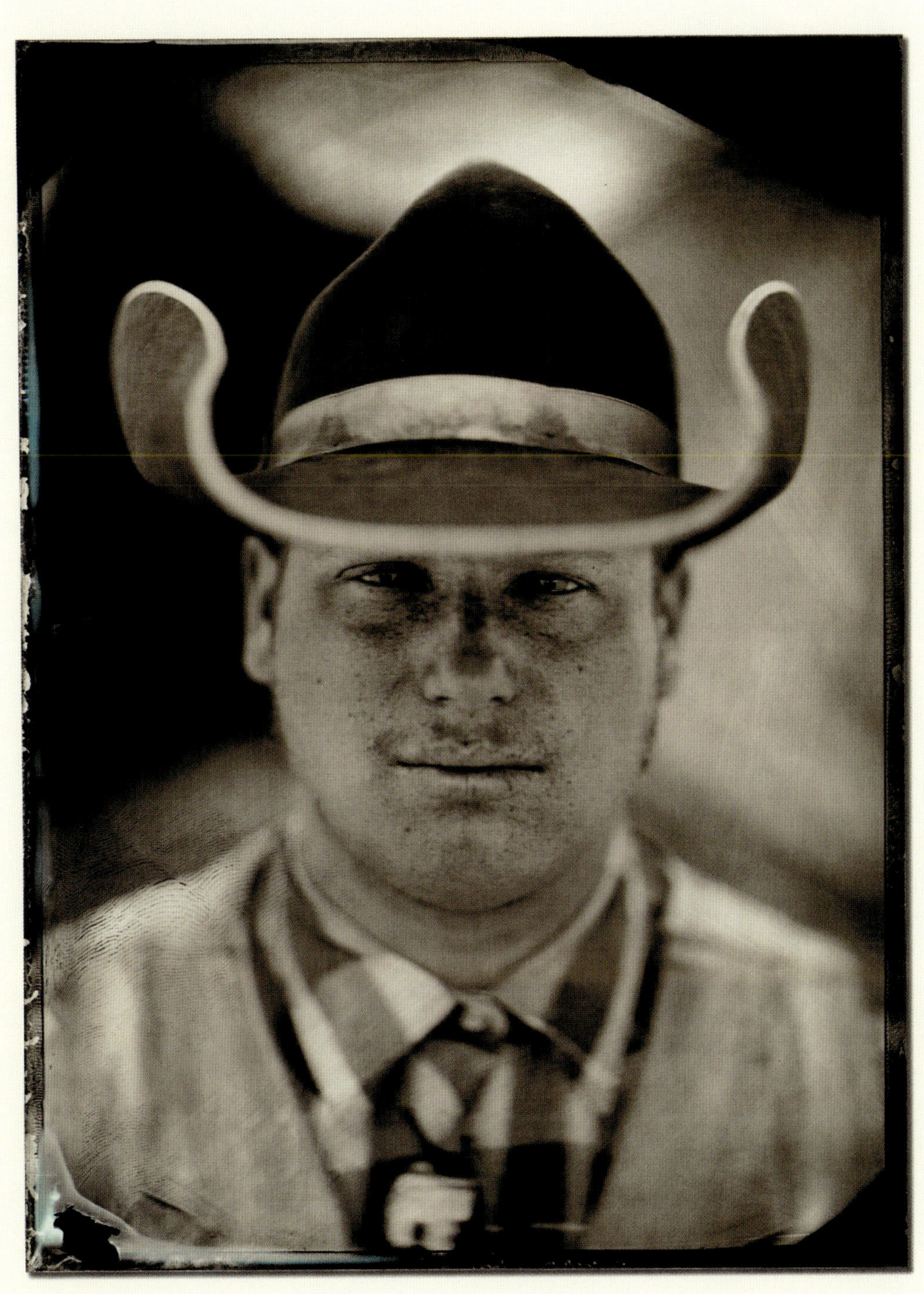

PLATE 58

RONALD LEWIS

6666 RANCH

Ron went to work cowboying 47 years ago and hasn't looked back since. "Saw photos of my granddad who was a cowboy and knew that's what I wanted to do. Never had a doubt."

He says staying horseback is what he's passionate about. He'd do a lot of what he does without pay, and he doesn't want to quit. "I'm going to keep cowboying as long as I'm pulling my weight and not a burden on those I'm working with. Cowboying is my retirement plan."

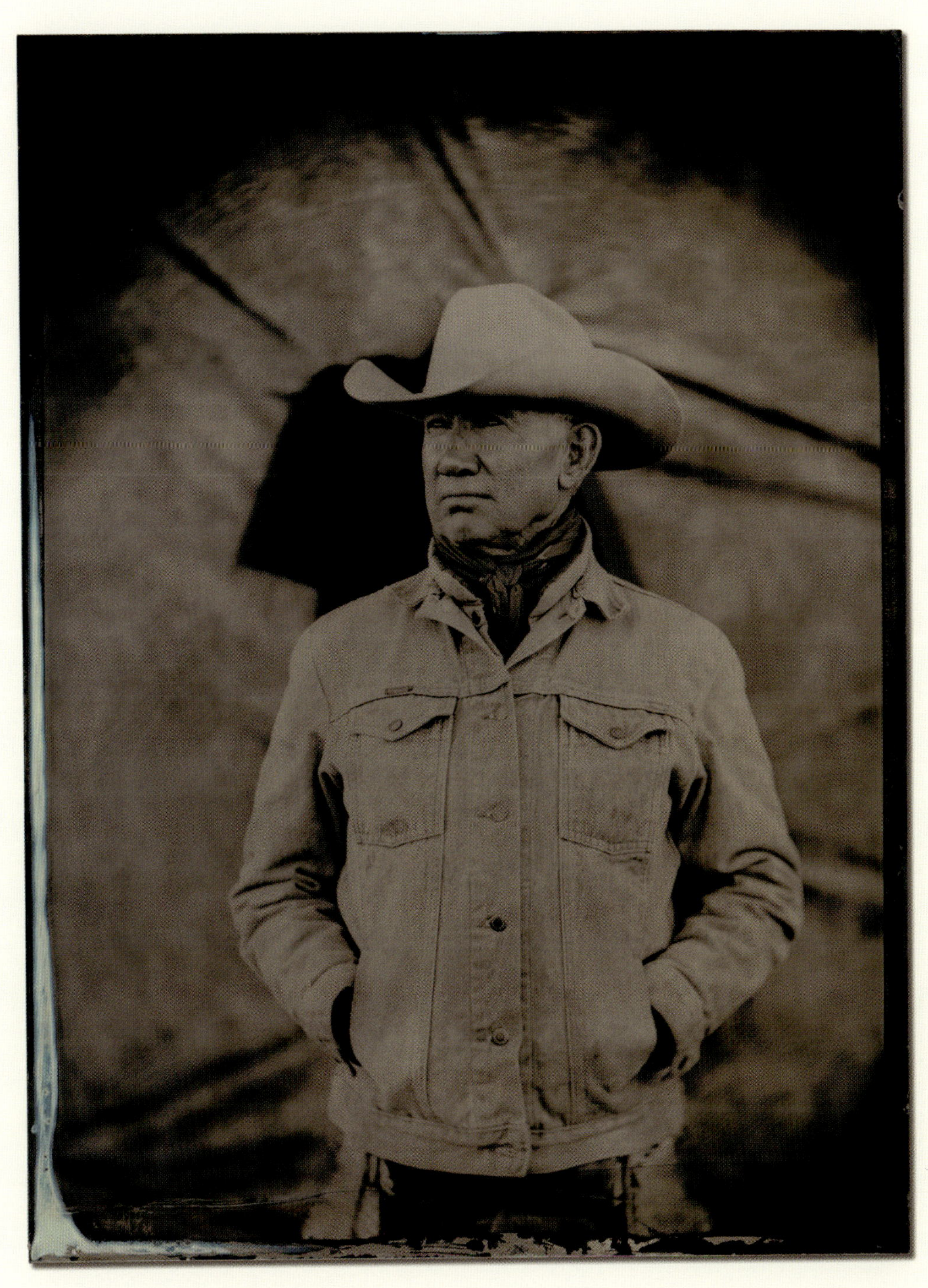

PLATE 59

FRANK GALVAN

PAISANO RANCH

"I'm a fortunate person," says Frank. "I enjoy my life. That's rare today and I feel lucky every day." He loves the challenge of working cattle. "There's a personal victory every time when you get cattle worked."

He loves the outdoors, and horses too. "The bond that grows through working with your horse is one of my top satisfactions. When other people compliment a horse you've worked with and made, it's gratifying."

Generosity, he says, is a way of life where he comes from. "Ranch people will give you the shirt off their back."

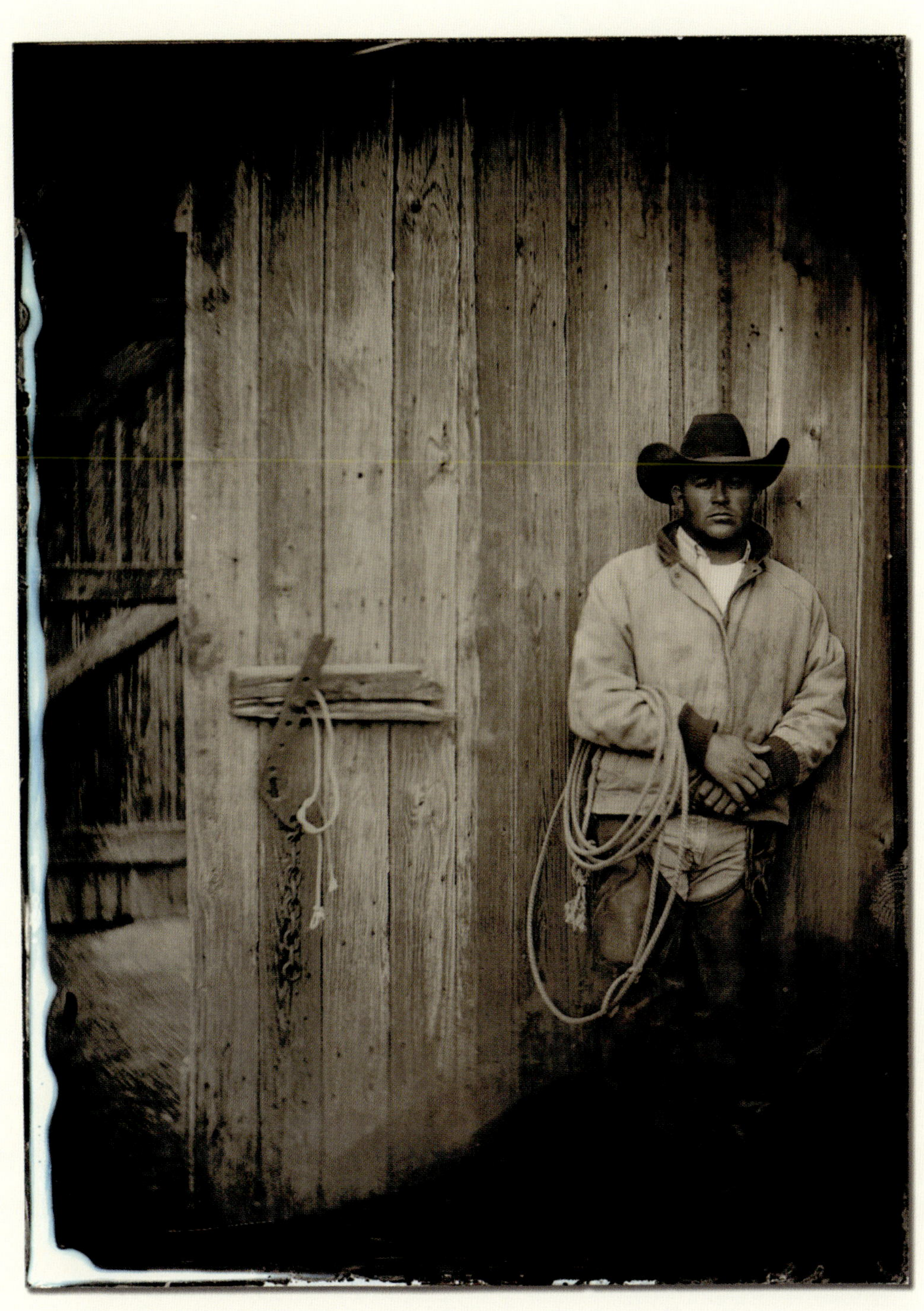

PLATE 60

JASIQUE HUGHES

LA ESCALERA RANCH

Jasique started riding colts when he was 15 and has always enjoyed being around horses. At 18, he started day working. Worked in California, Arizona, and now in Texas. One of the things he likes best is learning something new every day.

"You'll never know everything about punching cows. But a man will always continue to grow as long as he keeps his mouth shut and his eyes open."

At 23 years old, Jasique seems confident he's found his life's calling. "Don't think I'll ever have the need to do anything else."

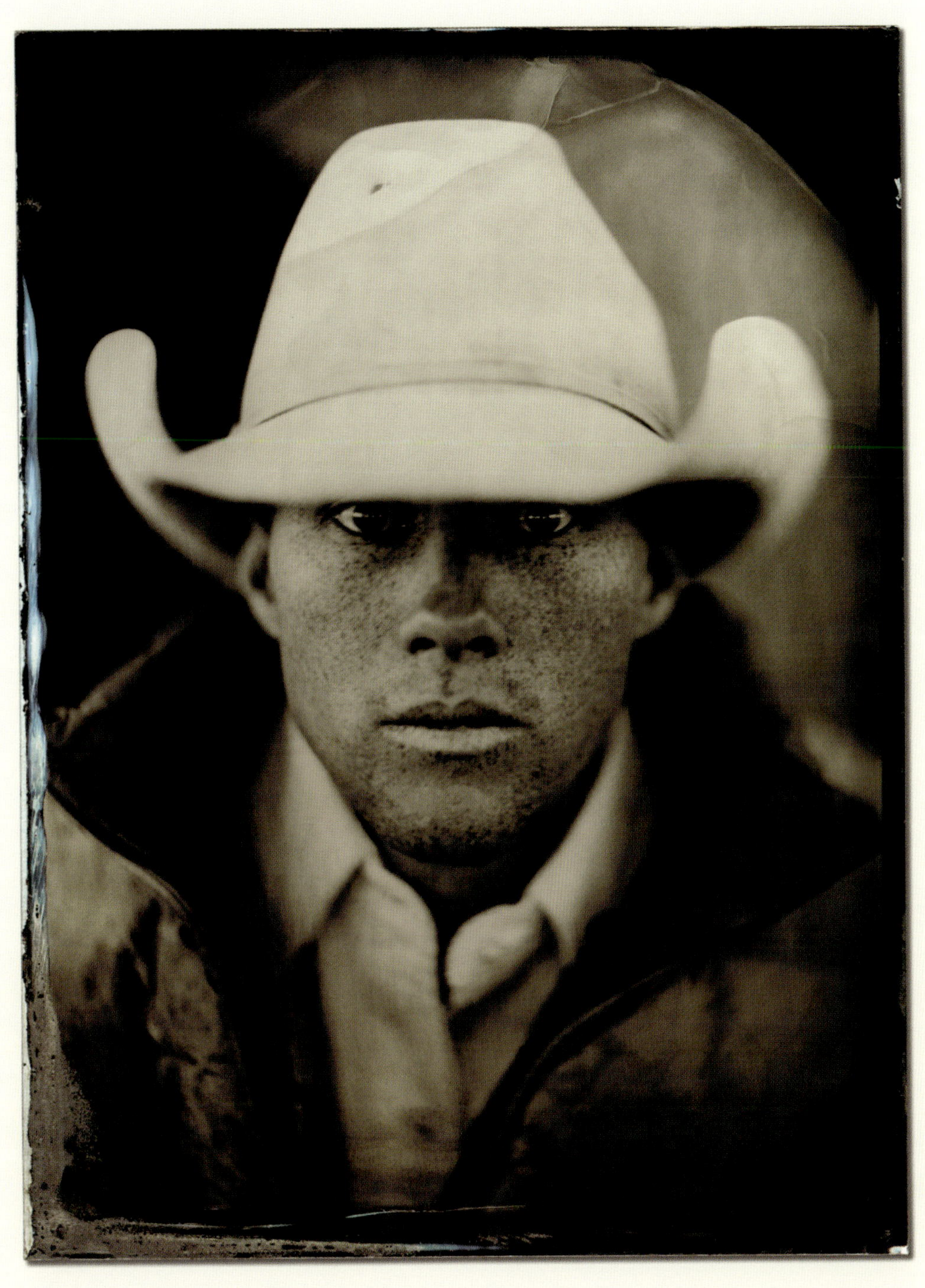

PLATE 61

DOUG DANCER

DAYWORKER

Horses. Freedom. These are the first words that come to Doug's mind when he thinks about what he likes best about cowboying. "It's hard work, but when you love what you're doing it's just part of the package."

Even less-than-cooperative weather.

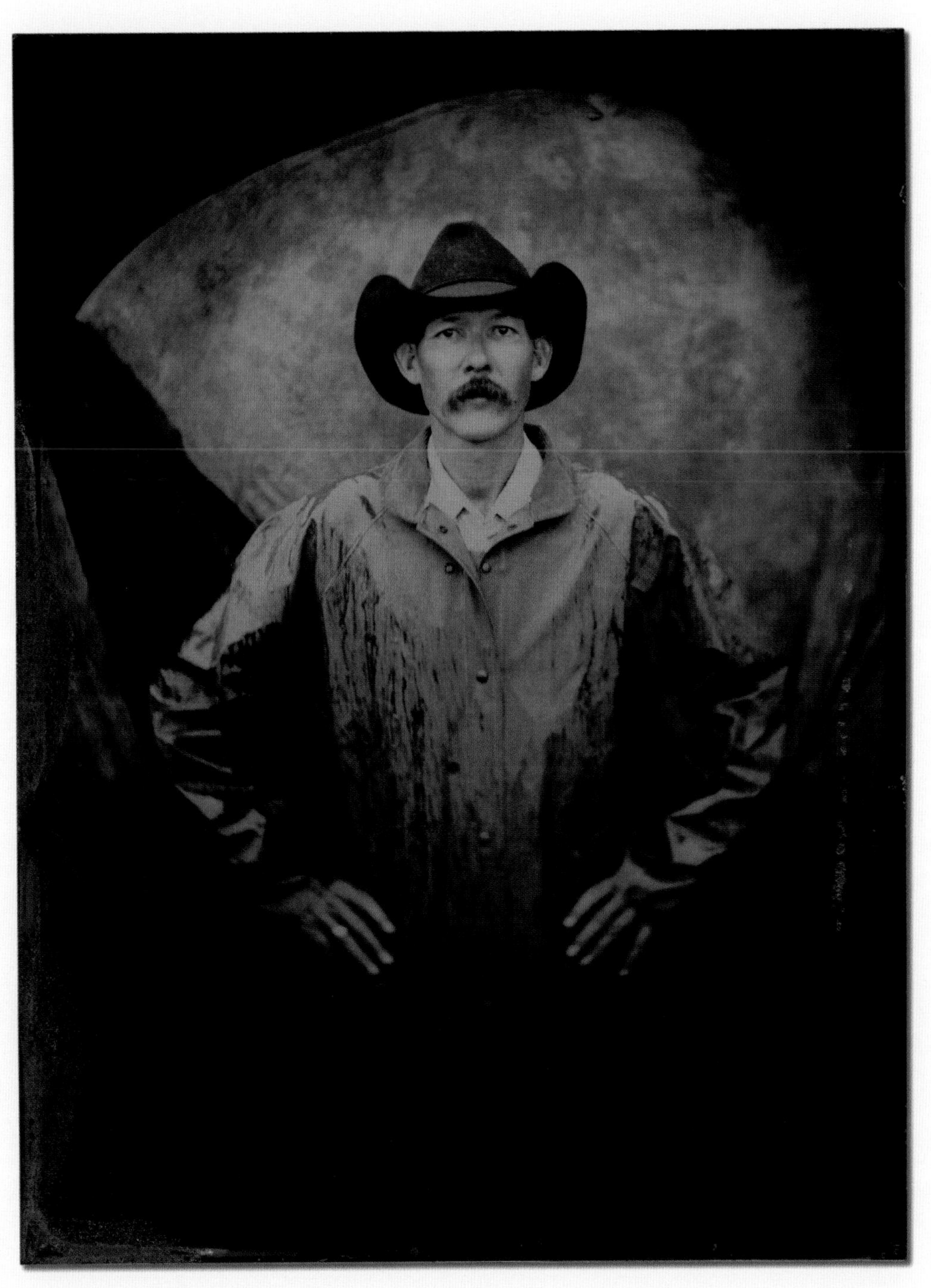

PLATE 62

KYNN PATTERSON

PATTERSON RANCH

"Cowboying is ingrained in you from the get-go."

For Kynn, that feeling began three generations ago, with his great-granddad. "My great-granddad settled in Texas in the 1800s. He was on his own at 13 when his father died. He came back and brought his brothers and sisters out." That's how Patterson Ranch began.

Working his family's ranch has by no means been an easy ride. "All I've inherited was opportunity." He says life is yours to make what you want. "You either improve your lot, maintain things, or you lose ground."

He measures success not by how much money he makes. "The job you do has to be more important than what you're making financially. Any money you make over what you really need usually becomes a burden."

The supply of cowboys in the world is something Kynn isn't too worried about. His son lives in Sweden, teaching roping and Western-style riding. "There's a lot of wanna-be cowboys out there. So there should never be a shortage in this country."

"As long as cows still run on rough country, there will be cowboys."

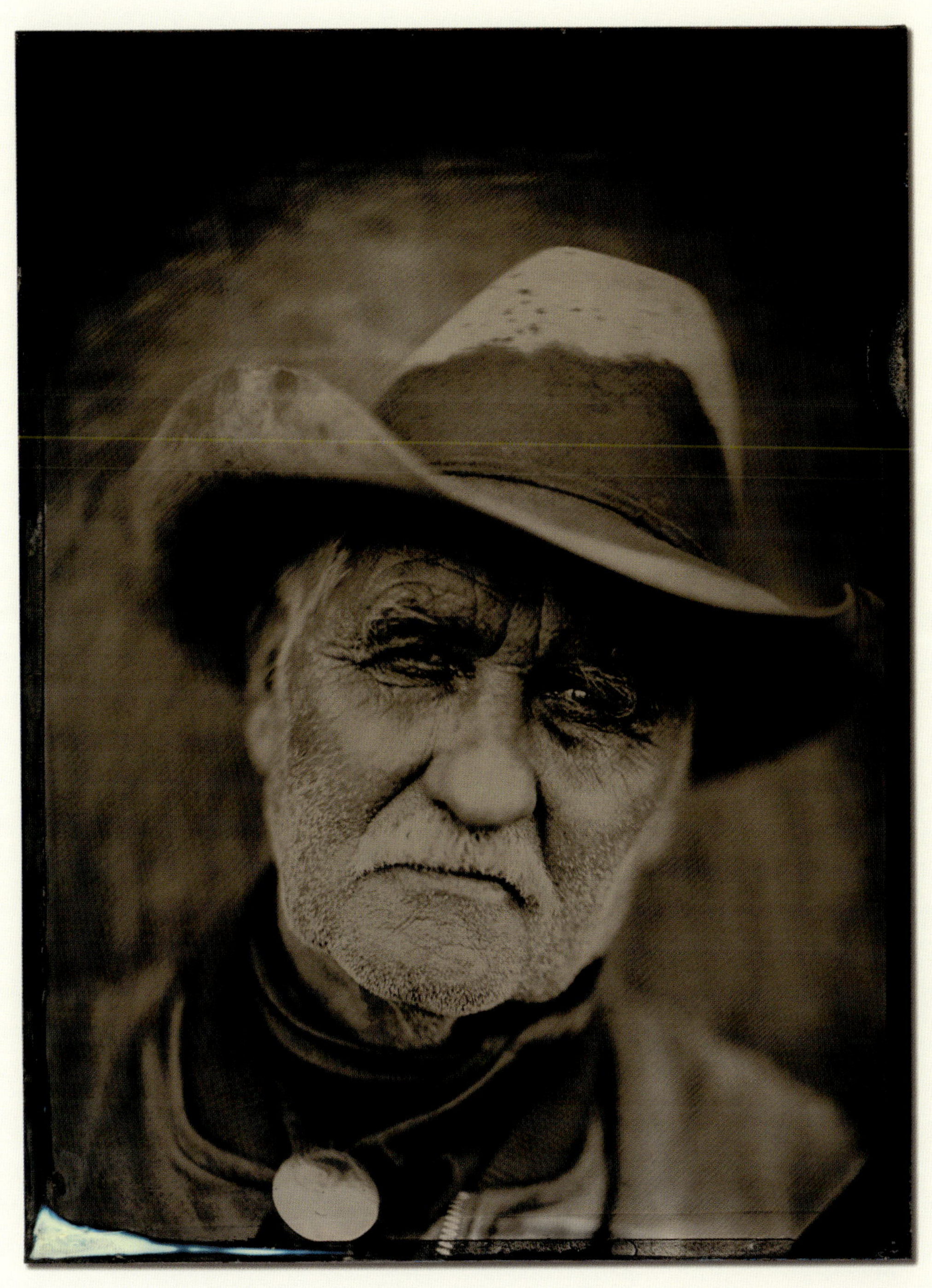

PLATE 63

ZACH DAVIS

KING RANCH

Zach is 24 years old and thinks he's got the greatest job in the world. "The way I see it, my office has the best view."

To him, a typical 9 to 5 job is unnatural. "You can't close a man in with four walls. You need the open space to appreciate the nature of our country. This is true freedom and the American way of life."

"Take a man's freedom, and you take his heart."

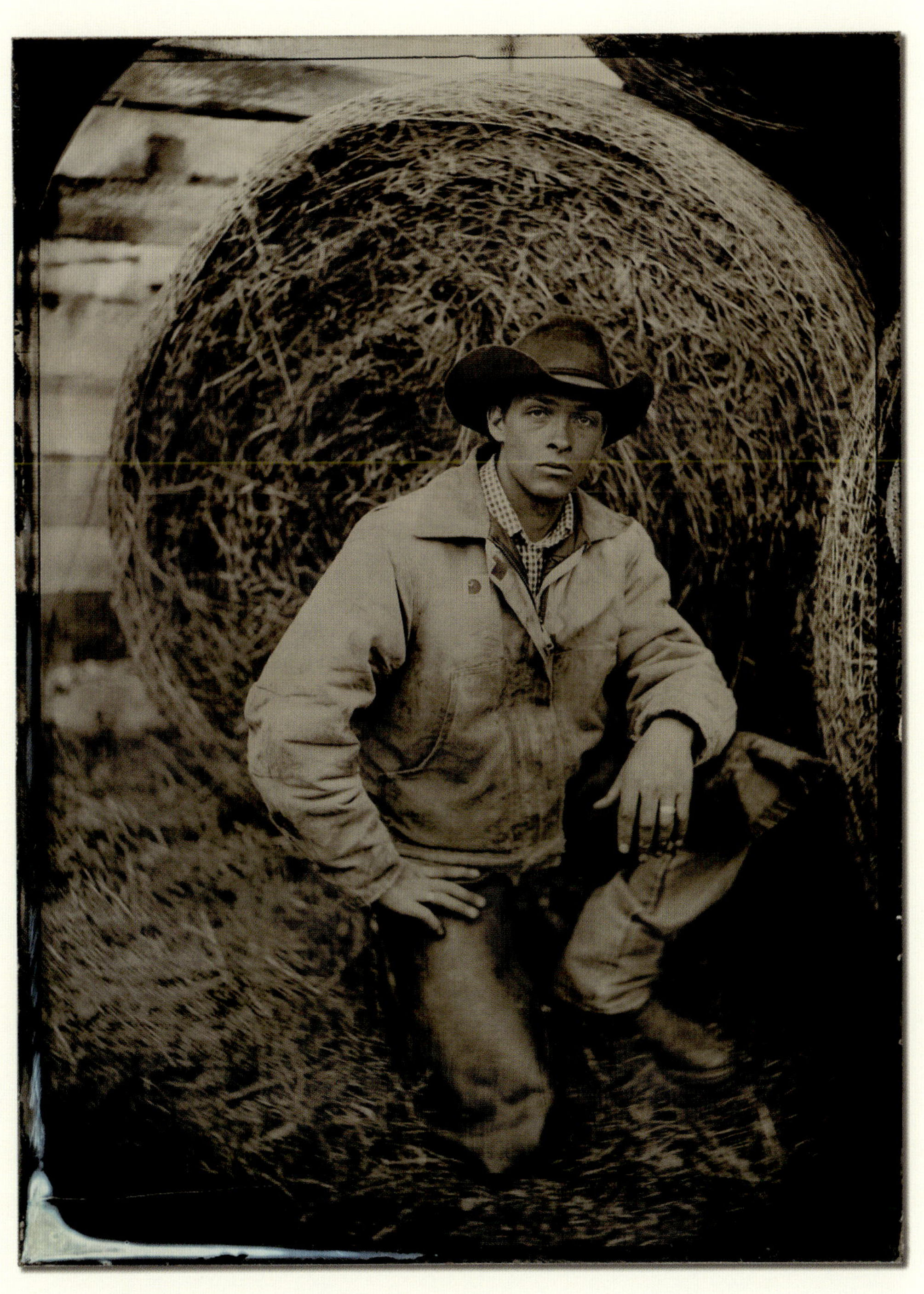

PLATE 64

JAKE WAGNER

RA BROWN RANCH

Jake doesn't cowboy for the money. He does it for the life.

"I don't think I could ever put up with office politics. On a ranch, as long as you pull your weight and get along with the other hands, you'll have a job."

For him, it's a profession unlike any other. "Cows are our customers, and unlike customers in other businesses, you can speak your mind to the cattle and they can't talk back to you."

Every single day of his life is filled with new experiences and challenges.

"If you are open-minded, you'll learn something while you're out here. You could spend your whole life cowboying and you'd never learn it all."

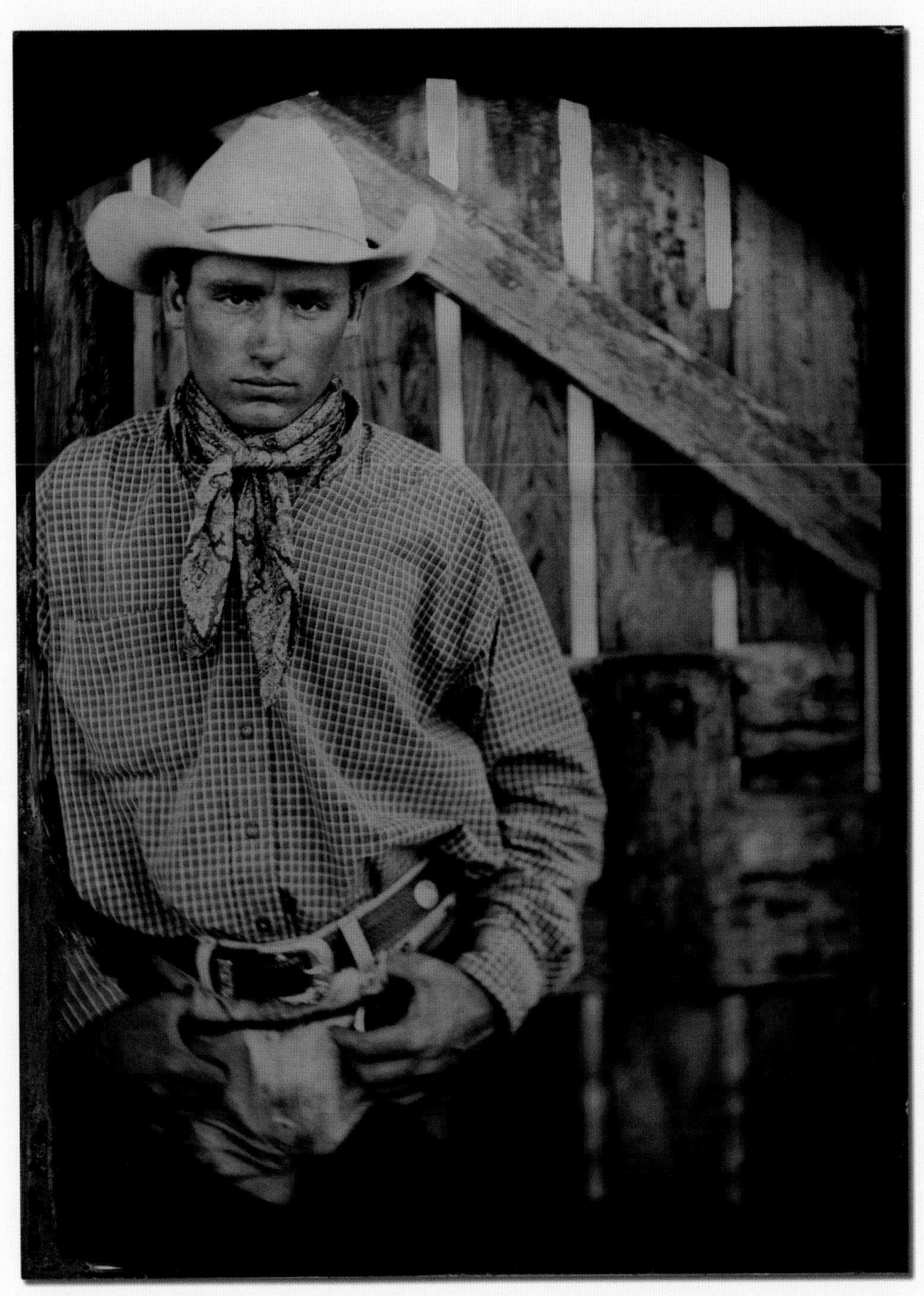

PLATE 65

MORRIS TIMMONS

TRIANGLE RANCH

Morris was born at Sand Creek on Mill Iron Ranch, east of Wellington, Texas. Then lived on another part of the ranch between Estelline and Turkey. His parents own a small place around Northfield, Texas, and run a few cows.

"I have lived in this area most of my life and worked on most of the ranches around here—6666's, Bird Ranch, Pitchfork Ranch." He has lived at the Triangle Ranch for the last 20 years.

"I have tried to do other jobs while trying to rodeo, but the ranch life always called me back."

He has been married 29 years, with two boys and two girls. All gone, and all but one married. Two grandchildren.

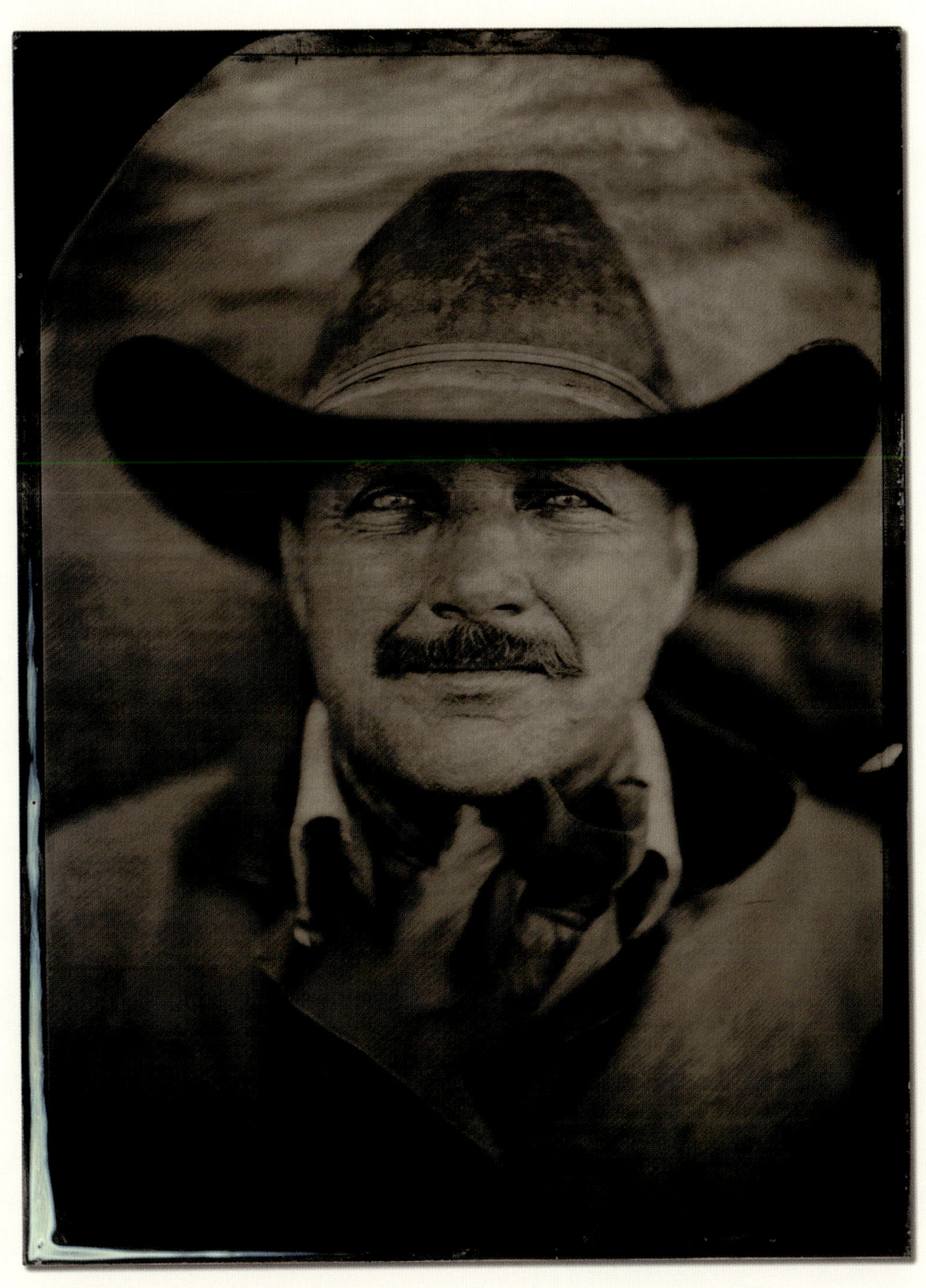

PLATE 66

INES SEGOVIA

JONES ALTA VISTA RANCH

"I find myself here on the Jones Ranch at a job and a way of life that I was raised in."

Ines left the ranch nearly 10 years ago to find work in Rio Grande City, Texas. After working numerous jobs, he headed back. "I have discovered that the ranch is my home."

He splits time between working on the ranch and spending time with his family. "During the week, my cousin, who also works for the ranch, lets me bunk with him and his family. As Friday comes, I catch a ride back to Rio Grande City to spend the weekend with my wife."

For Ines, the best part about the job is being able to work around his friends, being outside, and knowing every day will bring a different job to accomplish. The hardest part about the job would have to be the hours. "A regular workweek is from 7 a.m. to 5 p.m. and five days long. However, when the coritha starts you can often put in a full day before lunch and we may work 30 days before you get a day off. This can last several months."

Tough hours aside, Ines lives this life because it matters. "We are just as important to the animals we raise as a doctor is to humans. At the end of the month, I have done more than just earning a paycheck."

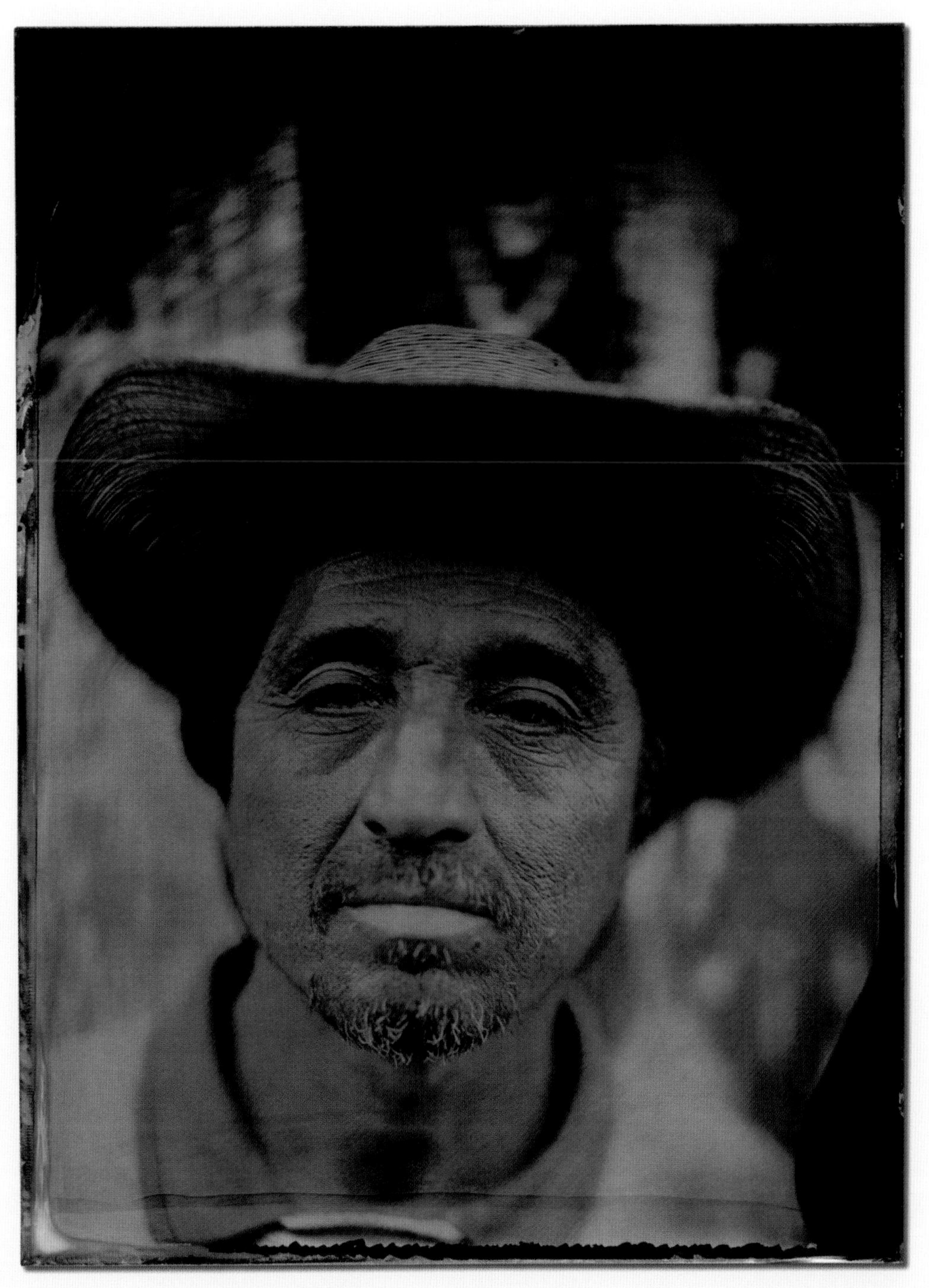

PLATE 67

KELLY WELCH

SILVERBROOK RANCH

Kelly has worked on the Silverbrook, where her father is ranch manager, for eight years. Loves to ride and work cows. She and her twin sister Kate have been hearing impaired since they were born. But that doesn't slow Kelly down any. Horses are her love. Branding and gathering cattle are fun for her too. "Actually, everything involved in ranching is fun," says Kelly.

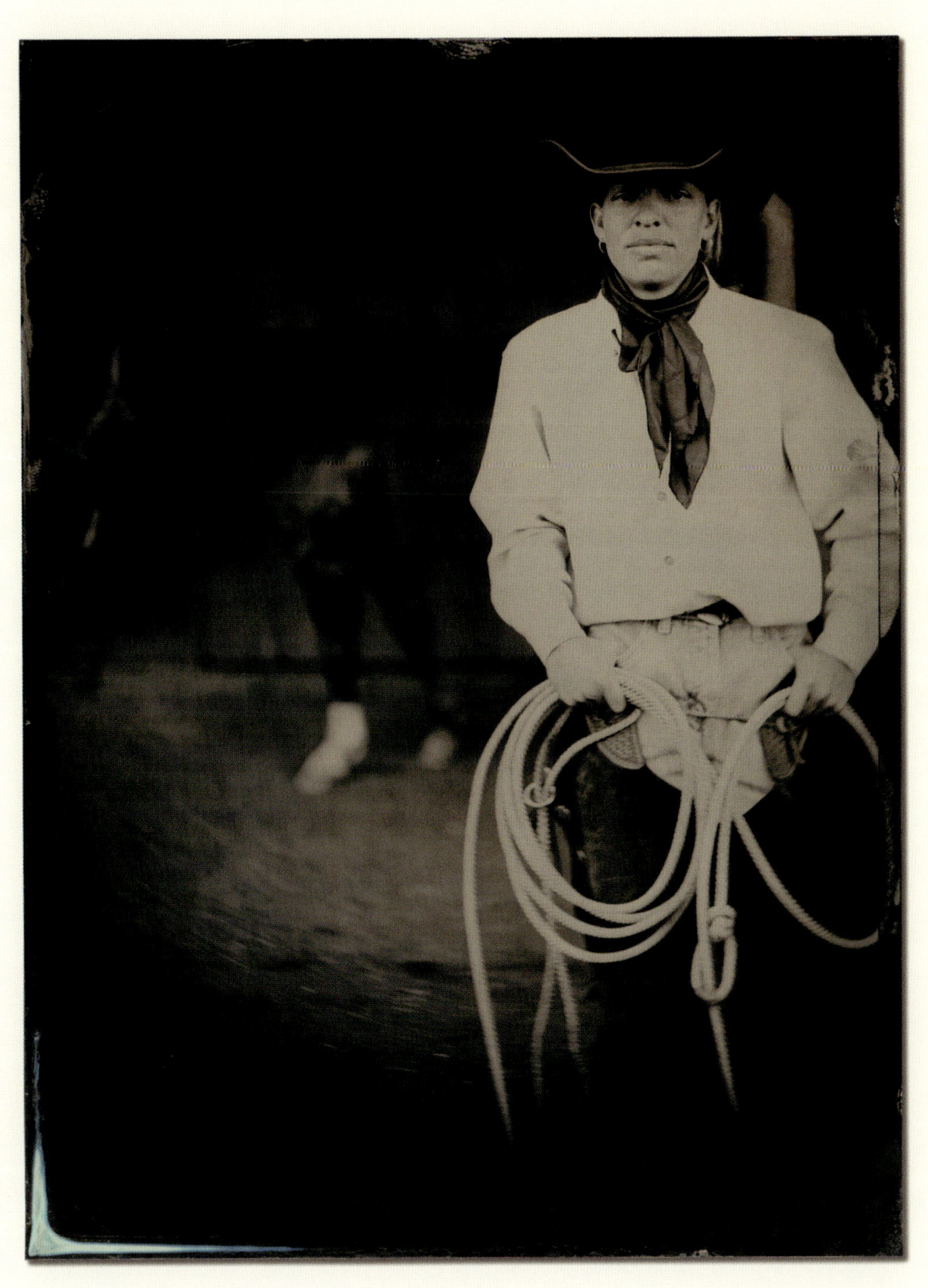

PLATE 68

DOUG L. HARNEY

SCRIBE M RANCH

He may not own the operation, but Doug runs Scribe M Ranch. With regard to the owner, Doug says, "he gives me latitude to run it as I see fit."

He enjoys the responsibility of being his own boss, and making decisions that create good results. But most of all, he just likes being outside.

"The freedom of being out in open country is unlike any other feeling. You can't trade that feeling for money."

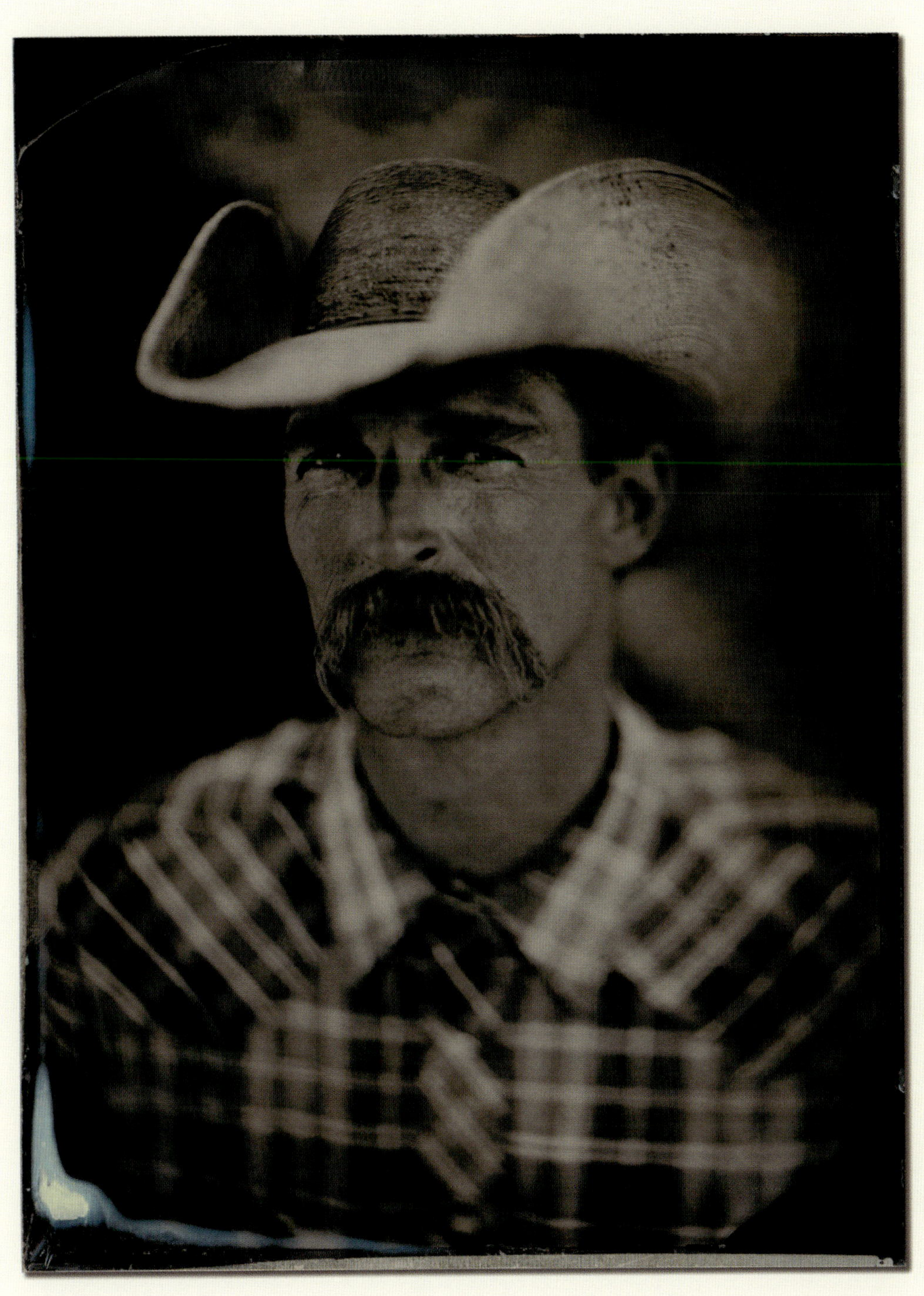

PLATE 69

HEGAN LAMB

SAUNDERS RANCH

Hegan has two reasons for wanting to be a cowboy. "To be free to do what I want to do. To be close to God when I'm on a horse."

It seems simple to him. "I've been raised that way all my life, since a kid."

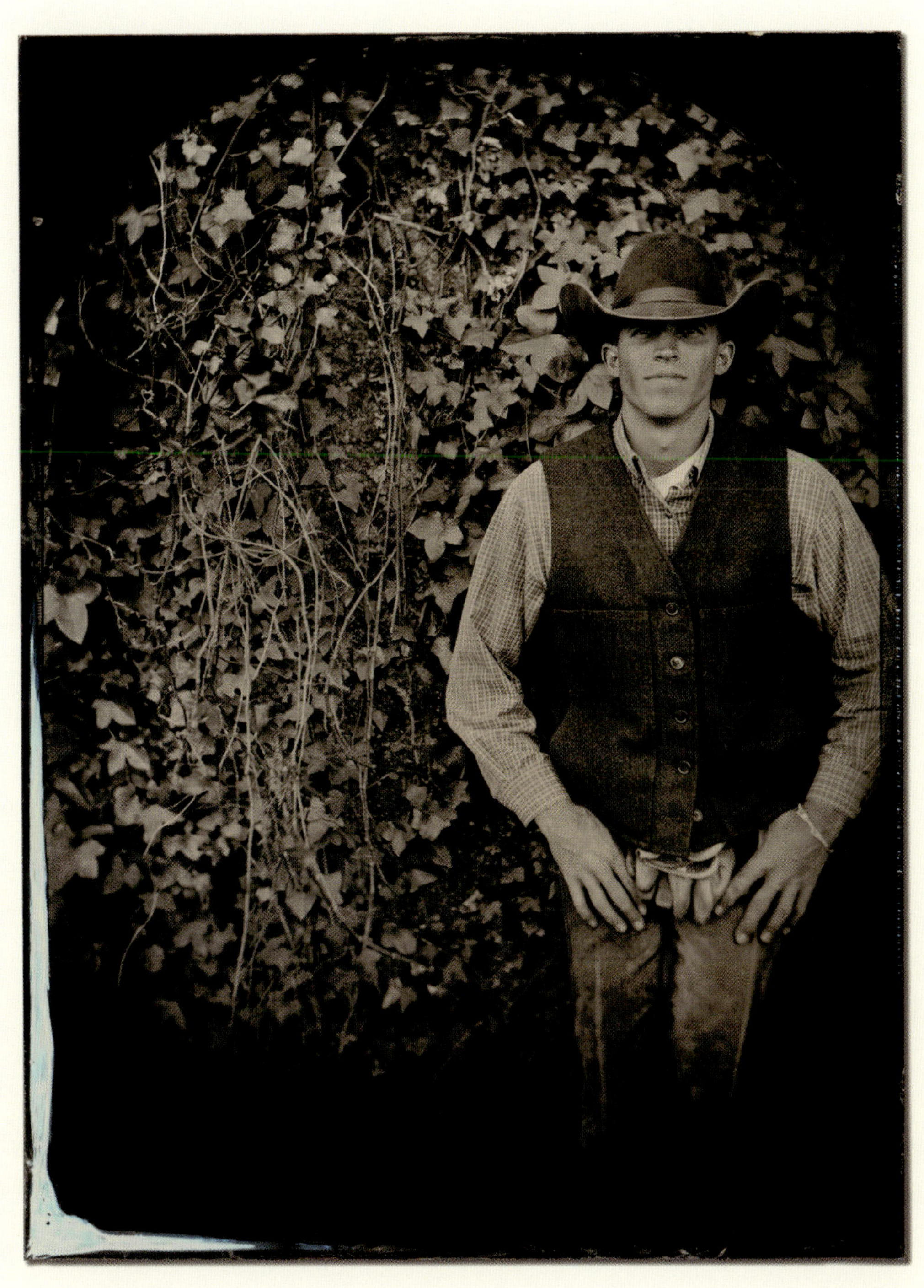

PLATE 70

WILL HUMPHREYS

GUITAR RANCH

Will has been around ranching all his life. Went to school for it as well. Got a B.S. in Range Management and a B.S. in Animal Science from Texas Tech. "What I learned in school, I'd experience in day-to-day work, but school gave me some specifics."

He says the satisfaction of accomplishing hard work and doing it right makes you proud. "It'll make you sleep well at night."

One of the great joys about Will's job is getting to work with his father. "I learn things from my father every day. He's a great inspiration. We work 16,000 acres together, and the open space keeps a man's head clear."

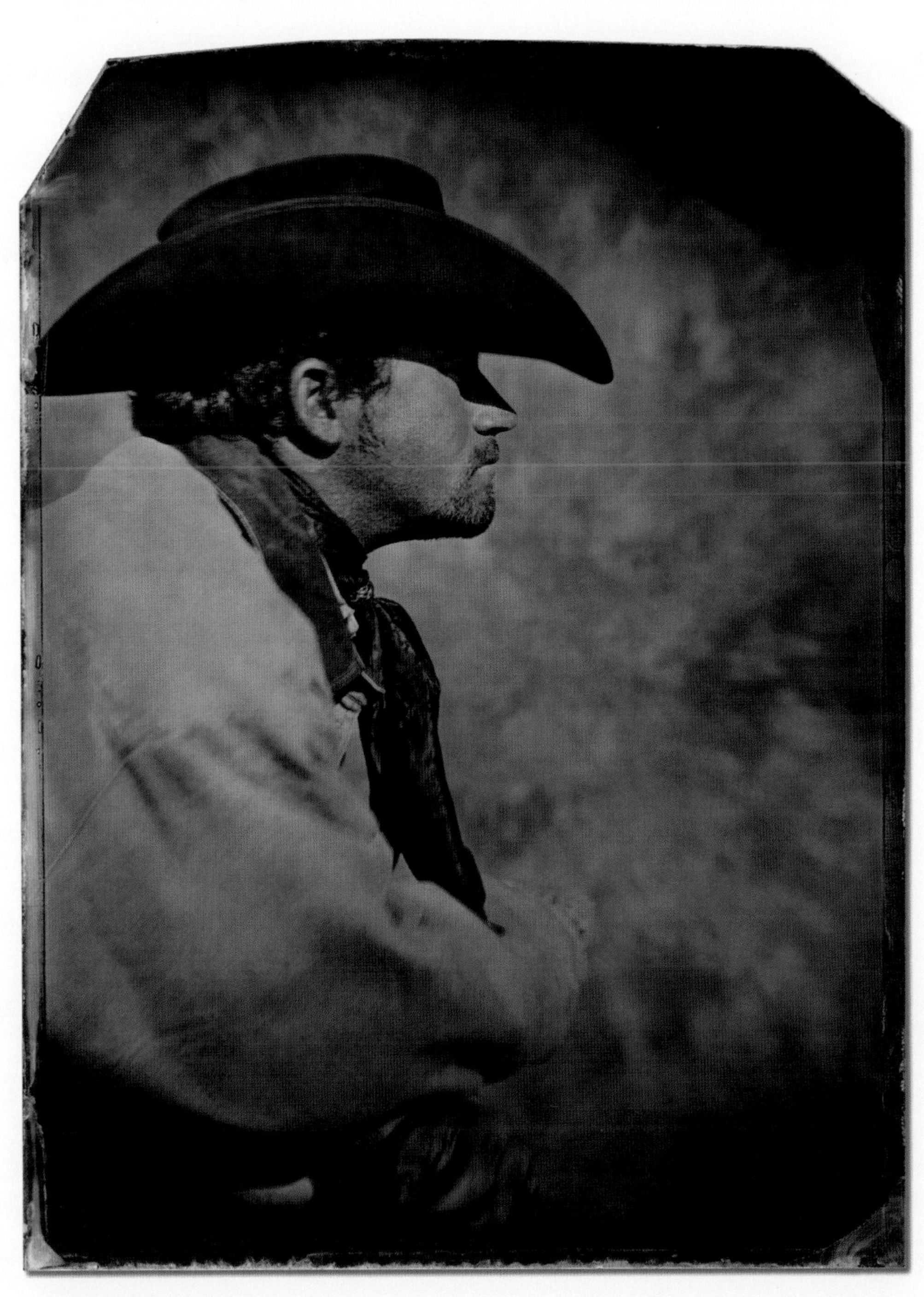

PLATE 71

JOSÉ LUJAN

MEANS RANCH

José has been a cowboy for 30 years, all at Means Ranch. He learned to ride a horse when he was only seven or eight years old.

"I used to ride in small rodeos in Mexico, but not anymore."

Even without rodeos, however, he likes the life for himself and his family of three children.

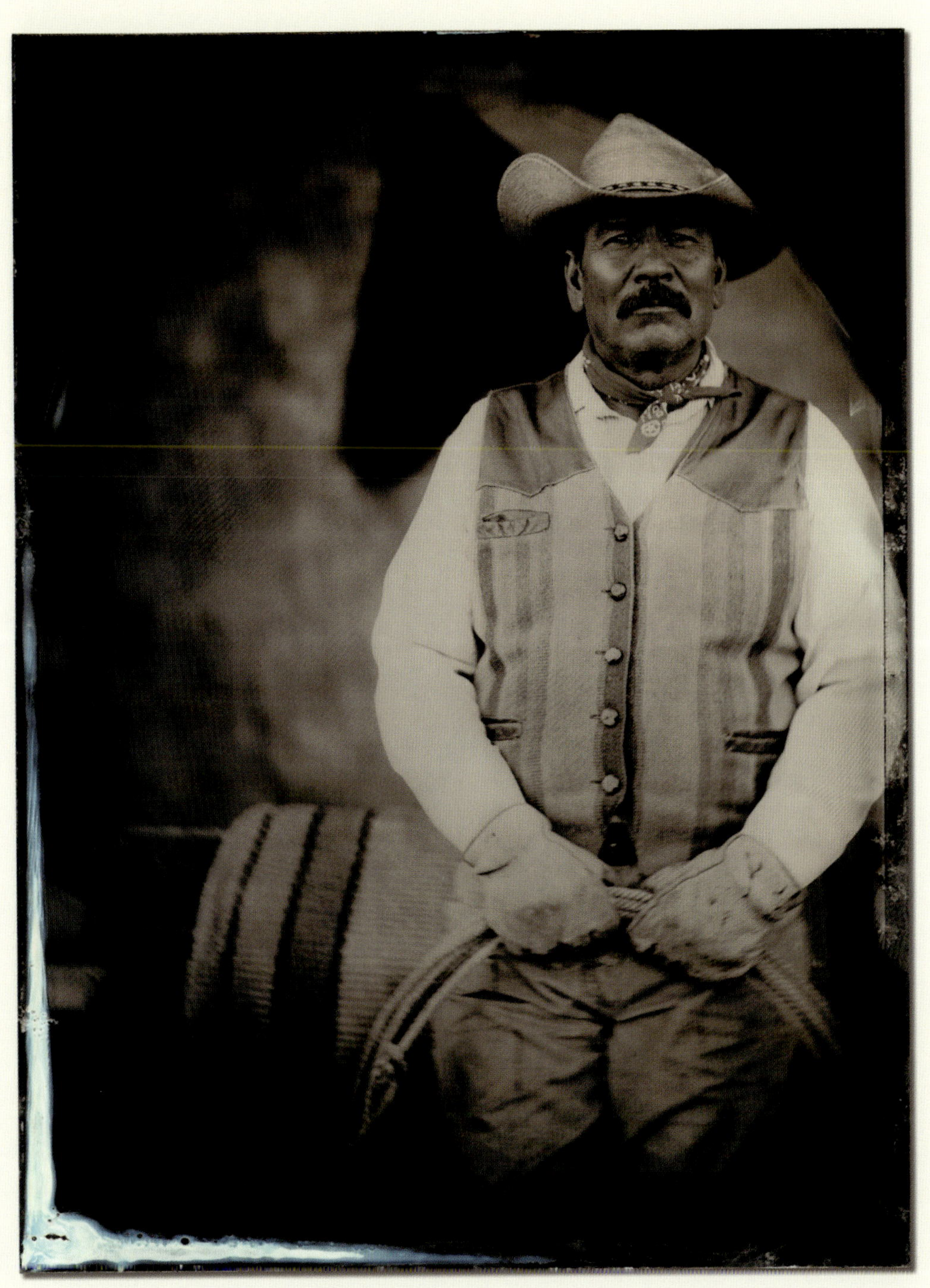

PLATE 72

TOM BELCHER

LAMBSHEAD RANCH

Tom was born a cowboy and just grew bigger. "The sense of freedom on a ranch was a fond memory when I was a boy. When I was five years old and big enough to handle a horse, I knew I wanted to cowboy."

Some might look at Tom's life and think it's nothing but toil and sweat. But not Tom. "Being out with hardworking men, doing hard work, and seeing nature every day doesn't seem like work to me."

Plus, for him, there's no better place in the world to bring up a family. "Raising my family on the ranch is the best foundation they can get. The values and responsibilities associated with ranch life can prepare them for most anything in the world."

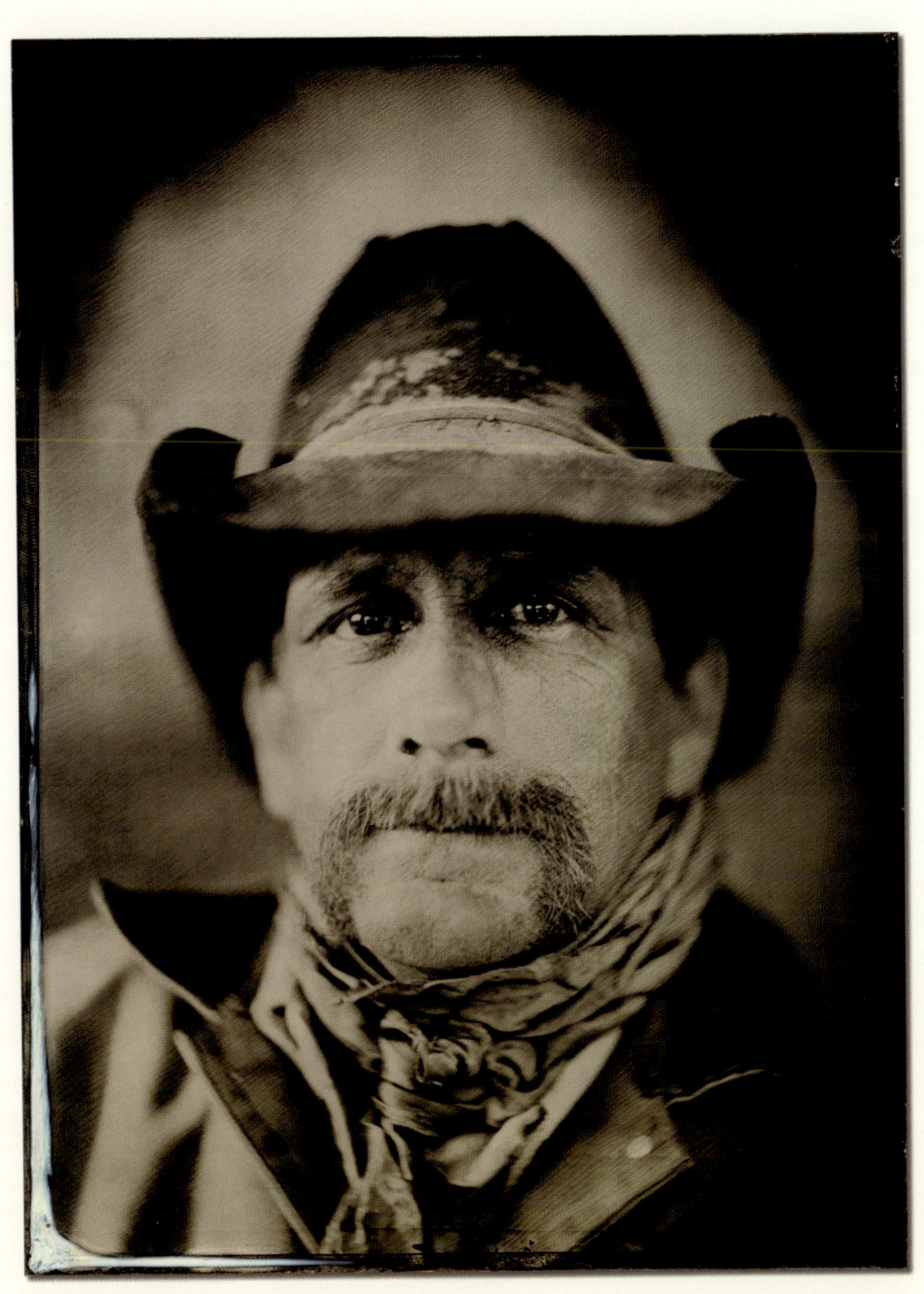

PLATE 73

BUCK McLAIN

JA RANCH

Buck is 27 years old. "When I leave the house, I don't go to work. I go to live life."

His favorite part of cowboying is getting a close-up view of the country he's responsible for. It's what Buck calls "prowlin'."

To him, working with other great hands, who have similar values and work ethic, makes the hard work easier.

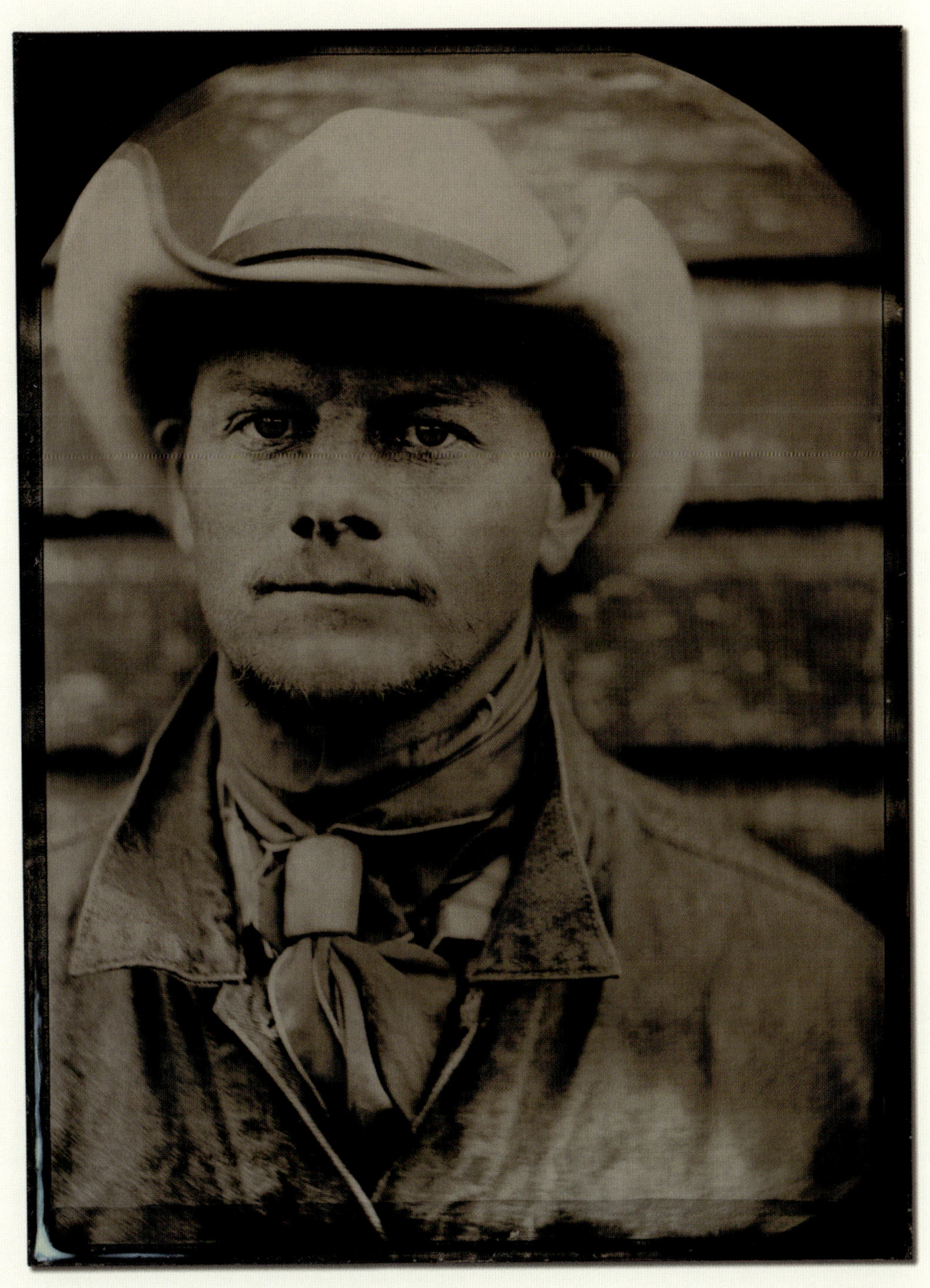

PLATE 74

JOHNNY STEWART

BAR CROSS RANCH

At eight years old, when most kids were learning how to ride a bike, Johnny was learning how to rope. Soon after, he got into training horses. Broke his first horse when he was just 12. Named him Gizmo.

Nowadays, Johnny says he likes to ride with his friends. He's got a lot of buddies who live in town. They come out and ride on the land, get a little taste of the freedom Johnny has.

Rain doesn't bother Johnny. Burning heat neither. To him, whatever the weather is like, "work is fun."

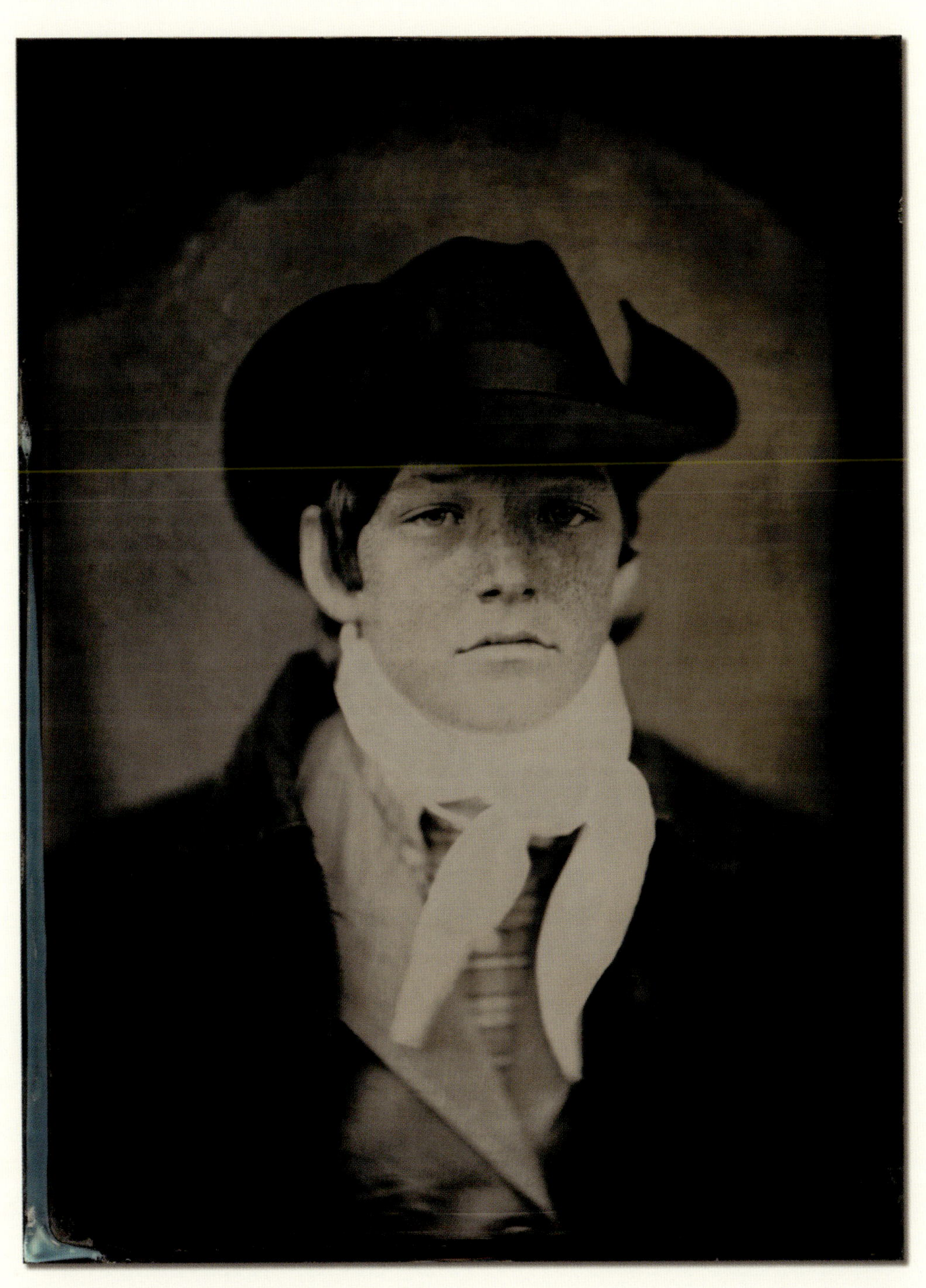

PLATE 75

TY SMITH

TONGUE RIVER RANCH

Ty was raised on a ranch and wanted his family to have the same experience. "Your kids learn responsibility in raising animals, helping with family duties, and respect in general."

He says a ranch is a good place to discover new things about life. "If you're open-minded, you can learn something new, even if it's a small thing, every day."

He says that when you work with people you like, all those hard jobs that aren't your favorite can become fun. "The hours don't matter much when you love what you do."

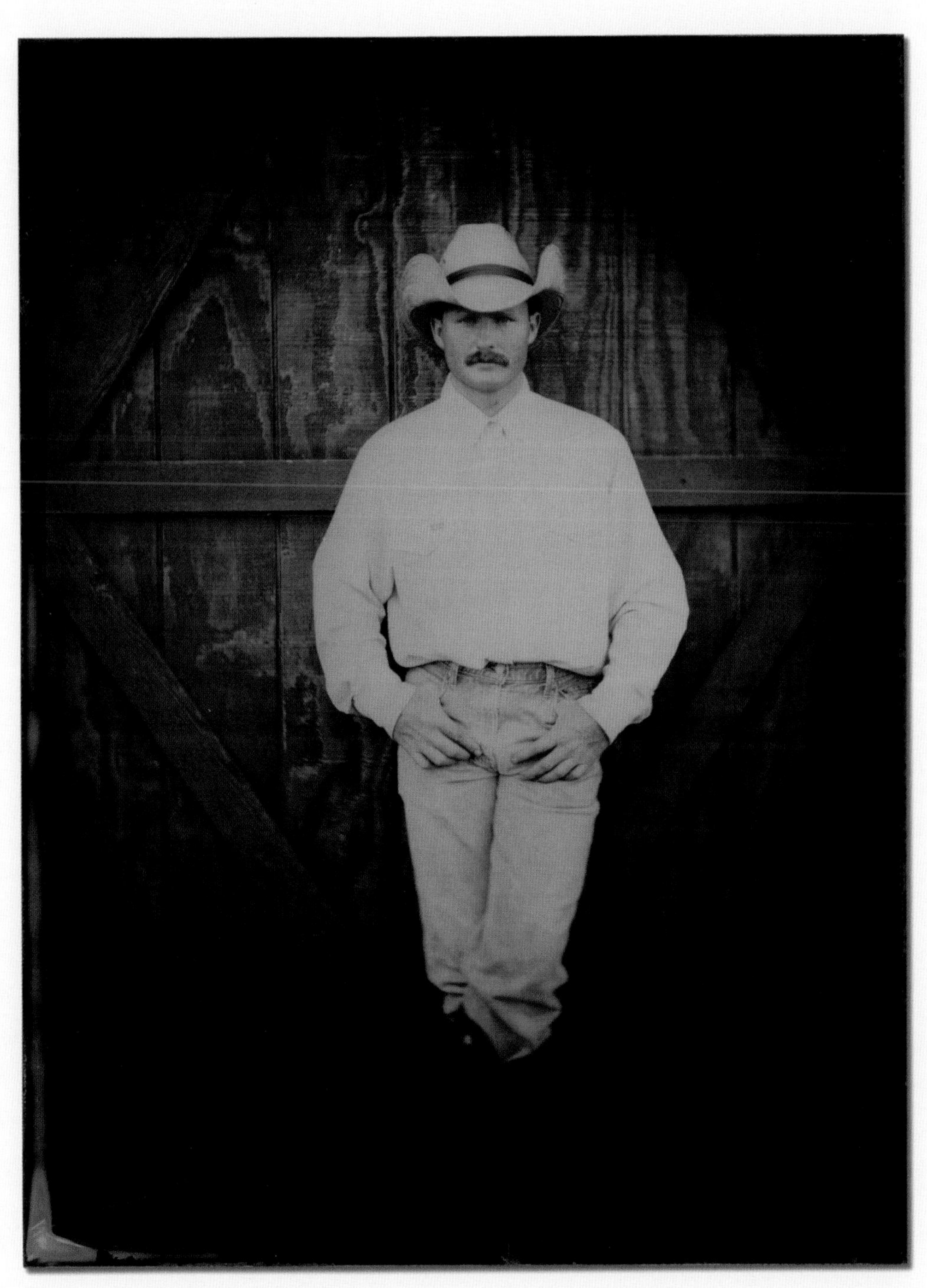

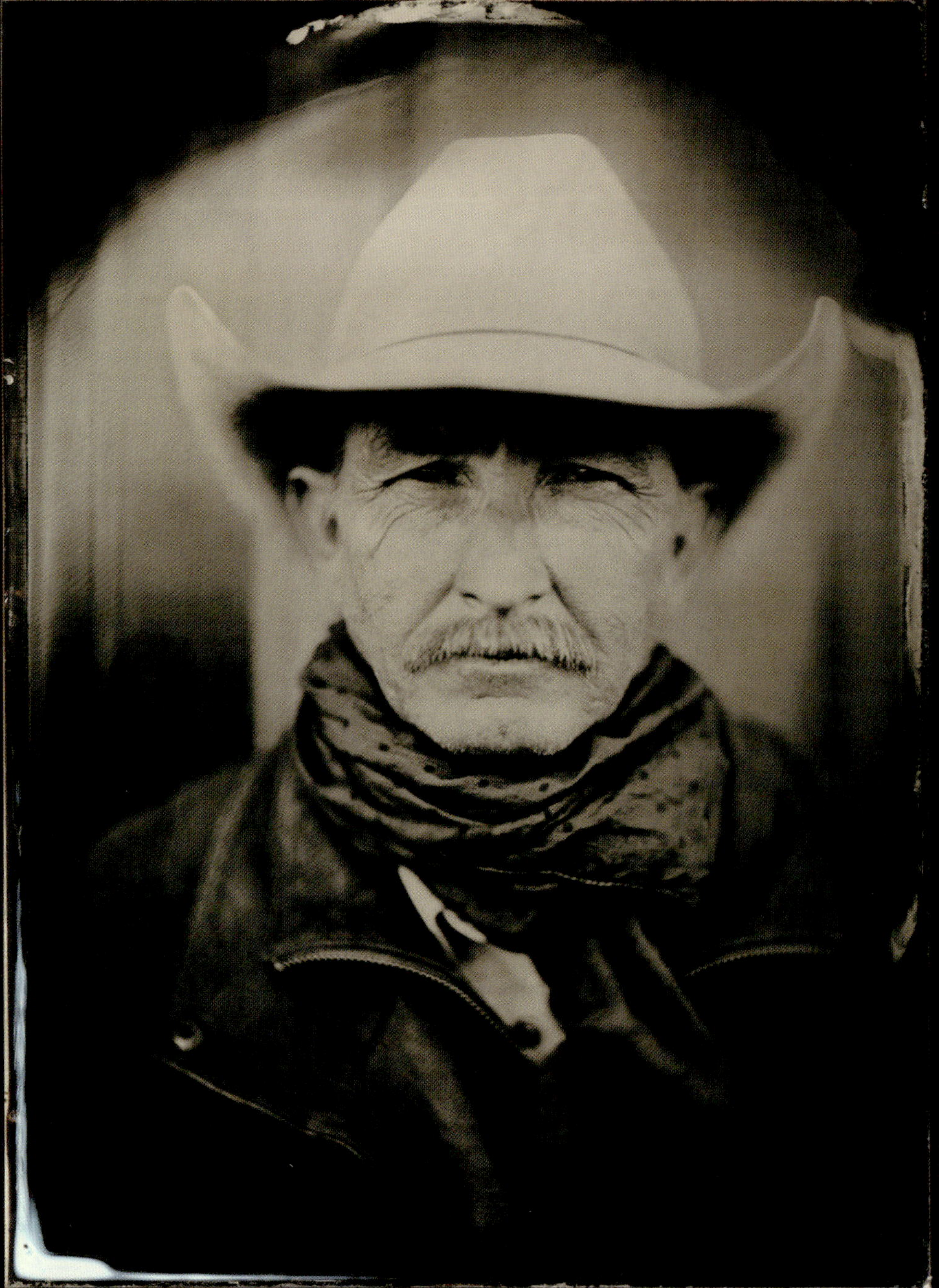

21ST-CENTURY TINTYPES

by MARGARET BLAGG

In 1856, HAMILTON L. SMITH OF OHIO PATENTED A NEW PHOTOGRAPHIC METHOD THAT CAME TO BE KNOWN AS TINTYPE. THESE ONE-OF-A-KIND IMAGES ARE MADE DIRECTLY ON A THIN IRON PLATE THAT HAS BEEN COATED WITH CHEMICALS, EXPOSED IN A CAMERA WHILE STILL WET, AND DEVELOPED ON THE SPOT. BECAUSE THE PLATES ARE IRON, NOT TIN, THE MORE PROPER TERM IS FERROTYPE, BUT THE PHOTOGRAPHS HAVE BEEN COMMONLY CALLED TINTYPES FROM THE BEGINNING.

The process, less expensive than daguerreotype and more durable than other earlier methods of photographic portraiture, became very popular during the Civil War and remained so into the 20th century until newer processes that could produce multiple images took over.

Robb Kendrick is one of a handful of people nationwide who knows how to make a tintype in the original method. Having collected them for a number of years, he sought out John Coffer, a historical re-enactor and tintype photographer who lives in up-state New York, for a lesson a few years ago. After a bit of practice and time to collect the necessary equipment, materials, and chemicals, Robb was ready to make tintypes of his own.

For this project, Robb traveled in a crew-cab truck with a slide-in camper in the bed, pulling a 7′ x 12′ portable darkroom trailer—mandatory since tintypes must be exposed when wet and developed immediately. The trailer also allowed him to carry 40 gallons of fresh water and to store tintypes on drying racks. It has air conditioning and heating and a vent fan to remove the fumes from the chemicals used in the process. Extreme temperatures and the humidity level can affect the chemicals and how they work. The optimum temperature is 68° F, but on this project Robb has shot in temperatures ranging from 21° to 103° F.

All the chemicals Robb uses to make his tintypes were historically used in the 1850s. Prior to departing on any trip to shoot tintypes, it takes him about seven hours to mix chemicals and prepare the darkroom trailer for the trip.

THE CHEMICALS HE USES ARE:

COLLODION (GUN COTTON AND ETHER) – the emulsion on the plate that holds the image.

SILVER NITRATE – used to sensitize the plate so it will be light-sensitive.

IRON SULFATE/EVER CLEAR MIXTURE – used to develop the plate after exposure.

POTASSIUM CYANIDE – used to fix the plate and turn it into a positive.

LAVENDER VARNISH – used after the plate is washed and dried to protect the plate and give it a rich tonality and sheen.

A typical day of shooting begins at 5:30 a.m., when Robb and his assistant, Jason Bryant (himself a blossoming documentary photographer) make coffee, grab a bite of breakfast and then depart for the ranch they will work

PRECEDING PAGE: JOE LEATHERS, 6666 RANCH DIXON CREEK

ROBB'S PROCESS

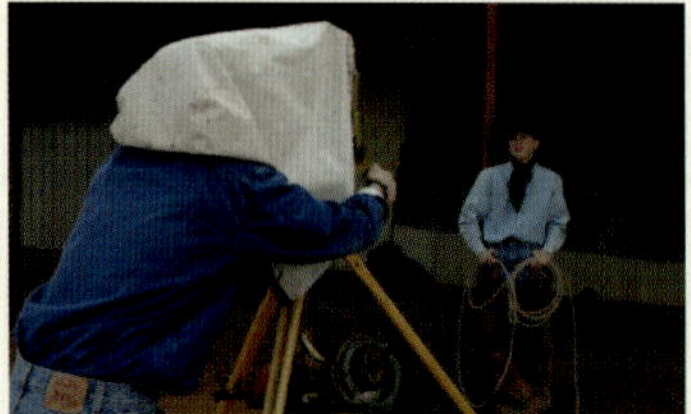
Setting up the shot

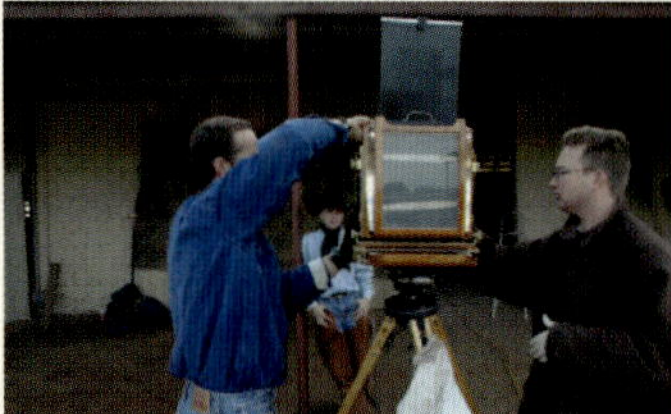
Making the exposure

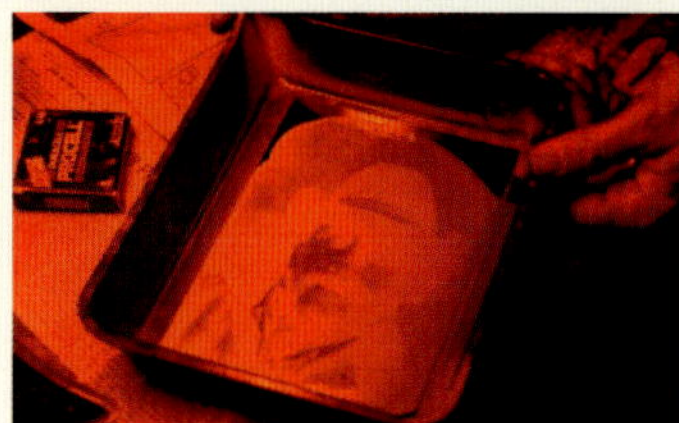
Plate in the developer

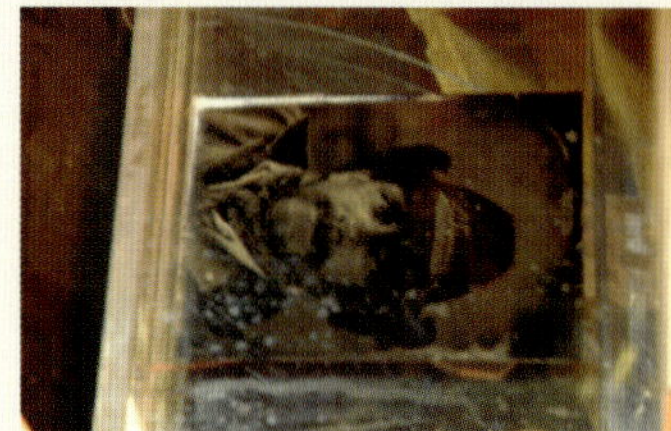
Turning positive in potassium cyanide

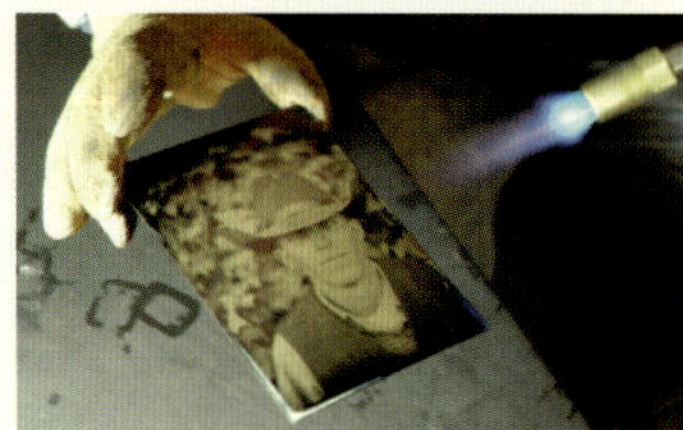
Torching the plate

on for the day, arriving usually by 7 a.m. While Jason sets up the darkroom, Robb talks about the project with the cowboys, showing them tintypes and establishing a rapport with them prior to shooting. He photographs them in whatever clothing and gear they are wearing that day for work. Photographing begins around 8:30 a.m., in a collaboration that requires total concentration and commitment from both the subject and the photographer. The subjects of the tintype portraits cannot move during the exposure, which is usually one to seven seconds long (although Robb has done exposures as long as 14 seconds). The 19th-century lenses Robb uses have a very narrow depth of field, so moving even 1/4 of an inch will affect the portrait. Robb usually exposes several tintype plates per subject, then asks the cowboys to enter the darkroom trailer to watch the plates develop. He says that unfailingly he and the cowboys experience the moment the image comes up in the fixer as "pure magic." All the posing, plate preparation, exposing, and developing can take 30–60 minutes per person.

In Robb's own words, here is how the process goes from start to finish:

I first flow the collodion onto a blackened tin plate, then place it in silver nitrate for four to six minutes. While the plate is sensitizing, I check focus on the camera and get the camera ready as well as the subject, also determining—based on light conditions—how long to make the exposure. Next I remove the plate from the nitrate tray, dry off any excess silver nitrate, place it in the holder (which is light-tight), and bring it out to the camera. Once removed from the silver nitrate, the plate must be exposed and developed in four to nine minutes—hence the name "wet-plate photography." I place the holder in the camera, pull out the darkslide, which has been protecting the plate from light, and remove the lens cover to make the exposure. Then I replace the lens cover, push the darkslide back down, remove the holder from the camera, and go back to the darkroom trailer. Once inside, I flow the collodion onto the next plate and place it in the silver nitrate (to save down time). I then remove the plate that was just exposed from the holder and place it in the developer for 15–25 seconds; then I place it in three trays of water for 20 seconds each to stop the development process and wash out any developer that might be in the emulsion. All the above steps are done while under amber safelight conditions. At this point I can turn the light on and place the plate in potassium cyanide for 30 seconds. The tintype transforms from a bluish image on a plate to a positive in the clear tank. It really is magical every time. After the cyanide fixer, I must carefully clean off any residue of silver nitrate from the image so the wet emulsion is not scratched. I wash the plate thoroughly, dry it, and put it up into the drying rack.

After a full day of shooting, we wrap up by breaking down the darkroom, filtering all chemicals before the next day's shoot. We then have dinner, drive to our next shoot, park where we are going to camp for the night, and then I usually go into the darkroom trailer to varnish the plates. I heat each tintype with a torch and pour a lavender varnish onto the surface of the plate, tipping the excess back into a bottle. I hold the plate and heat it with a torch for two minutes to dry the varnish. After shooting 30–40 plates in a day, it takes about three hours per night to varnish the plates. The plates are then rack-dried for two days to cure the varnish. At that point they are ready to sleeve.

What Robb Kendrick produces in this labor-intensive labor of love are unique images—handmade photographs that are more akin to paintings or drawings than to the

THIS PAGE AND FOLLOWING: DOCUMENTARY PHOTOGRAPHS BY WATT M. CASEY, JR. FOLLOWING PAGE: BOBBY PAUTSKY, COWAN & PAUTSKY RANCH

infinitely reproducible photographs common today. The tintype process does not produce negatives; hence there cannot be multiple tintypes of a single image. (The images in this book result from scans made of the tintypes.) Some 19th-century cameras had multiple lenses that allowed duplicate tintypes to be made, but these were used in a commercial enterprise in which they were finished as uniformly as possible.

In contrast, Robb takes great care in composing and finishing each tintype. The arched framing or uneven borders in some of the tintypes are the result of how Robb flows the collodion emulsion on the plate when he first prepares it to receive the image. As an artist, Robb conceives the composition as he surveys the setting and talks with each cowboy prior to posing and shooting. He then prepares the plate, making a uniform coating of the emulsion or perhaps—as just stated—pouring the collodion in a more artistic manner. Invariably, there is a buildup of collodion along one edge as he pours off excess emulsion. A reaction in this area between iron sulfate and potassium cyanide during the developing process produces the color that is seen along the edges of many of his tintypes.

Similarly, at the end of the process, Robb can enhance the image in a number of ways. Using a torch to dry the lavender varnish, he can create certain effects. Torch marks are seen in some images as burn patterns. Sometimes, if an image has been over-exposed, Robb scratches the surface to put more contrast onto the plate and frame the face of the sitter.

A final challenge in the process of tintype making is worth mentioning. Robb uses an 8 x 10 camera mounted on a tripod with a hood. When Robb ducks under the hood to look through the lens to compose and focus the shot, he is looking at an image—projected onto glass by the lens—that is reversed and upside down. He must right the image in his mind and imagine how the final tintype will look—all this in just a few seconds, for the plate is being sensitized in the darkroom trailer and will not wait—then make adjustments to the pose of the cowboy before putting the lens cap back on and dashing back into the darkroom trailer to get the plate. To see Robb Kendrick work is to see a man in constant motion and in focused concentration.

Because the exposure is made directly onto a plate, the resulting tintype photograph is a mirror image. There is no negative to reverse the image as we are accustomed in modern photographs. Many say tintypes look more real than modern photographs, because "this is the way we really look," meaning that this is the way we see ourselves in the mirror. A tintype is a permanent mirror.

Robb Kendrick's tintypes, however, are much more than a surface mirror. The collaboration necessary between subject and photographer and the trust and mutual respect that quickly develop between them lead to images that reveal depths of character in carefully recorded faces.

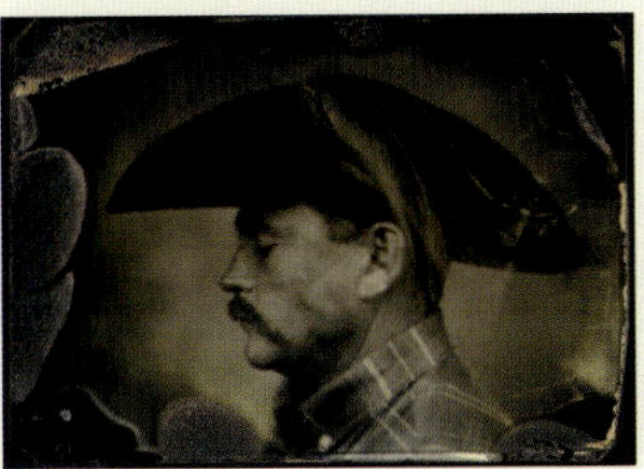

"Similarly, at the end of the process, Robb can enhance the image in a number of ways. Torch marks are seen in some images as burn patterns."

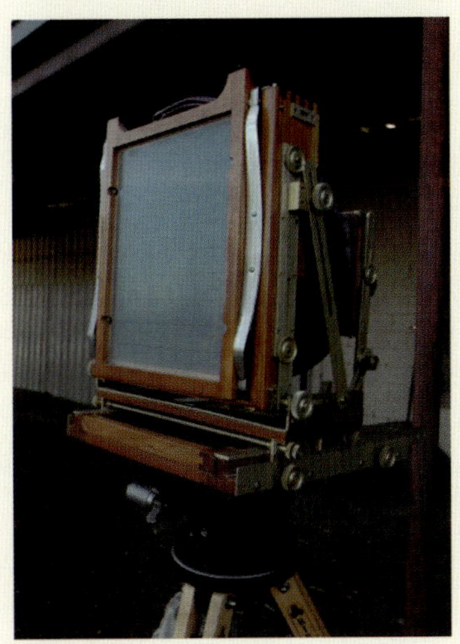

Robb Kendrick's 8 x 10 camera

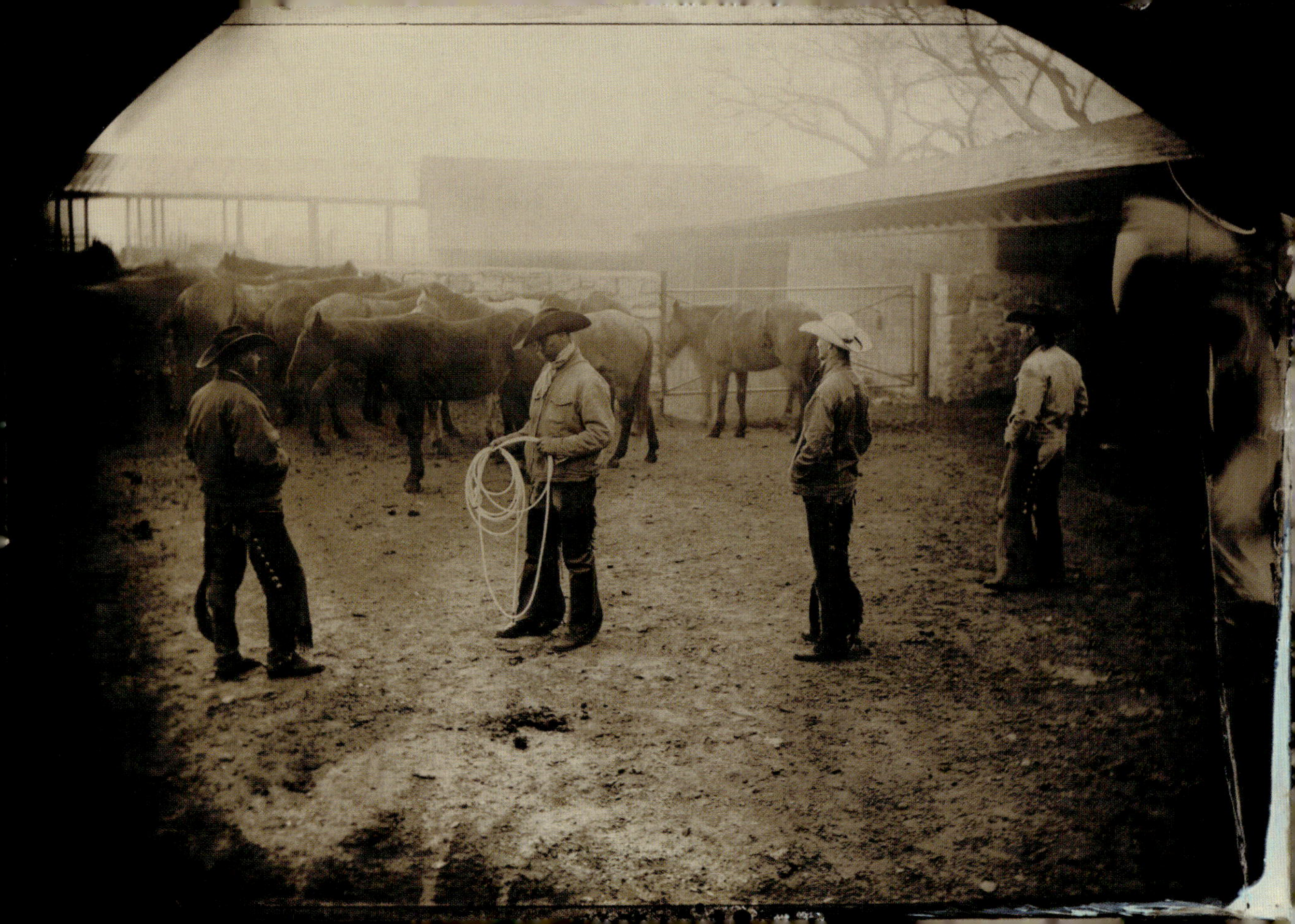

AFTERWORD

by BUSTER MCLAURY

The DEMISE OF THE COWBOY HAS BEEN REPORTED SINCE THE END OF THE TRAIL-DRIVING DAYS ALMOST 120 YEARS AGO. THE ODD FACT IS THAT JUST LAST WEEK I SAT IN THE COOKHOUSE ON THE PITCHFORK RANCH AND ATE DINNER WITH A WHOLE CREW OF 'EM. ON MY WAY HOME, I DROVE THROUGH THE 6666 AND SAW THEIR CHUCK WAGON CAMPED IN THE TACKETT PASTURE NOT FAR FROM THE HIGHWAY. THEIR CREW WAS BUSY WITH SPRING BRANDING. TODAY IS APRIL 8, 2005.

I was born and raised on big cow outfits in West Texas. I grew up in the company of men who worked and cared for hundreds of horses and tens of thousands of cattle on hundreds of thousands of acres of cow country. I thought nothing of seeing 150 head of horses in a remuda, of seeing 500 head of cattle in a roundup. Cowboys living at a chuck wagon for weeks or months at a time was a way of life.

If ever anyone was bred and born to be a cowboy, I was. My daddy and both my granddads were cowboys. I never remember wanting to be anything else. Since there were plenty of 'em where I was, I'd never heard of anyone thinking cowboys were extinct.

When I graduated from high school, I was valedictorian of my class and had a scholarship to go on to college. But when I sat in that classroom, I could hear limbs cracking and rocks turning over during a wild cow chase. So when they turned me loose, I loaded my saddle and bedroll and headed for the 6666. I got a job in the bronc pen.

When Sheryl and I married, I moved her 25 miles out in the country to a dilapidated trailer house on a cow outfit. We were making $350 a month. A year later, we changed outfits for a $25-a-month raise. After three months, we got another $25-a-month raise. Didn't figure we'd ever see another poor day. We had thousands of cattle to see after and work, and my mount of horses was five head of three-year-old broncs that were loco-ed (literally).

Some cowboys prefer the activity around a ranch headquarters. Others prefer the solitude of camp, where, as my friend Tommy Vaughn put it, "There ain't somebody standin' there ever' mornin' pointin' their damned finger at ya."

So why do cowboys cowboy? It sure ain't the money. There's never enough. It's not the glory. There ain't none. There are a million different reasons why a cowboy abuses himself and his family to do what he does, and most of them couldn't be put into words. They are things that are inside a feller, such as pride in a job well done, the challenge of a constantly developing set of skills with horses and cattle and nature, and self-discipline that manifests itself in integrity.

No small thanks should go to his family. My wife has lived at the end of many dirt roads. Out there, you don't just run to town right quick when you need a loaf of bread or a gallon of milk. You make do with what you have. She's made a home in some pretty questionable old ranch houses for us and our daughters, Tiffany and Misty. I dedicate my essay to these cowboys' families. Without their support, there'd be no pictures in this book.

PRECEDING PAGE: JA CORRAL

RANCHES

1 6666 RANCH
GUTHRIE

2 6666 RANCH DIXON CREEK
BORGER

3 ARMSTRONG RANCH
ARMSTRONG

4 BAR CROSS RANCH
LYTLE

5 CINCH RING RANCH
COMANCHE

6 COLLINS CREEK RANCH
ALBANY

7 DACUS LIVESTOCK
ALPINE

8 DOUBLE HORN RANCH
BLUFF DALE

9 EASY LAND & CATTLE
ALBANY

10 ELLIS CATTLE CO.
SINTON

11 GUITAR RANCH
SPUR

12 HART RANCH
MUNDAY

13 HASKELL FARMS RANCH
HASKELL

14 I BAR RANCH
GROOVER

15 JA RANCH
CLARENDON

16 JONES ALTA VISTA RANCH
HEBBRONVILLE

17 KING RANCH
KINGSVILLE

18 LA ESCALERA RANCH
FT. STOCKTON

19 LAMBSHEAD RANCH
ALBANY

20 LONG X RANCH
KENT

21 MEANS RANCH
VAN HORN

22 MOORHOUSE RANCH
BENJAMIN

23 PAISANO RANCH
MARATHON

24 PATTERSON RANCH
BENJAMIN

25 PITCHFORK RANCH
GUTHRIE

26 QUIEN SABE RANCH
CHANNING

27 RA BROWN RANCH
THROCKMORTON

28 SANDHILL CATTLE CO.
EARTH

29 SAUNDERS RANCH
WEATHERFORD

30 SCRIBE M RANCH
HASKELL

31 SILVERBROOK RANCH
CROSS PLAINS

32 SPADE RANCH
CANADIAN

33 SPIKEBOX RANCH
BENJAMIN

34 TONGUE RIVER RANCH
GUTHRIE

35 TRIANGLE RANCH
PADUCAH

36 W. H. GREEN RANCH
ALBANY

37 WAGGONER RANCH
VERNON

38 XI RANCH
CANADIAN

39 Y-SIX RANCH
VALENTINE

FOLLOWING PAGE: GEOLOGICAL SURVEY MAP *of* TEXAS—1844—COURTESY OF THE LIBRARY OF CONGRESS

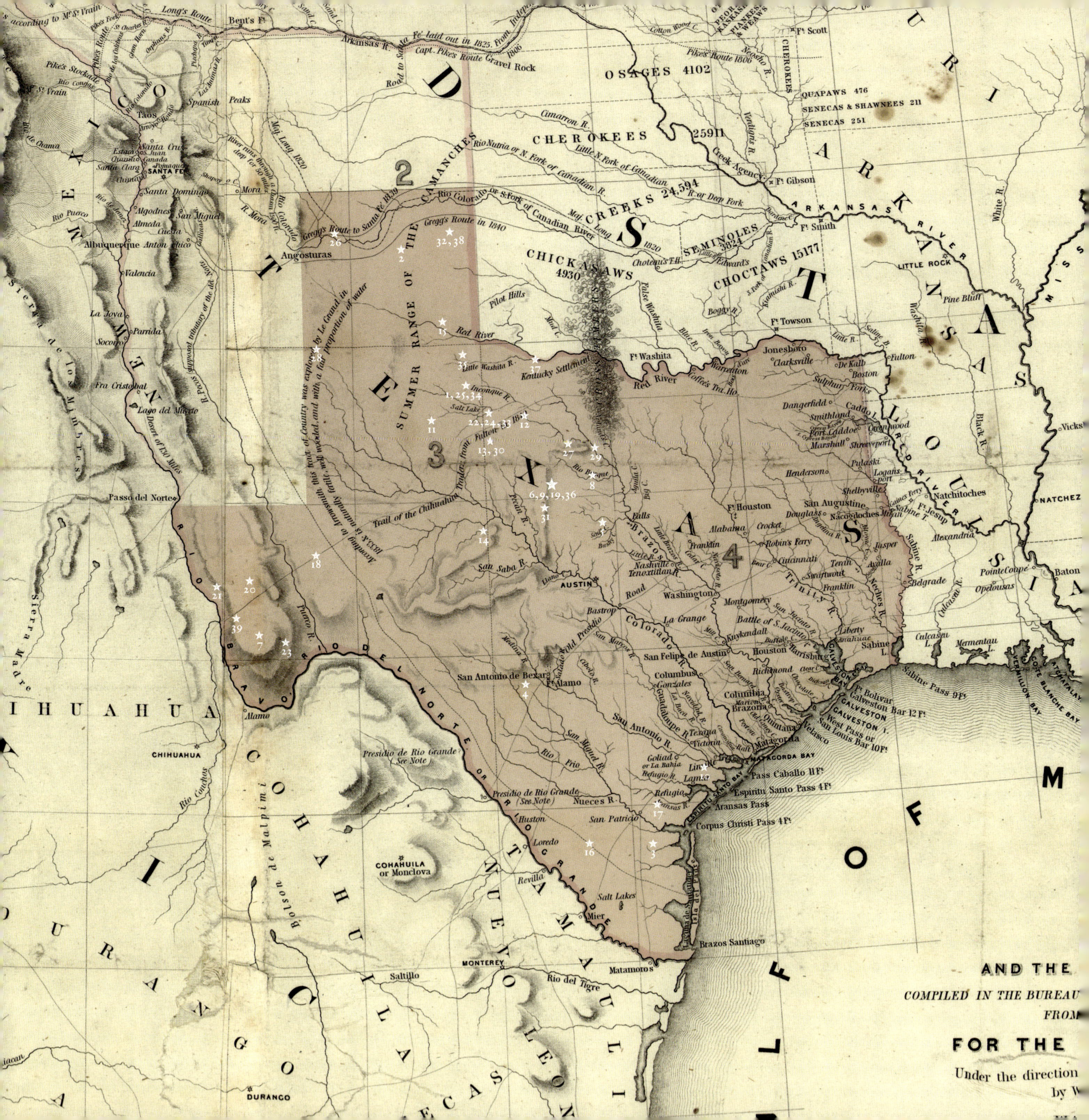

Long's Route
Bent's Ft
Arkansas R.
Santa Fé laid out in 1825.
Capt. Pike's Route Gravel Rock
Pike's Stockade
Taos
Spanish Peaks
Santa Fe
Santa Domingo
San Miguel
Algodnes
Almeda
Albuquerque
Anton Chico
Valencia
La Joya
Parrida
Socorro
Fra Cristobal
Lago del Muerto
Desert of 130 Miles
Passo del Norte
Sierra de los Mimbres
Sierra Madre
Angosturas
Mora
Maj. Long 1820
Gregg's Route to Santa Fe 1839
Gregg's Route in 1840
Rio Colorado or S. Fork of Canadian River
Rio Nutria or N. Fork of Canadian R.
Cimarron R.
Cotton Wood C.
Pike's Route 1806
Ft Scott
OSAGES 4102
CHEROKEES
25911
Creek Agency
Ft Gibson
QUAPAWS 476
SENECAS & SHAWNEES 211
SENECAS 251
CREEKS 24,594
SEMINOLES 3824
CHICKASAWS 4930
CHOCTAWS 15177
Ft Smith
Little Rock
ARKANSAS RIVER
Pine Bluff
Ft Towson
Washita R.
Red River
Ft Washita
Jonesboro
Clarksville
De Kalb
Boston
Fulton
Pilot Hills
Kentucky Settlement
SUMMER RANGE OF THE CAMANCHES
Little Washita R.
Salt Lakes
Trail of the Chihuahua Traders from Fulton 1840
Dangerfield
Smithland
Port Caddo
Marshall
Shreveport
Caddo L.
Pulaski
Logansport
Henderson
Shelbyville
San Augustine
Nacogdoches
Douglass
Natchitoches
Natchez
Ft Jesup
Alexandria
Ft Houston
Alabama
Crocket
Robin's Ferry
Franklin
Cincinnati
Swartwout
Jasper
Sabine R.
Belgrade
Pointe Coupé
Opelousas
Baton
Nashville
Tenoxtitlan
San Saba R.
Pecos R.
AUSTIN
Washington
Montgomery
Bastrop
La Grange
Battle of S. Jacinto
San Felipe de Austin
Houston
Harrisburg
Liberty
Sabine L.
Columbus
Gonzales
Richmond
Columbia
Brazoria
Velasco
Quintana
Matagorda
MATAGORDA BAY
GALVESTON
Ft Bolivar
Galveston Bar 12 Ft
Sabine Pass 9 Ft
San Luis Bar 10 Ft
Pass Caballo 11 Ft
Espiritu Santo Pass 4 Ft
Aransas Pass
Corpus Christi Pass 4 Ft
Victoria
Goliad or La Bahia
Refugio
Linnville
San Antonio de Bexar
Ft Alamo
San Antonio R.
Guadalupe R.
Colorado R.
Medina R.
Rio Frio
San Miguel R.
Nueces R.
San Patricio
Presidio de Rio Grande (See Note)
Laredo
Revilla
Mier
Salt Lakes
Matamoros
Brazos Santiago
RIO BRAVO DEL NORTE OR RIO GRANDE
Puerco R.
Alamo
CHIHUAHUA
COHAHUILA
COHAHUILA or Monclova
Bolson de Malpimi
Rio Conchos
MONTEREY
Saltillo
Rio del Tigre
TAMAULIPAS
NUEVO LEON
DURANGO
ZACATECAS
MEXICO
TEXAS
DISTRICT
ARKANSAS
LOUISIANA
GULF OF M
Calcasieu
Mermentau
Vermillion Bay
Cote Blanche Bay
Atchafalaya Bay
AND THE
COMPILED IN THE BUREAU
FROM
FOR THE
Under the direction
by W

INDEX OF SUBJECTS